DEATH DEALER

DEATH DEALER

*How Cops and Cadaver Dogs
Brought a Killer to Justice*

KATE CLARK FLORA

NEW HORIZON PRESS
Far Hills, New Jersey

Requests for permission should be addressed to:
New Horizon Press
P. O. Box 669
Far Hills, NJ 07931

Kate Clark Flora
    Death Dealer: How Cops and Cadaver Dogs Brought a Killer to Justice

Cover design: Wendy Bass
Interior design: Scribe Inc.

Library of Congress Control Number: 2014930465

ISBN 13: 978-0-88282-476-5

New Horizon Press

Manufactured in the U. S. A.

18   17   16   15   14   1   2   3   4   5

Dedication

To the brave officers who stand between us and evil
and to Maria's courageous family and friends

Author's Note

This book is based on the author's experiences and reflects her perception of past, present and future. The personalities, events, actions and conversations portrayed within this story have been taken from interviews, research, court documents, letters, personal papers, press accounts and the memories of some participants.

In an effort to safeguard the privacy of certain people, some individuals' names and identifying characteristics have been changed. Events involving the characters happened as described. Only minor details may have been altered.

Acknowledgments

M aine Warden Service Lieutenant Pat Dorian's comments that I might find this story interesting led me to Miramichi, New Brunswick. This book would not have been possible without the generosity of the Miramichi police, especially Deputy Chief Brian Cummings, Chief Paul Fiander, Constable Dewey Gillespie, Sergeant Jody Whyte, Retired Chief Earl Campbell and Greg Scott. Maria Tanasichuk's family and friends were invaluable in helping me understand her, especially her sister, Sharon Carroll, and dear friends Darlene Gertley and Cindy Richardson.

I have also had the privilege of learning about search and rescue dogs and cadaver dog training from the Maine Warden Service, especially from Specialist Deb Palman and Warden Roger Guay, and about mapping from Lieutenant Kevin Adam. Maine Search and Rescue Dogs (MESARD) volunteers, including Cindy Attwood, Jennifer Fisk, Michele Fleury, Spencer Fuller, Leslie Howe and Nancy Troubh, were kind enough to invite me to observe their training, as was the Warden Service K-9 unit.

I have been well advised.

Table of Contents

Prologue

Sudden light from outside, triggered by motion sensors, stabbed through the blinds and roused the detective from fitful sleep. In an instant, he was fully awake and on his feet, sweeping up his gun from the head of the bed. Keeping a loaded gun by the bed is against all police training, as is keeping a loaded gun anywhere in a house with small children. But when a vicious killer may be stalking your family, all the rules change.

In the shadowy kitchen, he shoved his feet into waiting winter boots, felt for the step and let himself quietly out of the sleeping house. Outside, he found an unlit corner of the deck and stood staring out into his snowy yard, holding his breath and listening for anything that varied from the usual night sounds. He was a hunter as well as a cop. He knew about listening. He knew what the night should sound like.

There were no streetlights in the quiet neighborhood. Beyond his security lights, the black was absolute. He was in his underwear and without gloves, but pumping adrenaline kept the cold at bay as he moved off the deck to check around the garage and the cars. His gun was up and ready. Checking. Listening. Checking. Something moving triggered those lights and he had reason to believe it could be more than a wandering animal.

The clear night was silent but for the occasional damp plop of snow knocked from a branch by the light wind and the crackle of a few dry leaves that hadn't fallen yet. Across the neighborhood, an animal gave a single sharp cry and a dog barked in response. Out on the highway, a truck engine roared as it crossed the Miramichi bridge, up-shifting as it labored uphill and headed away toward Moncton. The hair on his neck prickled as he searched the dark shrubbery for a human shadow's different darkness, then scanned the perimeter of his house for something that didn't belong by turning his head slightly to let his peripheral vision detect movement. He waited and watched as the cold lifted his skin into goose bumps.

Only a few weeks into the investigation into Maria Tanasichuk's mysterious disappearance, he wasn't sleeping much. It was supposed to be a relaxing night. At home for once, instead of on surveillance, and in bed not long after midnight. Able, for a short time, to silence the lists and what-ifs that plagued his mind, the constant second-guessing that hounded any complex investigation. But their suspect was a seasoned hunter. A gun nut. Deft with a bow and arrow. And he was nocturnal—as comfortable moving through the night as any sly and dangerous predator.

Their intelligence was that the suspect had become explosively angry at having the focus of the investigation so relentlessly turned on him, frustrated that his superior intelligence and the framework of lies he had spun had failed to divert the police from their constant concentration on his movements and their pressure on his friends. They had heard that he planned to retaliate against their families. It was information they had to take seriously.

They were trying to watch him so they would know where he was, but continuous surveillance by such a small police department in a quaint, quiet city, especially during the brutal cold of a Canadian winter, was difficult. Doubly hard when he was as likely to be traveling the hundreds of miles of hiking and snowmobile trails on foot or his three-wheel ATV through the surrounding woods as on the city streets.

The detective continued on around the perimeter of his house. Moving. Stopping. Listening. The cold gun in his hands was heavy and he steadied it, hoping he wouldn't have to use it. Hoping that if he did, it wouldn't be like the scene in his recurring nightmares—his gun jamming instead of firing or dribbling the bullets uselessly onto the ground as the bad guy raises his gun and fires.

Inside the house, his pretty, dark-haired wife and two small sons were sleeping. His boys. He'd be the first to tell you that the days they were born were two of the most important days of his life. He could accept the threat to himself. Personal danger is part of what he took on thirteen years ago when he made his decision to become a police officer. He accepted risk as a given in his life. The threat to his family was something new. It upped the ante and complicated everything.

Almost from the beginning, the investigation into Maria Tanasichuk's disappearance had been proceeding on two fronts. First, to amass enough evidence to arrest their suspect and take him off the streets in a case where they had no witnesses, weapon, crime scene or even a body, only their certainty, based on experience, that Maria was dead. Second, to find Maria's body before her killer could move it someplace so deep within the surrounding forests that they'd have no chance of finding it. Before the spring thaw came and the murderer buried it. Before scavenging predators destroyed it. They were desperate to find it so that they had definitive evidence of the crime they were certain had been committed and closure for her suffering family and friends.

Yet a new dimension had been added. Each time the phone rang—and his phone already rang at all hours of the day and night—it might be a new witness or a known witness who had recalled something vital; it might be the news that one of their searches had finally turned up Maria's body or it might be his wife or Paul's wife or Dewey's wife with the desperate message: "He's here!"

The threat to his wife and his boys was not acceptable.

The detective continued his circuit of the house, eyes watering in the cold wind, moving slowly enough to do a thorough search, even though the last of the bed's warmth had blown away and the night's chill was penetrating to his bones. There was nothing out there that he could see or hear, the hunter who had become the hunted.

He watched the motion sensor lights fade out. At last, having done all he could, he went inside. He placed the gun back at the head of the bed, where it would stay at night until their suspect was securely behind bars. Then the detective slid, shivering, back into bed and tried to resume his interrupted sleep.

Part 1

Maria Is Missing

Chapter 1

A Legacy of Terror

The Canadian city of Miramichi, in northeast New Brunswick, Canada, hasn't been a city very long. It was cobbled together in 1995 by combining the towns of Newcastle and Chatham, which lay on opposite banks of the Miramichi River, with the smaller towns of Douglastown, Loggieville, Nelson, Chatham Head, Nordin, Moorefield and Douglasfield. Although they have been one city for several years, each of the towns still retains its own character, its own downtown and its own stories, including a long-standing rivalry between Newcastle and Chatham that started in the "fighting election of 1843" and resulted in skirmishes between rival factions in the streets. Although Miramichi is small in population, it is the third largest city in the province of New Brunswick.

It's a hardscrabble area where many people still make their living off the land and it was hit hard by the closure of the region's two large paper mills, which resulted in an employment migration where many of the men traveled to western Canada for work, leaving their families behind.

The population is a mixture of Acadian, Scottish and Irish and nearly two-thirds of the area's residents are Catholic. Although the region is legally bilingual, almost 90 percent of the population is English-speaking. The area has an aging population and old-fashioned values. It is still the kind of a place where children roam freely between houses and people invite you home for dinner and serve homemade pickles. If you're lucky, at the meal you'll also get fresh-caught Miramichi salmon.

The Miramichi, or the 'Chi, as some residents call it, is a world-famous salmon fishing river, with a long tradition of families coming to fishing camps along the river every summer, often renewing their connection with the same river guide or family of river guides for generations. Although there are often significant economic disparities between these visitors and the local residents, the river exerts its sway on everyone.

As its many branches come together, the beautiful river widens as it winds its way through the city and makes its final approach to the ocean. The area's residents are passionate about their river and their region. Locals don't so much speak of being from a particular town as they speak of their region, of being "on the Miramichi," "in the Miramichi" or just "on the river." The geography and character of the area gets into people's blood and holds them there, making it hard to leave and drawing those who grew up there back when they do.

In the middle of the river, just southwest of the town, is Beaubears Island, where, during the British expulsion of Acadians in the mid-1700s, a small, desperate party of Acadian settlers retreated and starved through a long, harsh winter as they waited for a rescue that never came. The survivors were eventually driven away, though a few remained, permitting some residents of the region to trace their ancestry back to that dreadful winter on Beaubears Island. The island is now a historical site, with a visitor's center and a ferry.

Although the murder rate is less than one per year, some of Miramichi's murderers have been particularly memorable and dramatic. In 1979, there was Robbie Cunningham, known as "The Miramichi Axe Murderer" for the brutal way he killed Nicholas Duguay. At the time, some people fought to clear Cunningham, claiming he was innocent. Despite the clamor, officials refused to release him before his time was served. About nine months after his release, he committed another murder.

The area still struggles to live down the nickname, MurderMichi, that it got back in 1989 when one of Canada's worst serial killers, convicted murderer Allan Legere, known as "The Monster of the Miramichi," escaped from prison guard custody during a hospital visit and terrorized the region for seven months. While he was on the lam, Legere sexually assaulted then brutally killed three elderly women and he also tortured and murdered a priest.

Residents still talk about that uncertain time, when children played soccer outside under the watchful eyes of parents but could suddenly be called inside as a carload of Mounties pulled up and headed out into the woods. Doors remained locked. People who lived by themselves moved in with others. Gun sales rose and weapons stayed close at hand. The year that Legere was on the loose, Halloween was canceled. Few people went out after dark and any sound in the night was a cause for panic.

Even with Legere convicted and housed in a maximum security prison, residents remained uneasy, their fears periodically flamed by reports that he might be moved to a less secure facility where he would have a greater opportunity for escape. Many believed that Legere kept a list of those on whom he wanted revenge.

Almost fifteen years later, as snow fell on the city, the fear of a killer lurking in their midst was about to return. A call came in to the quiet, semi-dark Miramichi Police Emergency Dispatch Center on January 26, 2003, a snowy Sunday afternoon. David Tanasichuk reported that his wife, Maria, was missing.

David told dispatcher Joanne Young that he and his wife had been having marital problems and they had decided to spend some time apart. To enable that, Maria had taken a bus to the city of Saint John, three hours away, to stay with a friend. He stated that Maria had been gone since January 14, and that since her departure, he had not heard from his wife and he'd become concerned.

It had been an unusually dry January, but on the 26th, as if Mother Nature was making up for lost time, snow was pelting down and weathermen were predicting eight to ten inches. While civilians were buttoning up and settling in and snowmobilers, cross-country skiers and snow-shoers were jumping for joy, the police were gearing up for a miserable day of fender-benders and slogging through the streets to answer calls. There is no such thing as a snow day for a police department.

At approximately 2:30 in the afternoon, dispatch sent Constable Cheryl Seeley to meet David Tanasichuk at his residence to take his statement. The apartment was only a short distance from the police station.

Upon entering the apartment, Constable Seeley said, "Hi, David, I understand that you haven't seen your wife since January 12?"

Tanasichuk replied, "Yes."

He went on to explain that his wife, Maria, was extremely possessive and clingy and wanted them to be together 24/7. He said that Maria cross-examined him about where he was going whenever he left the house and watched him through binoculars when he walked down the street. He said that he and Maria had been married since 1993 and he had tolerated the togetherness because she had waited for him during his time in jail and so he felt she deserved his attention. Lately, however, he had been feeling oppressed by her scrutiny. Maria watched him every minute. She repeatedly called when he was at friends' houses to check on his whereabouts. She quizzed him when he returned.

As a result of Maria's anxiety and his feelings of oppression, David told the constable that Sylvette Robichaud, the counselor they had been seeing at an addiction counseling service for help with David's drug problem, had suggested they spend some time apart. Initially, he told Seeley, he had suggested to his wife that he would go to Moncton to stay with his brother, but Maria didn't like his brother's girlfriend and she thought there would be too many women around. Alternatively, he had suggested that he could go to Saint John and stay with his mother and another brother, but Maria had objected to that too, saying again that there would be too many females there. She suggested that he stay in Miramichi, where there would be fewer people to distract him and he would have time to think, and she would go to Saint John instead.

In trying to explain his wife's state of mind at the time she left Miramichi, he said that her behavior had become so difficult that his mother, who usually came for three weeks at Christmas, had left after five days. In response to the constable's questions, he told her that Maria was not angry when she left, but might have been a little upset. To illustrate his wife's controlling nature, he described an incident four years earlier when Maria had threatened to slash her wrists while he was out with friends if he didn't immediately return home. He told the constable that when he did return home, she had cuts on her wrists covered with bandages.

He also told Seeley that Maria had recently found out that she had Hepatitis C and believed that she had gotten it from him due to his drug use. She had been very angry when he tested negative and said, "Why would I have Hep C and you wouldn't?"

David said that he didn't know what time Maria had left, as he had been at a friend's house working on his bike between 10:00 A.M. and 4 P.M. on the 12th and when he returned she was gone. As they had no car, he assumed that she had taken the bus. He was unable to describe what clothing and footwear Maria had taken with her, stating that she had clothing from one end of the house to the other. He said she would have had $800 with her that she had taken from their safe, money they had been saving up for their headstones.

He was unable to give Constable Seeley the full name, address or phone number of the friend in Saint John with whom Maria had gone to stay, saying only that it was someone named "Cathy." He did give the constable the names of several friends and family members who might be able to help the police in locating Maria. Seeley said that she would contact them and advise him of what she learned. David said that he would also be contacting people. As Seeley was leaving the apartment, David Tanasichuk began to cry.

In her report, Seeley noted that during the interview, David appeared to be in an impaired state. Although his speech was not slurred and he was aware of his surroundings and able to provide the requested information, his eyes were shiny and dilated and he seemed to be in a daze.[1]

Large city police departments see a lot of missing person reports and usually have developed a standard operating procedure for handling them. Miramichi has a population of only around 19,000, and such reports are infrequent and generally handled more informally, often by a police officer who is already familiar with the person reporting and/or the one who has gone missing. It is generally true that in most small cities, the majority of persons reported missing eventually turn up, often with explanations for their disappearance involving alcohol, money, drugs, sex or mental health issues and often expressing surprise that anyone was concerned.

Therefore, the report of a missing person is typically not regarded as requiring immediate attention unless the missing person is a child or vulnerable adult or if the police have reason to believe the person might be at risk. In this case, there *was* cause for concern: Maria Tanasichuk had been gone for two weeks.

Seeley instructed David Tanasichuk to go to the police station the following day to give a formal statement, so that the police could gather as much detail as possible to aid them in searching for Maria. Then she gave David her business card and went back to headquarters.

Upon returning to the precinct and beginning to write up the report of her interview with David, Seeley realized that she had made a mistake in noting the date that Maria had left for Saint John. In his call to dispatch, David had reported that he'd last seen his wife on January 14. When she spoke with him about Maria at his apartment, she had erroneously said January 12, and David had agreed to that date. She immediately tried to reach him by phone to determine which date was correct but she was unable to contact him.

Around 6:00 P.M., Miramichi Police Dispatch received a call from David Tanasichuk for Constable Seeley. He left a message saying that he would be leaving for Saint John in fifteen minutes to look for Maria, and he left his mother's phone number in case Seeley needed to reach him there. Because clarifying the discrepancy in dates was important in initiating any inquiry, Seeley tried to return his call and when she couldn't reach him she immediately returned to his apartment, which was dark and he was apparently already gone.

While she was at the residence, Dispatch received another call from David. About twenty minutes later, he called Seeley and reported he was en route to Saint John, because he wanted to be involved in the process of finding Maria. Seeley then asked him to clarify the date Maria had left for Saint John, and he responded that Maria had left on the 12th.

During her conversations with David, Seeley had informed him that while the police would be looking into the matter, her work schedule would be changing and she would next be at work several days later. He had responded by asking if it would be all right, if he had questions in the interim, to contact Detective Brian Cummings, with whom he and Maria had developed a relationship recently during the events surrounding the violent death of Maria's only child. Seeley agreed that she would transmit the information to Detective Cummings.

Because Seeley knew that Detective Cummings had established a relationship with the Tanasichuks, she contacted him at home to inform him of the situation. She imparted some of the details of her conversations with David Tanasichuk and her concerns about the discrepancies in the date he said Maria had gone missing, as well as her observations about David's behavior and impairment that suggested possible drug use.

By then it was Sunday night. Detective Cummings had just opened a beer and was about to watch the Super Bowl with a friend. He advised her to take good notes on her conversations with David and in any follow-up interviews she might conduct with any of the people he'd suggested might have information about Maria's whereabouts. Cummings told her that he would review the file in the morning and begin looking into the matter.

The following morning, Detective Cummings was across the river at the courthouse (the main police station is located on Water Street on the Chatham side of the river and the courthouse is on the opposite side of the Miramichi in former Newcastle), attending to a case, when he saw David's former sister-in-law in the lobby. Knowing that she was Tanasichuk's former sister-in-law through a relationship with one of his brothers, he thought she might be familiar with the details of Maria's departure, so he struck up a conversation. When Cummings asked what she knew about the Tanasichuks' situation, she told him that she had stopped in at their residence a few days earlier, on January 24. Maria hadn't been there and David's appearance—slurred speech and "whacked" eyes—made her think he was high on drugs. During that visit, David had told her that Maria had gone to Saint John. David's former sister-in-law also told Cummings that word on the street was that "something bad" had happened to Maria.

Although he didn't expect to find David Tanasichuk at home, since David had told Seeley the previous night that he was on his way to Saint John, Detective Cummings headed right over to the Tanasichuks' apartment when he was finished with his business at the courthouse. Much to his surprise, when he knocked on the door, David called out, "Come in," and Cummings entered the apartment.

Cummings was shocked at what he found. The apartment was in an extreme state of disarray, a marked change from its usual tidy state and something Maria, who was a meticulous housekeeper, never would have stood for. He sat down with David and attempted to learn more about Maria's departure, probable whereabouts and why her husband had been concerned enough to call the police and report her disappearance.

Chapter 2

It Takes Two to Tango

When Brian "Bull" Cummings (Cummings's nick-name, because of his shaved head and large size, was based on Nostradamus "Bull" Shannon, a character on the TV series *Night Court*) first came into Miramichi and joined the Newcastle Police Force, there was sometimes a kind of "wild west" feel to policing in the area. Drug dealing was rampant on the river. The custom of work-men celebrating the weekend's arrival with heavy drinking was the norm; fights and brawls were common. A lot of police work involved breaking down doors to serve drug warrants. On Saturday nights, a constable could be reasonably certain that he was going to mix it up with someone before the night was over, and it was pretty likely that he'd wake up hurting on Sunday.

Early on, his fellow officers had warned him about the Tanasichuk brothers. They were a rough bunch, he was told, and one of them had expressed a deep desire to kill a police officer, so he'd better watch his back. Over the years, though, while one or another of the brothers occasionally crossed his path, he only had sporadic contact with David and did not know Maria.

Although Cummings had had little interaction with him, David Tanasichuk was well-known to the Miramichi police and to other police agencies in the province as a deeply angry man with an explosive temper and a reputation for violence. He was considered a bad man to cross, and many people were afraid of him. At the time he reported his wife missing, Tanasichuk was thirty-six, with a criminal record stretching back twenty years that included possession of stolen property, assault, breaking and entering, theft, escape, fraud, assault on a police officer and multiple convictions for possession of a restricted weapon.

In one significant case, his rage over an undercover drug operation which resulted in his prosecution had led him to plot the assassination of the presiding judge, the crown prosecutor and a police officer who had participated in the operation. Although, as a convicted felon, he was prohibited by law from owning a firearm, he had obtained a sawed-off shotgun to use in carrying out his plot.

In a rural hunting culture such as that on the Miramichi, guns are commonplace in most homes. Although, by law, guns are supposed to be registered, registration is considered a hassle and an expense, so it is common practice to simply fail to mention guns in the house, acting as though they don't exist and thus the law isn't violated, rather than go through the trouble of registering them. With guns everywhere and a ready supply of people in need of money, it's not difficult for someone looking for a gun to obtain one. Sawing off a shotgun is an easy way to convert a readily available hunting tool into an easily concealed and extremely lethal weapon.

Once he'd obtained the sawed-off, David Tanasichuk had wrapped his altered weapon in a tarp to protect it and hidden it in the woods just inside the city limits, in a spot where it could be easily retrieved when he was ready to execute his plan. Unfortunately for him, and fortunately for his intended victims, he had confided some of the details of his scheme to a fellow drug dealer who, it turned out, was working with the police as an informant.

As reported by the local paper, *The Miramichi Leader*, on October 27, 1993, the presiding judge, Judge McNamee, called the plot "a plan of wholesale slaughter" and, recognizing its lethal potential as an easily concealed weapon, he described the sawed-off shotgun as "the most sinister weapon imaginable." Noting that it had the potential to do untold damage, he observed: "These individuals [the targets of the plot] would have no way of knowing the seriousness of this or the timing. One could only imagine what they must have gone through because of this threat...The thought of the use of this weapon almost makes one's blood run cold."[2]

David Tanasichuk was an on-again, off-again drug dealer who was suspected of having grown marijuana in the woods outside the city and of having a "back door" clientele who bought drugs from his house. Although he was prohibited from having guns and despite the fact that they occupied the same residence, Canadian law did permit Maria to have her own guns in the house. David was an avid hunter. Employing Maria's guns and perhaps others he had secreted in tarps in the woods, he hunted deer, moose and bear, in and out of season. Despite their tight financial circumstances, he didn't hunt solely for the meat. He hunted for the pure pleasure of stalking and killing, sometimes leaving the animals he killed lying where they died.

Also, he was an avid bow hunter.

Provincial records show that at one point in May 1989, during a period when he and one of his brothers had escaped from prison and were on the run, his path crossed that of the Miramichi region's most notorious serial killer, Allan Legere. He was even briefly considered as a possible suspect in one of Legere's murders, that of Annie Flam, but authorities quickly decided the Tanasichuk brothers were too disorganized. According to prison lore reported by the corrections department's internal information system, he was fascinated by Legere, although he considered himself smarter, and therefore superior, to Legere, whom he criticized for having killed only women and old men. Some who knew him suspected him of having provided food and support to Legere during the months Legere was terrorizing the region.

David was tall and had a physique that showed his fondness for working out with weights. He had eyes described by one investigator as "shark's eyes"—cold, gray and expressionless. His torso was covered in tattoos, primarily guns and anti-police slogans. At the base of his throat, he had tattooed the words "смерть дилер." He refused to tell Maria or her friends, or even the tattooist who did it, what it meant. He had teardrops tattooed at the corner of one eye, and photographs taken of him over the years chart the progression of those teardrops from one to four.

The story was that the Tanasichuks had met when Maria was visiting her fiancé at the Springhill correctional facility. Once she met David, that engagement was off and ever after, David Tanasichuk was the only man in the world to her. It was, by all reports, a very strong attachment. Friends and relatives who spent time with David and Maria together said it was like a match made in heaven. The two of them shared a passion for outdoor activities, for hunting, fishing and riding through the woods on their three-wheelers. Sometimes they would be seen walking around Miramichi, holding hands. They did everything together. When they fought, friends reported, they cried, kissed and made up. Afterward they were closer than ever.

David nurtured a deep hatred for the police and this was something the Tanasichuks shared. Maria had escaped from a harsh family life in her early teens and had become involved with drinking and drugs, stealing and men who liked young girls. That behavior had gotten her sent to a reform school for girls as a teen. Her early experiences soured her on the criminal justice system and left her as hard-edged and suspicious as her husband when it came to dealing with the police. She rarely talked about her time in custody, even with close friends or family, except to tell her sister on the occasional home visit that it was an experience no one would want to have. She was adamant that she was never going to be incarcerated again, a resolution her relationship with David would ultimately cause her to break.

Maria's sister, Sharon, describes a childhood in a poor family with eight children that was largely devoid of love and affection. Many homes in Miramichi in that era still had dirt floors. Catholic families had many children, the economy was poor and the financial and emotional costs of alcohol abuse were common problems for families trying to get by with too little. Maria's family life was harsh and spare, in a home where her father, though kindly, had nerves damaged from the war and her mother was frustrated by poverty and overwhelmed by so many children. Care and attention came only when a child was sick and even that was meager at best. Pleasure was rare and presents even rarer.

According to Sharon, they usually got nothing for Christmas and they had learned not to expect anything. But one magical Christmas, when they were around eight and nine, both girls got their first dolls. During that long winter, they spent countless hours loving them and playing with them. To mark the specialness of these rare gifts, Sharon and Maria not only named their dolls, they also gave each other new names to use as they became loving mothers whose babies laughed and cried.

By her mid-teens, like many other young girls in the province, the strong-willed Maria had little supervision or correction. After a stint in reform school beginning around the time Maria was fifteen, she didn't return to Miramichi but moved to the larger city of Saint John to stay with her brother. There she became romantically involved. At fifteen, she was hardly more than a child herself when she had her son, B.J., and she spent seven years in a common-law relationship with B.J.'s father.

The relationship was reportedly abusive, due in part to the father's temper and in part to Maria's sometimes careless mothering. As a very young mother without the support of her family, Maria struggled with the challenges of rearing a child while desiring the partying, drinking and drugs available to unencumbered friends her age.

During those years, she became close to B.J.'s father's family. Her former sister-in-law, Cindy Richardson, remained a good friend to her over the years and was devoted to B.J. Cindy described Maria as always lively and fun—people describing Maria often used the word "bubbly"—but said that because of Maria's drinking, drugs and partying, the family became concerned about B.J. when he was tiny and asked social services to become involved.

Eventually, Maria left the relationship and Saint John and moved back to Miramichi to raise her son away from the larger city's temptations and be nearer to her family and her closest-in-age sister, Sharon. She had had enough of city life and looked forward to quieter times in Miramichi. By then, she had met David Tanasichuk and, wanting to become a better mother to B.J. and knowing she needed to be clean and drug-free to be allowed to visit David in prison, she weaned herself off drugs through sheer willpower. Living on public assistance was a severe, barebones existence, but Maria saw that her son was always well dressed and well fed, even if it meant that she had little money for her own needs. Like a lot of people on the Miramichi, they didn't have much, but despite their tough circumstances Maria and her sister, Sharon, shared food when they could.

With Maria's return to Miramichi, the two sisters were able to resume the friendship they had had as children, a comfort to Maria during the lonely years when David was incarcerated. Sharon's daughter and B.J., who were close in age, became good friends.

Maria was an attractive woman, medium tall, with lovely long brown hair, large brown eyes and carefully shaped brows. Until despair over her son's death rendered her depressed and couch-bound, Maria had been slim. She wasn't a fashion plate; even if she could have afforded fancy clothes, she was far too outdoorsy for that. Even as a child, she'd been a tomboy and preferred fishing and climbing trees to more girly activities. She favored the comfort of jeans or tracksuits and sweatshirts, but she was very particular about her appearance and was absolutely passionate about her jewelry. Maria had a large collection of gold chains, necklaces and rings that had been gifts from David. She regularly wore a lot of her jewelry, and she took great pleasure in showing her friends each new piece. Even in casual pictures, she can be seen wearing a lot of gold. It was always gold for Maria, not silver. She loved to look good when she went out.

The Tanasichuks lived mostly on public assistance and the profits from drug sales. David only occasionally held down a job and Maria never worked. Some friends speculated that this was because the Tanasichuks' reputation in the community was such that Maria thought it would be useless to even bother to try and find a job, as no one would hire her. Although they—and Maria in particular—had close relationships with friends, family and neighbors, in the wider Miramichi community they had a reputation. Maria's best friend, Darlene Gertley, illustrated that reputation with the story of an encounter shortly after she moved to Miramichi and had her first child: "One time, I went down to the [gas station] and the lady asked how I was getting along and did you make any friends. And I said, yes, Maria and Dave Tanasichuk, and the woman said, 'Oh, stay away from them.' And I asked why. And she said, 'They're bad news. They've been in jail more than church.'"

At the time that David Tanasichuk reported his wife missing in January 2003, the longstanding adversarial relationship between the police and the Tanasichuks had changed. In the Fall of 2000, Detective Brian Cummings had met Maria Tanasichuk for the first time under tragic circumstances. That September 1st, a large group of teens—literally hundreds of kids—had held an end-of-summer, off-to-college party in the woods where they would be out of the public eye. During the course of the evening, a fight broke out between Maria's son, B.J. Breau, and another young man. As kids stood around cheering and jeering, B.J. was knocked down. While he lay on the ground, the other boy began kicking him viciously. One blow struck B.J. in the chest and severed his aorta. He died before he could be taken to a hospital.

As a result of the investigation and legal proceedings arising from B.J.'s death, the Miramichi police, in particular Detective Sergeant Paul Fiander, head of the detective bureau, and Detective Cummings, developed a new relationship with

David and Maria. No longer did the police come to the door of the small apartment as potential opponents inquiring about drug dealing or stolen goods; now they came as compassionate public servants dealing with the grieving family of a murder victim. B.J.'s death was devastating to both David and Maria. He was Maria's only child (she lost her only pregnancy with David to an ectopic pregnancy) and he was like another son to David. David had a son of his own from a prior relationship, but it was his stepson who lived with him and he had helped raise B.J. for a decade.

In his iconic book on homicide procedures, *Practical Homicide Investigation*, Vernon Geberth describes the important relationship between investigators and the victim's family this way:

"Secondary victims are those persons left behind when a...child...is prematurely deprived of their life due to a homicide. These persons are the survivors. The homicide detective has a profound duty and an awesome responsibility in dealing with the surviving family in the murder investigation process."[3]

Then he lists the duties of the responding detectives. They include dealing with the emotions of the surviving family, establishing a base of inquiry which does not further traumatize the survivors, providing information about the circumstances of the death and the progress of the investigation and guiding the family through the complicated and confusing criminal justice system. The detective, Geberth says, becomes an advocate for the deceased and the surviving family throughout the process.

It was through this role that the new relationship between the Tanasichuks and the police was born. Because of their concerns about David's fierce temper and consequent fears that he would be tempted to avenge his stepson's death by taking matters into his own hands rather than letting justice take its course, the police were more closely involved with the Tanasichuks than with the families of many crime victims. It was also true, though, that Miramichi is a small city where people tend to know each other. Often, there is not the same distance between police and citizens that sometimes exists.

Over the course of their dealings with B.J. Breau's family, certain members of the Miramichi police, typically Detective Cummings and Detective Sergeant Fiander, spent a great deal of time with David and Maria. Both officers, themselves fathers deeply devoted to their own sons, were very sympathetic to the plight of parents trying to deal with the devastating loss of a child.

As she struggled to comprehend the loss, they saw Maria's demeanor begin to change. Through her upbringing, her personal experience with the criminal justice system and her marriage to a convicted felon, Maria had developed a resentful and suspicious attitude toward the police. As she experienced their kindness and support during her awful grief, a softer woman emerged.

It was impossible to be unmoved as they watched this lively, fun-loving, dynamic woman become couch-bound by depression. In the months following B.J.'s death, Maria began spending her days huddled under her special "sooky" blanket and cuddling the small, stuffed red devil bear that had been her last gift from her son.[4] Some days she never got out of her pajamas.

The detectives also understood how ordinary citizens can struggle to comprehend the slow and oftentimes infuriating mechanisms of the criminal justice system. In the case of B.J.'s death, that included such decisions as whether the perpetrator, who was just shy of his eighteenth birthday, should be charged as a juvenile or an adult. Supporters had collected 1500 signatures on a petition for the court to have B.J.'s attacker, who had allegedly threatened to "get him" earlier in the evening, tried as an adult. The authorities chose not to take this route. It became the task of the police to explain these decisions to the Tanasichuks, support them through the resulting horse-trading that went on regarding the nature of the sentence and then through the sentencing itself, always with an awareness of David's impulsive nature and his potential for a violent reaction. Many who knew him expected violence from David.

In the real world, the criminal justice system is not as swift as it appears to be on TV shows. Cases take time to make their way slowly through the system, a pace that—with multiple hearings, continuances and adjournments—can be agonizing torture for the family, who must go to court repeatedly, confront the perpetrator and appear as representatives of the deceased.

Over the period of nearly a year between B.J.'s death and when his assailant was finally sentenced, Brian Cummings found himself becoming quite close to David and Maria. Their apartment was only a short drive from the police station. Sometimes his visits would be to update them on the case. At other times, it would be a "wellness check," just a quick stop in to wish them the very best. Occasionally, because their finances were tight, he would bring them treats, dropping by around suppertime with a lobster for Maria to cook, because he knew that she loved lobster. He'd bring chicken or steak for David, who didn't like lobster. Occasionally, if time permitted or the need seemed great, he might stay and eat with them.

The relationship was close enough, in his mind, that Cummings even briefly considered inviting them to his wedding, until he realized that the presence of a convicted felon would mean friends of his in the justice system would then be unable to attend.

At some point in the process, David Tanasichuk took a surprising step to demonstrate his good faith and his willingness to rely on the judicial process to secure justice for his stepson. He wrote a letter to the local paper, *The Miramichi Leader*, affirming that he would abide by the law and not seek revenge on B.J.'s killer, as many expected him to do.

In a letter that appeared in the September 12, 2000, edition of *The Miramichi Leader*, he began:

"As me and Maria mourn the loss of our son, B.J., I feel compelled to write this letter to express some of our thoughts."

David went on to assert that although his son did not lead a life of privilege and had limited career options, "...Let me tell you, Mr. Cadogan, B.J. may not have come from your upper class rich family, but we did provide him with everything within our means, and anyone who knew B.J. could tell you, we did without so he would not. Do you really judge a person's worth by the amount they or their families have, or by the love they give or receive?"

David continued, "The next issue I want to bring forward is the fact that Billy-Joe's murderer has been given bail. Our son is dead, and *he* walks free waiting for trial. I'll quote the judge in this case, 'The accused has a right to an education.' That makes me want to vomit. What about B.J.'s rights? I just wonder if this is a prime example of the justice we will get in this case. If this is true, then may God have mercy on us all."

He then confronted a widespread assumption head-on: "...For the hundreds of people out there who are spreading this rumor that I may take the law in my own hands, I say to you all, 'give it a rest.' I truly believe that this is not what B.J.

would have wanted me to do. B.J. would have wanted justice to run its course. So that is what I shall do.

"I just pray that there is justice for B.J. Because if there isn't, may Satan have mercy on our souls [Tanasichuk considered himself to be a satanist]. Because that is where we'll all be, in Hell. I'll be waiting at the gates."[5]

Another example of how changed the relationship had become between an angry felon who hated cops and sold drugs out his back door and the local police detectives concerned B.J.'s burial plot. B.J. Breau was buried in St. Michael's Cathedral graveyard, within walking distance of the Tanasichuks' house. Maria went there regularly in the harsh winter weather to shovel a path to her son's grave. Then she knelt and tenderly cleared the clinging ice and snow from the letters on his headstone.

B.J. had been buried in one of the plots the church provided for those who could not pay. After B.J.'s burial, Maria went to the cemetery and tried to get the adjacent plot reserved so she could be buried next to him. There she learned that it was church policy to assign these burial plots in the order in which people died. When her attempts to secure the plot failed, the strong-willed Maria told her husband that if the only way she could be buried next to her son would be to be the next to die, then that's what she was prepared to do.

In a move that would have been inconceivable before B.J.'s death, David Tanasichuk went to the police station and approached Detective Cummings and Detective Sergeant Fiander, explaining that he needed to ask a particular favor. He told the detectives about Maria's ultimatum. Was there anything they could do, he wondered, to ensure that that plot could be reserved for Maria? In despair over the possibility of losing both his wife and his stepson, David cried when he asked the detectives if there was any way they could do this for him.

To David's great relief, the detectives were able to intercede on Maria's behalf and secure a promise that the adjacent plot would be saved for her. When David and Maria saw that they were going to get what they wanted, a thankful David returned to the police station to speak with Detective Cummings. He told the detective that if he and Maria were ever successful in becoming parents, they wanted Cummings to be the godfather.

That was the situation and the state of the relationship when Cummings went to the apartment to talk to David about his missing person report.

Chapter 3

Making Something of Nothing

A police officer may wear many different hats in the course of a single shift. He or she may go from investigating a robbery to dealing compassionately with someone mentally challenged, from interviewing a reluctant witness to trying to resuscitate a baby who's not breathing. All day, every day, police are making complicated mental and emotional adjustments. Individual officers' reasons for choosing police work will vary, but many are drawn by a need to preserve social order, a desire to serve others, a passion for righting wrongs and the hope, however often it is disappointed, in the possibility of goodness and redemption.

Because of the constant emotional demands of the job, police officers, as part of their training, are taught to maintain an objective distance from both criminals and victims. To do otherwise would make the job, with its frequent exposure to the horrific things people do to one another, too emotionally draining. All officers have cases that get to them, the cases they will carry for their whole lives. After the many contacts the department had with the Tanasichuks—with all the time and energy that had gone into helping them through B.J.'s death, the constant worry about David's potential explosion and the relationships that had resulted—Maria's disappearance was going to be one of them.

In many departments, standard operating procedure is not to act until an adult has been gone for more than twenty-four or forty-eight hours, unless that person is elderly or somehow compromised. Certain departments have levels of concern, from the more serious "Missing Person" to the more casual "Compassion to Locate" for cases where the primary reason was not fear of a crime but concern for a worried family. But Maria Tanasichuk was known to be a homebody who, according to her husband's report, had been gone for nearly two weeks. This, along with David's possible relapse into serious drug use, stirred concern for both husband and wife in the minds of the detectives who knew them best.

Although it is common in cases where a husband reports his wife missing to take a close look at the family dynamics, the Tanasichuk matter was not immediately flagged as a possible domestic incident. The Tanasichuks were not a couple known for their domestic problems; quite the opposite, they were fiercely protective of one another and known to be extremely close. They were a couple whom others envied for their loving relationship and the way they seemed to enjoy doing so many things together. Friends and neighbors alike spoke of their closeness and their devotion, particularly of Maria's devotion to her husband.

In an effort to explain the intensity of Maria's loyalty to David, B.J.'s aunt, Maria's former sister-in-law Cindy Richardson, described the following event: David had stolen some guns from a gun shop around the corner and hidden them in the apartment. When police searched and found the guns, David and Maria were both charged.

Cindy said, "...She ended up going to court. And the judge knew about Dave and his character. And of course, I didn't know he was this bad character as he turned out to be, and so they told Maria if she would stay away from Dave, she could have no time at all, but she said no, I'm sticking by my man. First, she was getting three months, but when she said she was sticking by Dave, the judge said he was giving her six months to think about it, because he figured she could start her life over without Dave. But she was in love and she was going to stand by her man, and she ended up going to jail in Saint John. And so she calls me from the courthouse, crying her head off, can I come and get Billy Joe, she's got no one to take care of him, her mum don't want him. So what else am I going to say? I said of course, Maria, I'll come get him. And she asks me to come get Billy Joe and get him in school and stuff, and of course I said I would, so in 1991, Billy Joe comes to live with me."

When Maria got out of jail, she went back to living in the couple's home, where David later joined her.

Detectives embarked on the investigation hoping that this would be a typical missing person case: that Maria, as David had said, had left to take some time off and visit with an old friend in Saint John. Officers who were fond of her genuinely hoped that she would soon reappear, puzzled that anyone had been alarmed, to rejoin her husband and return to her quiet domestic life.

Nevertheless, David's rather odd behavior and his former sister-in-law's comment about "something bad" having happened to Maria roused concern.

On the Monday following David's call, the Miramichi police began talking to Maria's friends to establish some of the basic facts pursued in any missing person situation: Maria's recent state of mind, her current domestic situation as observed by those who knew her best, the likelihood that she would have gone away, where she might have gone—Saint John or elsewhere—and with whom she might be staying. They were looking for which friends or relatives she might have told about her plans and, given David's conflicting state-ments about when she left, wanted to create a timeline of when she was last seen.

In a large, anonymous city, where people live isolated lives and frequently don't bother to know their neighbors, finding people with useful information can be difficult. But Miramichi is a small and old-fashioned place with an old-fashioned sense of community. Weddings, baby showers and wakes are community events. The Miramichi is still a place where kids run in and out of neighbors' kitchens, call home for permission to stay at a friend's for dinner and play outside in groups until dark falls and parents call them in. It's a place of homemade pickles and canned moose meat and salmon on the grill, a place where friends drop in on each other, share meals or go for coffee, regularly check in with each other by phone and keep up with each other's lives and news.

Maria Tanasichuk might live a humble life without even an automobile for transportation, but in one respect she was very rich in her abundance of close and caring friends. Friends who were regularly in touch. Friends who, even though it had been more than two years since B.J.'s death, understood her pain and were still attentive to her grief.

David had given two conflicting dates—January 14, as he'd stated in his initial phone call to the police, and January 12, which he agreed with Constable Seeley was the correct date on which his wife had left for Saint John on the bus. On the 26th, after reporting his wife missing, he told Seeley that he was traveling to Saint John, about three hours away, to look for her, getting his brother to drive him because he didn't have a car.

On the following morning, though, when Detective Cummings stopped by, David Tanasichuk was at his apartment. He said that he'd started for Saint John, his brother had had car trouble and he'd decided that, in any case, he needed to be on the Miramichi in case Maria returned or there was news of her.

When Cummings went to the Tanasichuks' residence to follow up on David's report, he planned, in the unlikely event that he found David Tanasichuk at home, to get David to come down to the station. There, a complete written statement could be obtained regarding the circumstances of Maria's departure: what she was wearing, what she'd packed, what she'd said, the state of their relations, contact information for the person she'd gone to visit. Cummings also wanted to obtain the names, addresses and phone numbers of people who might have useful information about Maria's whereabouts, both on the Miramichi and in Saint John.

He went to the apartment believing that he was on his way to see someone he knew well, someone he considered a friend, having visited the Tanasichuks frequently since B.J.'s death. What he saw when he entered the apartment shocked him. David Tanasichuk, a big, strong outdoorsman who, like Cummings, worked out with weights and prided himself on his physique, was thinner and haggard. While David didn't appear stoned and was able to carry on a conversation, he had the look of a "pill-sick" junkie who was suffering from withdrawal, something with which Cummings, from his years of police work, was very familiar. It seemed obvious to the detective that David, who had flirted with drug use on and off for years despite Maria's efforts to keep him straight, was back to using drugs. He was also edgy and appeared uncomfortable, lacking the easy familiarity usually present during their visits. While he was normally quite a talker, on that occasion he didn't seem to want to talk to Cummings.

The apartment, which Maria always kept impeccably clean, was in serious disarray, a state that Cummings knew would have upset Maria. Despite the fug of cigarette smoke, as the two were constant smokers, Maria was a proud and meticulous housekeeper who rigorously enforced her "leave your shoes at the door or else" rule.

David readily admitted that Maria had been heavily on him for his drug use and that she had been hiding their money so he couldn't get at it to buy drugs. When Cummings tried to gather information to aid them in searching for Maria, asking who Maria had gone to stay with and what clothing and other things she had taken with her, information that might help them gauge how long she planned to be away, David became vague. He reiterated that he thought she had gone to stay with a friend named "Cathy" in Saint John, but still couldn't furnish a last name, an address or a phone number.

David said he wasn't sure what she had taken but that her red and yellow kit bag was missing. Then David added that when Maria left, she had not taken her prescription pills with her.

Otherwise, despite his having expressed concerns serious enough to involve the police and ask for their help, David didn't seem to want to talk about Maria, but only about himself. He admitted to having had a few "setbacks" with drugs and said he was seeing Sylvette Robichaud at the addiction counseling service to deal with the problem. He said that he felt like he was on the verge of a nervous breakdown and like he didn't know what he was doing half the time.

After a few more unsuccessful attempts to obtain information about Maria's departure, Cummings told David that he would need to come to the police station to give a formal statement so they could get details to help them locate Maria. David said that was not a problem and agreed that he would come to the station the following day, January 28, to give a statement.

Cummings left the apartment feeling dissatisfied with the interview and hoping that he would learn more on the following day when David came in to give his statement. Cummings didn't know whether David's vagueness and his apparent lack of anxiety about Maria's whereabouts was the result of impairment due to drug use or a deliberate deception. He also left with very little to go on in terms of how to try and locate Maria.

What Cummings did know, though, from his time spent with the Tanasichuks, was that despite her rough edges and hard attitude toward authority, Maria Tanasichuk was a woman who made, and kept, deep friendships. If David didn't have useful information to offer, some of her close friends probably did.

Later that same morning, Cummings went to see Maria's sister, Sharon Carroll. Sharon confirmed to him that Maria had been increasingly voicing her concerns about David's drug use. Sharon said that during her last conversation with Maria, around the 10th to 13th of January, Maria had told her that she was tired of fighting with David. Sharon also said that Maria had never left before without telling anyone she was leaving and that such behavior would be very much out of character.

In contrast to David's assertion that he had volunteered to leave but Maria had insisted on going instead, it was Sharon's belief that Maria was extremely unlikely to leave the apartment for any length of time. It was the place where Maria had lived so long with her son, B.J. Sharon told him that Maria had a strong sentimental attachment to her son's possessions that were stored there. Stored, Cummings knew, was hardly the operative word. B.J.'s bedroom had remained essentially unchanged from when he had last slept there, except that Maria had turned the room into a shrine for her lost child by adding items including candles, flowers and a memorial Bible given to the couple at B.J.'s funeral.

Sharon also shared another reason why she doubted that Maria would be likely to go away without telling anyone. She said Maria was very excited because Sharon's daughter, Angela, was expecting twins and Maria was going to be the godmother. Sharon said that Maria's close attachment to Angela—although Maria was Angela's aunt, after B.J.'s death the two of them had become more like sisters—and Maria's concern about Angela's difficult pregnancy meant that Maria would be unlikely to leave without telling someone or to stay out of touch for any length of time. Sharon also reported that David and Maria had stood up with Angela at her wedding down in Fredericton, and upon their return, Maria had said that she didn't like being away from home and she was done with traveling.

Following their conversation on the morning of the 27th, Detective Cummings called David again that afternoon to see if there had been any word from Maria. He couldn't reach David, so he left a message confirming that they would meet the following day for an interview. While he waited to interview David, he continued to speak with many people who knew the couple. The nature of the information coming in, and David's unavailability, created an increasing sense of urgency.

After his visit to Sharon Carroll, Cummings went to speak with Maria's best friend, Darlene Gertley. Darlene and Maria had been close friends since becoming neighbors in

1998. They called each other "girlfriend" and normally either saw each other or spoke on the phone daily. There was even a chair in Dave and Maria's living room nicknamed "girlfriend's chair" which was where Darlene sat when she was visiting.

In the Fall of 1997, Darlene had moved to Miramichi from Prince Edward Island with her husband, who was a chef. Her husband worked long hours. She was pregnant and isolated, living in a new province and desperately lonely. Darlene and her husband rented an apartment next door to Maria.

"I used to look over, when I put my dog out, and I'd see this brown-haired lady tossing a bone to my dog," Darlene said. "And I was lonely and I used to think, 'Gosh, I wish you'd toss me a bone someday.' Then, after I gave birth to my son, when he was about six weeks old, I decided to take a walk down to the store on the corner, and I took my son in the stroller, and I walked down and I walked past their house and she said hi and I said hi and I looked down and didn't say anything more 'cause I'm really quite shy, and I was pushing the stroller up onto the porch and I dropped the baby's blanket and didn't notice that I'd done it, and I was unlocking the door and there she was with the blanket.

"From that day on, we became friends—would you like to go for coffee, let's go for a walk, you know. She was beautiful. She was thoughtful. She had a large heart. She loved her husband. She loved her son. She loved me as a friend. At that point, I had lost my twin brother. I'd lost him in a car accident, and Maria knew I needed friendship and someone to talk to. I'd moved to a French place, and I spoke only English. I was shy and housebound. Maria was the only real friend I had, and she was constant."

By the time she spoke with the detective, Darlene had become deeply concerned about Maria's well-being and had become convinced by David's behavior and his responses to her inquiries about Maria's whereabouts that something awful had happened to her dear friend. She had already shared those concerns in phone calls to Maria's sister, Sharon, and to Maria's ex-sister-in-law, Cindy Richardson, neither of whom initially shared her anxiety. Now, relieved that she finally had someone to share her concerns about Maria's absence with, she spoke very frankly with Cummings. She told the detective that she was deeply worried about her friend and had been for many days. As the days progressed, she had been making increasingly anxious phone calls to David and to Maria's friends about Maria's long absence. Then she shared the chronology of her last contacts with Maria.

She had been in Prince Edward Island (PEI) from January 10th to the 13th, visiting her terminally-ill mother, and she had borrowed money from Maria for a rental car to make the trip. She said Maria's relationship with David had been deteriorating recently because of David's increasing drug use. Because Maria was so very depressed and constantly anxious about her failing marital situation, Darlene had urged Maria to come on the trip with her and get a change of scenery. Maria had declined, saying she didn't want to leave her house or David, because she was concerned about David's drug use and thought she ought to be there in case he needed her.

On the day Darlene returned, January 13, she had stopped by Maria's at around 6:30 in the evening. David and Maria were both home and Maria was in her pajamas. On the 14th, Darlene had been next door visiting Maria's neighbors, and decided to drop in to see Maria. Maria was fine, but David was on the couch with one of his migraine headaches. There was tension in the air and it appeared that the couple was not getting along, so Darlene left.

Darlene told the detective that Maria had been quite depressed for about a month, because she felt that her relationship with David was worsening. David had been getting more deeply into drugs, they had been fighting about his absences and the money he was spending and Maria was doing everything in her power to stop him. Darlene explained that Maria had long believed that because she'd been able to kick her own drug habit through willpower, David could do the same with her help. Her lack of success was sapping her energy and she rarely left the apartment.

Darlene said that she had returned the following day, January 15, for coffee with Maria, at which time the two of them made plans for a shopping trip on the 17th to return some unwanted Christmas gifts. That evening, Maria was complaining about a sore thumb, the result of a scuffle she'd had with David over money the night before. On leaving, Darlene gave her a kiss and hug and promised to repay the money she owed when they got together on the 17th.

The following day, January 16, when Darlene stopped by to visit Maria, David answered the door. He told her Maria wasn't home and that she'd gone to a christening with Pauline and Sandy. David's statement puzzled Darlene. Maria had not mentioned attending any christening when they were together the previous day, though it was something Maria would normally have shared, and Darlene thought she knew Maria's friends and didn't know of anyone named Pauline or Sandy. At his request, she gave David a ride to his friend Donnie Trevors's house.

On the 17th, when they were scheduled to go shopping together, Darlene called Maria several times to make arrangements but got no answer. She left messages and when they weren't returned she went to the house but found there was no one home. She continued to telephone her friend or visit Maria's house daily, but Darlene's calls weren't answered and she never found Maria at home.

The interviews by Constable Seeley and Detectives Cummings and Dewey Gillespie in the days after David reported Maria missing produced numerous other dates and stories about Maria's schedule and the time of her departure. They also produced some disturbing revelations about David's behavior regarding Maria's property in the two-week interval between the date Maria allegedly left for Saint John and the date when her husband reported her missing. The Miramichi detectives hoped that the information they would learn from David's interview would explain the discrepancies and finally give them a set of hard facts to go on in their search for Maria Tanasichuk.

To improve their chances of locating Maria, at the same time that they were interviewing witnesses and trying to obtain a detailed statement from David, the Miramichi police sent Maria's description and what details they had about her disappearance to news media and police departments in Canada via CPIC, the Canadian Police Information Center. Her mysterious disappearance and recognition of the Tanasichuk name from prior cases involving David as well as the story of B.J.'s death quickly grabbed media attention. Stories about Maria's disappearance began to appear in newspapers and the Miramichi community grew more and more concerned.

Chapter 4

Till Drugs Do Us Part

Shortly before noon on the day scheduled for his interview, David called Detective Sergeant Paul Fiander to say that he was in Saint John, where he'd gotten a list of Maria's old friends and was planning to contact them to see if anyone had heard from her. He reported that he would be returning to Miramichi either late that night or on the following day. Later, he called the Miramichi dispatch and told them that if Detective Cummings was looking for him, he had gone to his mother's in Saint John. He left a contact phone number.

Later that morning, David called Maria's friend, Darlene, and told her he was in Saint John. Then he tried to convince her that she was wrong about the dates on which she had told police she had last seen Maria, and that she had last seen Maria at the apartment on January 12. Darlene reminded him that she was away visiting her mother on that date and also of their conversation on the 16th, when she'd stopped by and he'd told her Maria wasn't home because she'd gone to a christening. David disagreed, saying that Maria had gone to Amanda Malley's baby shower that day.

Concerned by the odd nature of the phone call, Darlene phoned Detective Cummings and repeated the conversation to him.

David also called the ex-husband of his upstairs neighbors and asked him to feed the Tanasichuk's dog while he was away. While David was in Saint John, he was contacted by a reporter from Global News, Dave Crase. Crase had seen the police press release about Maria Tanasichuk being missing and had recognized the names both from David Tanasichuk's past brushes with the law and from the events surrounding B.J.'s death. Crase contacted Tanasichuk and asked for an interview. At first, David refused the interview, but when Crase pressured him, suggesting that refusal would demonstrate his lack of concern about Maria's whereabouts and welfare, David agreed.

He gave the television interview to Global News from his mother's house in Saint John. It appeared on the six o'clock news on the evening of January 28. In the segment, David told the interviewer that things between himself and Maria were fine when she left. He described the day she left and said that he believed Maria had taken the bus to Saint John and he presumed that she had taken a cab to the bus station. David said that his concern for his wife began after he hadn't heard from her for four or five days, and he told the reporter that the police suspected some of Maria's friends were lying for her and helping her to hide. Then he made a plea to the general public for information about his wife's whereabouts.

With David out of town and unable to be interviewed, the detectives continued to speak with the Tanasichuks' friends and neighbors. They learned that what others were saying was inconsistent in many respects with what they'd been hearing from David.

Police officers have a motto (from former US President Ronald Reagan) that they operate by: "Trust, then verify." In any investigation, given the uncertainties, inconsistencies, faulty memories and the way that full information can often take repeated interviews to obtain, detectives like to have multiple sources to establish any facts on which they're going to rely. This meant that while David Tanasichuk was Maria's husband and therefore presumed to be the person closest to her and most likely to have the information they needed to help locate her, they wanted to check what he was telling them against what they could learn from her friends, relatives and the Tanasichuks' neighbors.

In this case, they were also forced to turn to other sources in seeking information useful in locating Maria, because despite the concern he had voiced about his missing wife, David had thus far been unwilling or unable to provide much of substance that the police could use in trying to locate her. They had no idea what she was wearing when last seen or what she'd taken with her. They didn't have a name and address for the friend she'd gone to visit. They needed an explanation as to why, if she had packed luggage to be gone for a week, she'd left behind something as important as her prescription medicines. Even something as basic as the day she'd left town was uncertain.

The investigators suspected that David's vagueness might be due to his admitted issues with drug use. A person under the influence of drugs can have a fuzzy memory and be unable to recall dates and times. But a person who expresses deep concern about a disappearance, yet seems unwilling to assist in investigating that disappearance, also raises suspicion. He had spoken about providing names and phone numbers but hadn't provided them. He had agreed to an interview but instead left town. He had said during his television appearance that he believed her friends were hiding her, yet the friends police had spoken with had not heard from her. The significant dates he was giving the police differed from those of other witnesses. And now, if Maria's friend Darlene was telling the truth, he was trying to persuade people the police might interview that their own recall of significant dates was faulty.

In his brilliant book about homicide detectives in Baltimore, Maryland, *Homicide: A Year on the Killing Streets*, David Simon observes the following from the police officers whom he has interviewed:

> It is a God-given truth: Everyone lies. And this most basic of axioms has three corollaries:
> A. Murderers lie because they have to.
> B. Witnesses and other participants lie because they think they have to.
> C. Everyone else lies for the sheer joy of it, and to uphold a general principle that under no circumstances do you provide accurate information to a cop.[6]

In truth, there are plenty of honest witnesses. But even with well-meaning witnesses, obtaining information and then determining if it is "truth" is a complicated business.

Good people tell the truth—or try to—or tell the truth as they remember it. Witnesses may tell as much of the truth as they think will reflect favorably on them and maybe leave out the parts that reflect poorly on them. Perhaps they were under the influence of drugs or alcohol and have poor memories of what happened. Sometimes, as with the case of a man with a reputation for violence like David Tanasichuk, they're afraid to tell the truth because of who the parties are and their fear of retaliation.

In some cases, witnesses may know something but they're actually unaware of the significance of what they know. Sometimes their memories are vague or unreliable and it takes multiple interviews to jog the information back into consciousness and coherence. Sometimes it can take more than one interview to build the trust necessary to get witnesses to talk freely and share what they know. Detectives are often forced to walk a fine line between re-interviewing in order to conduct a competent investigation and over-interviewing and risking the charge of harassing the witness.

All of these factors combine to complicate the investigator's task. In this case, the murky nature of the information available, combined with the deep concern and fear for her safety expressed by Maria's friends and relatives, made the detectives certain that Maria's disappearance warranted further investigation.

On January 28, after hearing David's former sister-in-law's ominous words at the courthouse about "something bad" happening to Maria and following his conversations with Maria's sister and best friend, Detective Cummings spoke with Amanda Malley, whose grandmother was the Tanasichuks' next door neighbor. It was her baby shower that David had told Darlene Gertley, in their telephone conversation, that Maria was attending on the 16th, as a reason why she wasn't at home when Darlene called.

Amanda said she considered herself a close friend of Maria's, seeing Maria a few times a week and speaking with her on the phone even more often. She told the detective that her baby shower had been held in November and Maria had been there. She had had her baby on January 7. On the 12th, she had spoken with Maria around midday and they'd made plans for Amanda to bring the baby for a visit the following day. Maria had congratulated Amanda on the baby and made no mention of any plans to go to Saint John. On the 13th, the baby was sick, so the visit did not take place.

Asked about the state of the relationship between Maria and David, Amanda told the detective that the last time she had seen Maria was on January 4 at the B.J. Breau Basketball Fundraiser, an annual event held in memory of Maria's son, B.J., to raise money for scholarships. For the first time, David, who enjoyed social events and loved being the life of the party, did not attend. Maria, who did attend, seemed sad and subdued and said that the couple was not getting along well because David was back on drugs again. Maria told her friend that she'd given David an ultimatum—either he got clean or she was going to leave him.

As an aside in their interview, referring to Maria's passionate attachment to her jewelry collection, Amanda Malley told Cummings that if any of Maria's jewelry was still in the house, he should consider it a serious problem, because Maria would never go away for any period of time and leave her jewelry behind with David.

After he left the interview, following a hunch born of his long experience with drug users descending into addiction, Cummings visited a pawn shop on King George Highway. The proprietor confirmed that on and around January 16 and 17, David Tanasichuk had been into the shop and, over the course of those visits, he had sold some jewelry outright and pawned a number of pieces of women's gold jewelry, including several rings and a chain with a pendant reading "#1 Wife."

It's a common thing and something Cummings had seen far too much of in his career—the devastation that drug use can cause a family. As the addiction takes hold and use becomes more frequent, the allure of drugs can become so powerful it outweighs duty to spouses and children, dragging users down until they've destroyed everything around them. First it's a bit of the grocery money, then money to pay the bills and the rent, all accompanied by tears and promises to stop, along with endless lies and deception. There is no liar like a drug user.

And it doesn't stop there. Far too often, a woman will come home to find the house missing a piece of furniture or that the television has been sold to buy drugs. As the need for the next fix comes to control the addict's life, he or she will sell the car, the washing machine, the children's beds, their clothes, occasionally even the children themselves—anything to satisfy that craving. And now Cummings was hearing that David was selling or pawning Maria's treasured jewelry the day after Darlene Gertley said she had last seen Maria at home in her apartment.

There was no way to ignore what he was hearing. Every interview, every report, every story that friends and neighbors were telling him increased the urgency of Cummings's need to sit down with his friend David and get the straight story.

David's initial statements and interviews with family, friends and neighbors had raised so many questions. What had been the true state of their marriage in recent weeks and months? What day had Maria actually left? What had she been wearing? What had she taken in her suitcase—clothes for a few days, a few weeks? Had she in fact taken her jewelry? David had mentioned prescriptions, so what had her state of mind and health been? Might she have told him she was going to Saint John and gone to stay with friends somewhere else? If she wasn't in touch with him, who might she have been in touch with? Could he provide the names and addresses of people she might have gone to stay with? Had he recalled Cathy's last name?

On January 29, at around 2:00 P.M., three full days after he'd first reported his wife missing, David Tanasichuk came to the police department and sat down with Cummings to give a statement. He had a miserable cold and requested a paper cup as a place to spit phlegm. Before embarking on his questions, to show Maria's husband that they were taking the situation seriously, Cummings showed David the reports in the provincial papers of Maria's disappearance, noting that usually the papers don't react to missing persons so quickly.

"It's out of character for her, we told them. Run this story," Cummings said. Then he asked David to start wherever he thought relevant and describe the circumstances leading up to Maria's disappearance.

David then described in detail how Maria would come with him to his counseling sessions with addiction services and how Maria was reluctant to give him any time to himself, so the counselor had proposed that one of them should get away from the other. He explained that initially he had wanted to stay at his brother Joe's house, but Maria disliked Joe's girlfriend and insisted that there would be "too many girls around." He had also suggested going to his mother's in Saint John, but again Maria believed that there would be a problem with too many women. Maria countered that she would travel to Saint John instead and stay with her friend Cathy.

David said he had phoned home on the 11th from the pay phone in the lobby of a grocery store to ask if he should get more dog food. She told him that they didn't need it, they still had half a bag and added that she would be leaving the following day on the bus. Initially, he thought that her threat to leave was just a ploy to make him come home, so he went back to their apartment. When he realized she was serious, they discussed her plan to leave. He told the detective that Maria thought it would be better for him to be at home where people were around who could look after him.

David said that the following morning, January 12, he brought Maria coffee in bed and they discussed her plans—how she was glad to be seeing her old friends and maybe she'd go drinking with them. She already had some stuff packed and she said she was leaving on the bus at 2:00. They promised to always be good to each other. Soon he left to go to his friend's house to work on his three-wheeler. When he got back around five, Maria was gone. She hadn't left any note, but she'd said she would be gone about a week and that she'd be in touch with his mother, who lived in Saint John, so he should call his mother if he wanted to contact her.

Cummings asked whether he had heard from her since, or spoken with anyone who had seen her. David said that the closest he'd come to any sighting or word about Maria was that Darlene Gertley claimed to have seen her on the 15th at their house. Since in his version of events Maria had already gone, he thought that this meant Darlene must have been taking too many prescription pills and only imagined it. And no, he told the detective, there were no bank cards or credit cards she might have used that could help track her because he had screwed up their credit.

When Cummings asked for more information about who the person was that Maria had gone to visit, David repeated that her name was Cathy and added that earlier in the month, Maria had had a call from an old friend named Cathy who lived in Saint John. When he'd gone down to Saint John to look for Maria, he'd spoken with a friend who had told him it was probably a woman named Cathy Penny.

Getting down to identifying details, Cummings asked what Maria was wearing on the day she left. David said she was still in her pajamas when he left, so he didn't know. He did describe her yellow and black winter jacket in detail and agreed that while he knew nothing about women's pants, he thought she was likely to be wearing jeans and hiking boots. He told Cummings Maria would have had over eight hundred dollars with her, money she had taken (David actually said that Maria had *stolen* the money) from their safe, funds they had been saving for their headstones.

Then he described Maria's tattoos. On her right breast there was an open locket that read "In Memory of B.J." and the date of her son's death, with his high school graduation picture. She had a pink bunny on her right shoulder, a trillium flower on her left ankle and the name "Billy Joe" on her left forearm.

Asked if he knew for sure that Maria had taken the bus, David said he'd considered calling the bus station, but decided that wouldn't prove anything because he'd taken the bus many times and knew you could buy a ticket on the bus. She probably didn't pre-purchase a ticket because she was a homebody who never left the house except for grocery shopping, bill paying or cleaning B.J.'s grave.

David described Maria's jewelry, saying that she wore a lot of it, often fifteen or twenty rings at a time, which Cummings agreed he remembered seeing in the past, and David told the investigator that he hadn't seen any of her jewelry around the house so he presumed she had taken all of her jewelry with her, including some rings that had belonged to B.J. that she wore for sentimental reasons. He described some of Maria's favorite pieces in detail.

Afterward, they discussed the idea of Cummings coming by the apartment and looking at pictures of Maria, to get a better idea of what jewelry she had and often wore. Later they did this, and David used some photographs of Maria wearing her jewelry to help remember what she usually wore, including her *90% Devil* pendant.

What she had left behind, though, was her prescription medication, David said, along with the red devil teddy bear that she called "Baby B" for her son B.J. and her "sooky" blanket that she wrapped around herself for comfort when she curled up on the couch. David told Cummings that Maria kissed the bear every night, made him kiss the bear and would not go to sleep unless it was on her pillow.

Because state of mind is such an important factor in evaluating any disappearance, they next discussed David and Maria's relationship at the time she left. Although the interview up to that point had been generally cordial, things got tense when the detective tried to explore the state of the relationship between husband and wife.

Cummings reminded David that he had told Constable Seeley that things hadn't been good between them because of Maria's refusal to give him space. David agreed, saying that things actually hadn't been good between them for years, but that it had gotten much worse after Maria was diagnosed with Hepatitis C back in late August or September. While the couple hadn't had physical fights, they had argued often about David's drug use. David resented her interference, which was persistent and stifling, even though he understood that she did it out of genuine concern for his health. Maria would tell him to go look in the mirror, because he was killing himself. But he couldn't see it, even after his son came to visit and his altered appearance made the boy cry.

David admitted sometimes injecting hydromorphone, readily acknowledging buying pills on the street as well. He had last used drugs, he told Cummings, about a week prior to the interview.

He had started getting worried after Maria had been gone for a week without him hearing from her, and around the 17th or 18th he began calling people, though he couldn't provide the names of the people he'd called, referring Cummings to the list he'd given to Constable Seeley and the people he'd contacted in Saint John. David said that he had a list of the people he'd contacted at home, pages and pages of them, which they agreed Cummings would come to the apartment to pick up.

David had brought to the interview two prescription bottles for pills prescribed to Maria. Both were dated January 6. The first was an antidepressant. The bottle had initially contained sixty pills and the label instructed Maria to take one half tablet daily for the first seven days. When Cummings later counted the pills, there were fifty-five and one half. The second prescription was for an anti-anxiety medication. That bottle was empty. The recent prescriptions led to a discussion of Maria's state of mind, and David said that she was tattered. Since her Hepatitis diagnosis, she'd been convinced that her life was over. Maria, he said, cared more about what happened to him than about anything else in the world.

When Cummings started going back through his notes of their conversation and writing out the details for a formal statement, David objected and became angry, stating that none of the stuff about their relationship or his drug use was going to help them find Maria.

In response to the question, "What do you think happened to Maria?" David admitted to being of two minds. A part of him thought she was staying with a friend, maybe had hooked up with someone, maybe was back on drugs herself. Another part worried that something might have happened to her. What he wanted, he said, was for someone to come and tell him she was all right.

When Cummings attempted to explore the possibility that something *had* happened to Maria, asking, "What if she's not all right?" David replied angrily and threatened to walk out. Then he began to cry.

After David's statement was reviewed, agreed on and signed, Detective Cummings then made the distraught man a promise. He said, "I want to find Maria as much as you do, okay? And I will find Maria, all right? I will."

Chapter 5

Four Heads Are Better Than One

Following David Tanasichuk's interview on January 29, Detective Cummings drove David back to his apartment. The next day, Cummings returned there to pick up the list of people David had contacted and to get the contact information for a friend of Maria's in Ontario who had been mentioned during the interview. The man he found at home that morning seemed to have undergone yet another dramatic change. This was neither the edgy man with glazed eyes the detective had found following David's phone call to report Maria missing on the 27th, nor the coughing, spitting, highly emotional, weeping and sometimes argumentative man he'd interviewed the day before.

On January 30, despite there being no new information regarding his missing wife, David Tanasichuk acted lighthearted and cheerful. He chatted easily about drug dealing on the river and then asked Cummings for a favor, saying he had a problem with which he needed help. He said two of his friends had given him a hydroponic plant-growing setup to hold for them because they were afraid they were about to be raided by the police. Then he'd grown nervous himself about the risks of being found with the equipment and had thrown it away, only to find that it was worth $5000. He was concerned, he told Cummings, that his friends might seek retribution. Would Cummings be willing to give him a fake appearance notice so that it would look like the materials had been seized by the police?

When Cummings complied and produced the requested appearance notice, David had another question. Since Maria was gone, he wondered, was he still allowed to have Maria's guns in the house? Cummings told David that, in his opinion, the guns were okay because Maria still lived there, but he offered to run the question by the department's firearms officer.

During the entire time that Cummings was at the Tanasichuks' apartment, despite the fact he was there to obtain a list of people who might have information about Maria, David never mentioned her except to inquire about her guns. Far from acting like an anxious husband deeply concerned about his missing wife, he acted like someone relieved that he'd gotten over a hurdle—like the police interview he'd been avoiding—who believed his responses had been satisfactory and he was in the clear.

It was at that point, based on David's bubbly, relaxed demeanor and conduct, that Cummings's suspicions about David as a suspect firmed up. A review of the information gathered thus far in the investigation reinforced that feeling.

After consulting with the department's firearms officer, Cummings returned later in the day to collect all the guns and ammunition in the house, to be held until Maria's return. David handed over four guns and ammunition, stating that that was everything they had.

Back at their offices, the detectives met in the conference room with their supervising sergeant, Paul Fiander,
to discuss the case, sharing the information each of them
had gathered from all sources, including David Tanasichuk's
interview, and testing the information David had supplied
against that which had come from other sources. Once it was
all out, they would decide how to proceed in their search for
Maria Tanasichuk.

In evaluating the state of the couple's relationship, the
detectives shared what they had learned from Maria's friends
and neighbors—that while David and Maria had been a couple seemingly very much in love, since B.J.'s death Maria had
experienced long bouts of depression, making her emotionally unavailable, while David had increasingly taken refuge in
drugs. His drug use, in turn, had made Maria hyper-vigilant
and suspicious. She wanted to know where he was going whenever he left the house. She had taken to inspecting his body, his
pockets and even his socks when he returned home, looking
for drugs, drug paraphernalia or signs of drug use. Maria was
willing to do anything to help the man who was, witnesses told
the investigators, the center of her universe. A man she had
been willing to go to jail for, even if it meant being separated
from her young son rather than end the relationship.

David's response to Maria's anxious questions and her
efforts at supervision had been to stay away from home,
often for days at a time, so that he could indulge his drug
habit without being questioned. His behavior and deteriorating physical condition deeply worried Maria and she had
taken to calling his friends to ask if he was with them. To
prevent him from using their scarce cash for drugs, she had
started hiding their money in her bra.

Despite her many years of total devotion to David,
recently Maria had seemed to be reaching a terminal point,

according to those closest to her. She told friends that she had grown sick of the arguing, the fights, David's absences, drugged-out hazes and deception. After David had been too stoned to get off the couch and attend B.J.'s memorial fundraiser on January 4, Maria announced she'd had enough.

Something detectives do when they're dealing with a crime victim, or, as in this case, where all they *knew* they had was a disappearance and thus a *suspected* crime victim, is to build a profile of the victim so that they know what would be her typical behavior, habits and routines. This profile, known as "victimology," is created by speaking with people who knew the victim, as well as from information learned from searching the victim's dwelling and reviewing phone, computer and other domestic records. In Maria's case, where they knew that she was housebound and didn't use credit cards, have an employer or own a car, their information came primarily from speaking with her sister, her niece, close friends who were regularly in touch and her neighbors.

From these sources, they had learned many details about Maria that didn't mesh with what David had told them. Maria's niece and her best friend both told investigators that Maria was deeply attached to the little red devil bear that had been her last gift from her dead son and would never leave home without it. David himself had said that Maria kissed it every night and couldn't sleep without Baby B on her pillow.

Multiple witnesses confirmed Maria's attachment to her apartment because it was where she had spent so many years raising her son. Because of her fondness for B.J.'s memory and his possessions, people told the investigators, she was very unlikely to be willing to leave the apartment for any length of time. Her niece reported that after Maria and David had journeyed to Saint John for her wedding, a trip on which Maria had taken her little bear and her "sooky" blanket,

Maria told people in Miramichi that she wasn't interested in ever going to Saint John again.

It was not just her attachment to the apartment that made Maria's reported decision to go to Saint John so suspicious. Maria's former sister-in-law, Cindy Richardson, told investigators that when she was at the cemetery visiting B.J.'s grave, it was untended. Maria had been very faithful about that.

Maria's next door neighbor, John Paquet, an avuncular former military man who hunted with David and was very fond of Maria, reported that Maria had explicitly told him that if one of them were ever to leave, it would have to be David, because the place held too many memories for her.

Cindy Richardson had told Cummings, "Darlene Gertley called me and said she was worried about Maria and had I heard from her? I'd called Maria on the 11th, because the week before was [the fundraiser] and I know she was in bad shape then, and she told me Dave was back on the shit again, and she wanted to get back home to check on Dave, to see if he was still home, worried that he'd taken off. So she didn't want to hang around and talk to people...Maria was real run-down looking. She had circles under her eyes and she was so stressed out and she hadn't slept for days and who knew if she ate? And I hugged her and kissed her and said, Maria, call me anytime, you know. I'll be there for you. So on the 11th, I called her, and that's the last time we talked.

"So Darlene and I figured it had been enough time, and the first thing I thought of was, "I'm calling Saint John. So here I am calling up Saint John...I think this was the 23rd or something. And I told mum Maria was supposed to have gone to Saint John, and mum said, 'Funny, I haven't seen her. If Maria's in town, she'll surely come to see me or [her brother-in-law].' So mum said she'd get [the brother-in-law] and Billy to go around and check up with old friends if any-one had seen her. And nobody had seen hide nor tail of her."

What investigators are looking for, in the case of a missing person, is whether she has departed in significant ways from her usual behavior. Nearly every aspect of the story David was telling them marked a significant departure. It seemed unlikely to the investigators that Maria, who spent days at a time huddling in her pajamas on the sofa and who was so strongly attached to her apartment, would suddenly decide to leave town. It seemed improbable that a woman who regularly spoke by phone to her sister, her niece and her close friends and visited with them frequently would leave town without a word to anyone, or that she would be gone for two weeks without being in contact with anyone she knew either in Miramichi or in Saint John, where she still had many friends.

It seemed suspicious that a woman who, only a little more than a week before her sudden departure, had con-sulted her doctor for medicine to help her with anxiety and depression would leave town without it; yet David had given the medicine bottles, one barely touched, the other empty, to Cummings and reported that she'd left them behind.

Investigators found no one who knew of Maria taking any trips without David; just a week before, despite her dis-couragement and depression and the fact that they had been arguing frequently, Maria had been fearful of leaving David alone when he might need her and she had refused to leave for a mere three days with her best friend, Darlene.

Given how attached to her jewelry collection her friends said that Maria was, they felt she would never leave her cher-ished jewelry behind. Even David had said she wouldn't do that. Yet immediately after the last date on which anyone had seen Maria, David had been pawning pieces of jewelry that he specifically told Detective Cummings that Maria had taken with her.

And then there was that small, but telling, comment that Paul Fiander had noticed while monitoring Tanasichuk's interview with Cummings from another room. During their discussion about Maria's jewelry, her attachment to it and her habits about wearing it, Tanasichuk had said: "...See, Maria was the type where one week she'd wear them all and the next week she'd wear none or just a couple." Maria *was*. David had not used the word *is*, suggesting a present connection, but *was*, suggesting that Maria, and her choices about what jewelry she would select and wear, was a thing of the past. This comment acquired greater significance when meshed with what they were learning about the fate of some of Maria's jewelry. In his book on statement analysis, *I Know You Are Lying*, Mark McClish observes, "One way that people's words will betray them is through verb tenses...It may also be that by talking in the past tense, a person will reveal he is being deceptive. Listen to the verb tenses being used in a statement. Inconsistencies in verb tenses can show you what a person is really saying."[7]

There was another disturbing piece of information that was distinctly at odds with the story David was telling. While Cummings was in that interview room with David, the detective bureau had received an urgent call from the addiction counseling service at Miramichi Hospital.

In his initial statement to Constable Seeley, David said his counselor at the addiction counseling service had told the couple that they needed to spend some time apart. David Tanasichuk had reiterated that information during the formal interview, explaining in detail the discussion that he and Maria had had about who would leave and where they would go to gain the time apart their counselor had recommended.

Detective Sergeant Fiander, who received the call from the addiction counseling service, learned it was prompted by the newspaper article about Maria's disappearance and the concerns it raised at the agency regarding Maria's safety. The addiction counseling service director told Fiander that at the beginning of his treatment, David Tanasichuk had signed a contract with his counselor, agreeing that if his wife or his counselor saw signs of "relapse, agitated, restless temper, aggression of voice, missed appointments without calling to cancel or of *risk to society*," he gave them permission to call the police.

The call was made pursuant to that contract and the counseling service's "risk to third party" policy. The caller informed the police that at prior appointments, David Tanasichuk had stated that sometimes he got so angry he wanted to hurt people, sometimes to the point where he felt like killing someone, and one of the reasons for his drug use was that it took away those urges. The addiction counseling service had received calls from Maria twice during December, expressing concern about David's drug use and her fear that he might hurt himself or someone else.

David had missed two appointments in January. When he did attend an appointment on January 23, he had come without Maria and didn't want to talk about his wife, ducking counselor Sylvette Robichaud's queries about Maria's absence. At that appointment, Robichaud observed that David seemed like a different man. He discussed with her his interest in writing an article on his drug abuse and his hopes that such an article might be helpful to other drug users. Despite his statement that he wasn't on drugs, Robichaud felt that he had been using that day and she terminated the session early because his impairment made further discussion futile. As he was leaving, he also violated the boundaries of such a session by attempting to embrace her. Robichaud further reported that she had never told the Tanasichuks that they needed to spend time apart, other than suggesting the occasional hour apart to give each other some space.

Because of the initial confusion about the date of Maria's disappearance, the investigators had been diligent in trying to find witnesses who could establish the last date when she had been seen in Miramichi. In their interviews, investigators had identified three people who had seen or spoken with Maria on January 15. Her next door neighbor, John Paquet, had spoken to her that morning when she came outside to see if the mail had arrived. He was certain of the date because Paquet was waiting for his guide's license, which arrived the following day. Maria's niece in Fredericton had spoken to her on the phone that afternoon, a call that had been interrupted by someone at the door. Finally, Darlene had had coffee with Maria that evening, and at that time the two friends had arranged a shopping trip for the 17th.

The investigators then looked at the information David Tanasichuk had given them about the date of Maria's departure. He had been very specific in detailing their conversations on January 11, the day before Maria left, and his activities on the 12th, the day she had allegedly taken the bus to Saint John. He had gotten up first and brought Maria her coffee in bed. She had not yet dressed at the time he was ready to leave for his friend Donnie Trevors's house, where he was going to work on his ATV. She had her bag open on the floor and had begun to pack. David had asked if she was really going and when she said she was, they had embraced and promised to always be good to each other and then he had left. When he returned, Maria was gone.

Why was it, then, that in subsequent days, her friend Darlene would have visited her at the residence twice? Why would Maria have made plans to go shopping with Darlene if she was planning to leave town? Why would she have failed to mention her planned departure to her sister, her best friend, to Cindy Richardson or to her niece, when they spoke on the phone?

Perhaps more interesting was the question of why David had told Darlene, when she stopped by on the 16th, that Maria wasn't home not because she'd left to go to Saint John, but because she'd gone to a baby shower. Why had he told her sister that she'd gone to Saint John on the 19th and would be back around the 25th? Why had he told another acquaintance that Maria had left on the 20th?

A question all of the officers raised, as they sat around the conference table, was why David had chosen the 26th, two weeks after her supposed departure for Saint John, to become worried enough to report Maria missing?

In part, their interviews suggested, the pressure had come from the increasing level of concern expressed by her sister, her friends and neighbors, who, as many days passed without a sign of Maria, had been phoning the apartment frequently or stopping by, looking for her. But another, more disturbing, explanation also presented itself to these seasoned outdoorsmen. The weather that January had been unseasonably dry. Between January 14 and January 26, the total snowfall was less than two inches. On the 26th, though, they finally had a significant snowstorm during which nearly nine inches fell. Another eight fell the following day. If, as they were beginning to suspect, David was responsible for something ominous happening to Maria and had disposed of her body somewhere in the woods surrounding the city, the tracks of his distinctive three-wheeler, his footprints and her body would still have been visible on the ground between the 15th and the 26th. After the 26th, those tracks would have been wiped out and the body buried under deep snow.

With no idea what they were looking at—whether Maria might have suffered harm at home or elsewhere—the detectives determined that they needed to search the Tanasichuks' apartment. Their decision to search had dual purposes: first, there was the possibility that the apartment might be a crime scene and second, even if a search suggested that harm had not befallen Maria there, her residence might yield further information about Maria's whereabouts, her mindset and what clothing and possessions of hers were present. A search would also help them identify what items were missing from the apartment—information which they could get from Maria's friends—which might corroborate or contradict the information they'd received.

They immediately went to work on crafting a search warrant and supporting affidavit. Not knowing what they were looking for made the task complicated, for they had to anticipate, and describe in enough detail to meet legal standards, a wide variety of items and areas (the apartment, out-buildings, trash cans, basement, common areas, the yard and the Tanasichuks' vehicles) to be included within the scope of the warrant. The investigation didn't stop while they were writing the warrant. While some of the team went to work on the documents, others went back out into the community to continue to interview witnesses who might have information about Maria.

Although the search warrant for the apartment had the highest priority, they also had to prepare warrants for Maria's jewelry and the pawn and sales records at the pawn shop. They had to prepare warrants for Maria's prescription records and arrange to interview her doctor. They needed a warrant for records at the addiction counseling service.

Someone also had to do a follow-up interview there and get a statement. They still had to decide, from a myriad of possibilities, where they should next focus their efforts to locate Maria Tanasichuk, while their current to-do list was already growing long.

At this point, the investigation was no longer regarded as simply an attempt to locate a missing person. Nor, though the police had to consider the possibility, did this look like a case of suicide, even though witnesses agreed that Maria had been depressed. The pattern of lies David Tanasichuk had told, coupled with the information received from witnesses and their victim analysis which suggested that Maria had departed significantly from all of her normal patterns of behavior, made the investigators feel strongly that they were looking at a potential domestic homicide, with David Tanasichuk as their primary suspect.

Chapter 6

The Focus

With a suspect, the investigation into Maria's disappearance and likely murder could get fully under way. At the center of the investigation would be the supervising officer in the criminal investigations division, Detective Sergeant Paul Fiander. Originally from Cape Breton, Paul Fiander was a tall, handsome man with that quiet air of confidence and authority that the police call "command presence." Colleagues described him as a natural leader and a man who was fundamentally fair. They respected his dedication to the job and his ability to put mission before ego, which led him, when the Miramichi police department was formed, to leave his job as chief in the nearby town of Blackville and begin again as a constable in the newly formed department. STRANGE THING TO DO

It would be Fiander's job to listen to each member of the team, assess their suggestions and direct the investigative strategy. It was also his job, with Greg Scott's assistance, to keep the files in the case. "Keeping the files" is one of those phrases that sounds so mundane and unimportant it makes a person's eyes glaze over, but it is in fact at the critical heart of any criminal case. Police personnel may come and go—they leave, retire, move away. Their memories fade. They die. Cases may take years to come to a final resolution. In the end, it is the quality of the work as reflected in the case files—that dated, signed, detailed and carefully reviewed compilation of interviews, photographs, videos, evidence, evidence lists and lab reports—that ultimately results in a successful resolution of a criminal case.

Brian Cummings might be a brilliant interviewer with superb people skills, but if he didn't document the interviews, create a legal paper trail for essential documents and get properly obtained statements from important witnesses, what he's done may not be available for the crown prosecutor's case months or years down the road or critical statements may not be admissible. Dewey Gillespie may know everyone in the province of New Brunswick by face, name and personal history (or so it sometimes seems), but if his endearing, easy ways get them to confide in him and then he doesn't record it and it doesn't go into the right box, all that talent and those long hours spent won't make any difference to the final resolution of the case. And if Greg Scott, that insightful document analyst and superb writer of warrants, doesn't find the necessary information in the files to persuade a judge to issue the warrant, his talents are wasted because he has nothing to work with.

Detective Brian Cummings was the lead investigator. Cummings was a tall man with shoulders so broad that if he bought an off-the-rack jacket to fit them, it swam on the rest of a body he kept lean through running and working with weights. He had a perpetual kinetic energy that suggested he was about to jump even when he was seated at his desk, and even when he was on the computer, he was usually also on the phone. A relentless practical joker and a chronic tease, he was also a superb interviewer, a keen observer and a natural leader. He was easy to talk to and easy to trust, a man who made witnesses feel safe talking to him and the bad guys think he understood them. He was a master at subtly weaving essential questions into a dialogue with a suspect so effectively that his subject didn't know what was happening. An instructor in interview and interrogation technique at the provincial police academy, Cummings could watch the video of an interview and pinpoint the moment when a subject decided to lie.

Working with him were Dewey Gillespie and Greg Scott. Gillespie was a large man with graying hair and deep blue eyes. He liked to present as an 'awe, shucks' kind of guy, not too smart, just one of the lads who wanted to help out and do whatever someone else needed done. It was a great act and many a bad guy fell for it. In truth, Gillespie was a walking encyclopedia. If he didn't know everyone in the province, he certainly knew many of them—their family stories, their history, their traumas and their damage. Cross the border two hundred miles away and they'd ask after Dewey.

He hated his cell phone and his gun. He frequently managed to leave them in the pocket of his jacket at the office when he was out in his car, or somewhere in his car when he was at his desk. Gillespie's lumbering gait belied a keen eye and fast reflexes: he was a crack shot and scored a perfect 300 at annual range qualifications on more than one occasion.

Gillespie had an immense well of concern and compassion, which made him the department's go-to guy for the delivery of difficult news. He was also the sex crimes investigator—a great choice because of his kindness and caring. He could make a traumatized person feel safe and comforted and willing to confide, but it was a job that left him with a lot of bad memories. He didn't like to go out in public, he said, because there were always people there who had been victims or perpetrators in cases he investigated.

Gillespie grew up on the river in a large family, his father one of the legendary Miramichi fishing guides, and when he talked about being on the river, he visibly transformed from cautious cop to ecstatic dreamer. He loved fly tying and wrote a book about famous fly tyers of the Miramichi. He and a friend wrote a series of children's stories about Gusbur Glaspie, a lad who grew up on the Miramichi.

Quiet, handsome Greg Scott was the least outgoing of the group. A thoughtful, insightful family man with a deep-seated passion for justice, he hated interviewing but loved working behind the scenes. His compulsive nature was helpful for keeping orderly files. He was the go-to guy for analyzing documents, especially financial documents, for surveillance and undercover work, and for writing persuasive affidavits and watertight warrants that conformed to the law and covered all the bases. Again, it's a job that might sound boring but is essential to the successful progress of investigations and to preserving the integrity of evidence at trial. Scott was described by the other members of the section as humble to a fault. They would also be the first to say that the section would be hard-pressed to function without him.

Once they focused on Maria's disappearance as suspicious and David as a suspect, the investigators acted quickly to draft a warrant, not wanting to let any more time pass during which he might clean up a crime scene or destroy evidence, aware that police were now focused on the situation.

Shortly after midnight on February 1, two days after David's interview at the police station, Constable Dewey Gillespie, accompanied by several patrol officers, knocked on the door of the Tanasichuk apartment. The outside

temperature that night hovered around -13 degrees Celsius
(9 degrees Fahrenheit). Police had been conducting surveillance on the residence so they knew that David Tanasichuk
was home.

When David answered, they presented him with a warrant to search the premises and arrested him for the culpable
homicide of his wife, Maria.

David told the arresting officers he didn't want a lawyer
and was then transported to the Miramichi West police station while investigators began a search of the premises.

There were two reasons for going into the house to conduct the search late at night as they did. The first was tactical:
when you're going to do an arrest and search on a suspect
who has a well-known history of violence, you look to minimize your odds of confronting that violence. Analyzing the
safety or danger of a situation is a critical consideration if an
officer wants to go home alive at the end of the day. While
they believed they'd collected all the guns and ammunition in
the house when they came to remove Maria's weapons—and
while David had said that he'd given them everything—they
couldn't be sure he hadn't hidden one. Nor were guns their
only concern. An avid hunter like David would also have his
bow and numerous hunting knives at hand. Getting to someone while they're dazed and sleepy helps to minimize the risk
of violent confrontation.

The second reason for the timing of the search actually
had nothing to do with tactics. When the warrant and affidavit paperwork was ready to be presented to a judge, the police
discovered that there was no judge available to sign it, because
all of the judges were away at a conference. A constable had
to drive the warrant to a judge an hour away to get it read
and approved. They couldn't proceed until it was signed and
returned.

Once David was out of the apartment, the search began. The officers didn't know whether they would find a crime scene, a body buried in the dirt basement (someone had phoned in a tip that Maria was buried in the basement; someone else had suggested she might be buried under the storage shed), other evidence of violence or clues that might suggest where her body was. They also needed to be attuned to evidence that might reveal David's state of mind or behaviors subsequent to Maria's disappearance, clues to where the body might be and the possibility of a murder weapon or stained or bloody clothing. They needed to be sure their search included looking for information about Maria's belongings. What might be missing? What was present that should be missing if she'd gone away for a week? Was her jewelry there?

Because they were proceeding with extreme caution to be sure they covered everything and because they were going in with such a broad set of parameters, the search ended up taking three days.

What was particularly frustrating and challenging about the investigation, right from the outset, was that because it involved a disappearance they were not operating under the usual rules. From the moment their suspicions hardened into the certainty that they were dealing with a homicide, their investigation necessarily took on a dual focus: on the one hand, finding evidence which would connect David Tanasichuk with the crime and lead to an arrest and a conviction, and on the other, the different and difficult challenge of finding Maria.

In most homicide cases, the investigation is initiated by the discovery of a body and a crime scene. Reading that scene, observing what is discovered there and what it can tell them, noting the apparent mode of death and what is subsequently learned from an autopsy of the body, gives the investigators essential information with which to organize their inquiries. Here, by contrast, what they had was a void, an absence, an unexplained and highly unlikely disappearance, coupled with a tangled web of conflicting stories about that disappearance. Nothing was clear, not even the day Maria disappeared.

They also had a prime suspect with a savage temper who was known for plotting to violently dispose of those who thwarted him, a suspect whose recent behavior suggested he was descending into the desperate and unstable world of a serious drug user.

Once David had gone quietly with the arresting officers, Detective Sergeant Fiander, who would act as the exhibit control officer, and Detectives Cummings, Gillespie and Scott, as well as Jody Whyte from the drug division, accompanied by Royal Canadian Mounted Police (RCMP) forensics officers from Bathurst, began to search the apartment.

A search doesn't begin, as one might see on a TV program, by storming into rooms, going through drawers and pulling books off shelves; nor do detectives conduct their search in the dark with flashlights. In real life, "searching in the dark" is metaphorical. A good search begins with the eyes, with standing quietly and taking in the surroundings— noting what's normal and what's not, what's out in plain sight and what its presence tells an experienced investigator. Eventually, yes, they will open closets and drawers, look under cushions and search shelves, too, but it will begin with observation and, often, photographing and recording the surroundings.

As Jody Whyte said, "You kind of got to empty your mind of 'okay, I'm going in to find the smoking gun or I'm going to find a big blood splotch'...you just look for everything. You've got to be methodical in your search, and when you look at it, you really look at it, to say okay, this could be used for this, or this is probably what that is used for."

Before anything is collected, it is photographed in place. Pawn slips, drug-related materials, items in wastebaskets. Items leaning against walls or stacked in closets.

In any police action, there's a lot of planning on the ground before the activity is undertaken; but how it is actually carried out depends entirely on the circumstances that arise as the operation unfolds. Going in, they thought there might be blood spatter in the apartment. Maria's friend Darlene had told them that she'd found David mopping the kitchen one day, shortly after Maria disappeared, behavior that struck her as significant because in all the years she'd known him, she'd never seen him do housework before. The detectives had to wonder whether he was trying to clean up a crime scene.

There was the possibility of a body within the apartment or in the dirt-floored basement below. There was also the possibility that the clues they would find would be minute. Subtle things that would tell them a story only if they kept their eyes open and listened carefully, evidence that could indicate whether or not Maria might actually have packed her bag and left. Evidence of David's activities before and after her departure. One thing that was immediately evident to Cummings was that the apartment had fallen into serious disarray without Maria there to keep things in order. The place was dirty and untidy. Drug paraphernalia lying on a dresser indicated that, freed from Maria's scrutiny, David had been openly indulging his habit. It also suggested that he didn't anticipate her return.

Sometimes small findings can be significant. In the wastebasket in the bedroom, they found Constable Seeley's business card. She had given it to David when she first came to the apartment to take his statement about Maria being missing, so that he could contact her with additional information and inquire about the progress of her investigation. The card had been torn in half and thrown in the wastebasket. In an apartment where papers were hoarded—the drawers and closets housed stacks of ancient bills, correspondence, legal documents, photographs and receipts—the fact that David had torn up Seeley's card and discarded it looked like a statement of deliberate unconcern about his wife's disappearance, a suggestion that the call and the report were pretextual and not heartfelt.

Similarly, the investigators found a large envelope with a packet of laminated "missing person" posters asking for information about Maria; however, not once since Maria's disappearance was it reported that anyone had seen any of these posters distributed around Miramichi or heard of them being posted elsewhere. On the computer on the desk, David had been composing a letter asking the public for help in locating Maria.

Searching the hall closet, investigators found over a thousand dollars hidden under some storage bins, money David apparently didn't know about or he wouldn't have been pawning Maria's jewelry. It left them wondering about the eight hundred dollars which David told the police Maria had "stolen" from their safe and taken with her to Saint John. Despite David's assertion that he had turned it all over to the police when they collected the weapons, they also found a container of mixed ammunition in the closet.

In the living room, resting on the floor against some furniture, they found two purses, one of which contained Maria's birth certificate and a brand new health service card dated January 10, 2003, a card she would have needed to have with her if she wanted to obtain medical services or fill a prescription while she was away, along with various recent store receipts suggesting that it was a purse in current use. Some minute blood spots were discovered which, when analyzed, proved to be deer blood.

Among the items the searchers found under the cushions of the couch and collected was Maria's little red devil teddy bear.

They approached the basement with a plan to take it slowly. As Paul Fiander said, "We knew there was the dirt floor in the basement, so, you know, you kind of keep your mind open…"

The basement didn't yield a body or any signs of recent digging. What it did contain, though, was more than a little spooky: in that dirt-floored space, festooned with cobwebs and dust because the dryer vented there, David had set up a satanic altar.

Once, according to Maria's sister, Sharon, he had taken Sharon's daughter down there and showed her the whole setup—pentagram painted on the wall, altar, black candles, a cape he'd stolen from a Catholic church and a satanic bible on the altar. He'd opened the bible and urged her to pray for Satan to come into her heart. The terrified girl had fled up the stairs and never gone down there again.

Although Tanasichuk had told the police about Maria leaving the bear behind, he had been more secretive with her friends, who would have understood the significance of that bear. In her interview with Cummings, Darlene Gertley had described going to the apartment after Maria disappeared. Making the excuse of visiting the restroom, she had peered into Maria's bedroom and seen the bear on the Tanasichuks' bed. Then she challenged David about its presence, asking, "Did girlfriend go without her devil doll?" David had told her that it wasn't Maria's doll, but instead a toy belonging to the children upstairs.

One reason the search went slowly was investigative caution. They didn't want to release the apartment back to David
until they were certain that they'd learned everything the space
could tell them. The search was also slowed by the logistics of
arranging to bring some of Maria's close friends, who were
familiar with her wardrobe and her possessions, to the apartment to assist them in determining whether any of Maria's
clothing or footwear was missing. David had described
Maria's preparations, stating that she'd laid out splash pants,
heavy splash suits and had them ready to pack. Her friends
agreed that everything she regularly wore still seemed to be
there, including her pajamas and the winter boots she would
ordinarily have worn when she left the apartment.

Also among the items found were two sets of house keys,
one on a lanyard with a picture of B.J. attached. One set was
determined to belong to David. A friend of Maria's identified
the one with B.J.'s photo attached as the one she had given to
Maria to help her keep track of her keys.

Without a body, a crime scene or sufficient other evidence to
charge David with killing his wife, the police could only hold
him for twenty-four hours. On Saturday night, mindful that
the legal holding period was ending soon, Brian Cummings
conducted another interview with David Tanasichuk, this
time with David as a suspect who had been given the proper
cautions. Nothing was gained from that interview and, at the
end of the evening, David was released.

David's release added a lot of tension to the situation.
Since they had not found any evidence in the house to suggest that it was the crime scene, they had to assume that
Maria had been killed in a place away from the residence,
and that her body was probably hidden somewhere in the
woods that surrounded the city. David didn't own a car; he

and Maria traveled on their three-wheelers or got friends to give them rides. There were hundreds of acres of woods surrounding Miramichi, crisscrossed with a vast network of woodland trails, many of them groomed, which served hikers, snowmobilers, snowshoers and cross-country skiers in the region.

Where would they even begin to search for a body? It seemed unlikely that David could have buried it—even though there hadn't been snow when Maria disappeared, it had been very cold and the ground was frozen—but he was so familiar with the surrounding woods from his many years of hunting in all seasons that he might have found a spot where the ground was sufficiently soft to allow a shallow burial. He might have dumped Maria somewhere in the woods and covered her body with snow and brush. She might be up in one of David's bear tree stands, or "crow's nests" as they're called in the region, the shelters he'd built throughout the woods as part of his passion for bear hunting.

Now that he knew he was a suspect, one of their biggest fears was that he would retrieve Maria's hidden body and move it to a location so remote they would never be able to find it. It immediately became a priority of the investigation to conduct surveillance on David, hoping he might lead them to the body.

Conducting surveillance on a suspect sounds like a perfectly straightforward investigative activity. However, they were facing surveillance in the depths of winter by a small police department on quiet streets, where most of the officers were already known to the suspect. It was a nightmare even to contemplate and even harder to put into effect. The investigation would soon take several twists and turns, as witnesses made some shocking revelations and David lost his famous temper.

Chapter 7

Skeletons in the Closet

E ven as some of the investigators were slowly working
their way through the Tanasichuks' apartment, documenting how unlikely it was that a woman like
Maria, particular about her clothing, dependent on her medication and worried about her husband, would have left town
without her purse, her clothes, her house keys, prescriptions,
medical card, money or her cherished mementos and comfort blanket, others were continuing to interview friends and
neighbors familiar with David and Maria.

Dewey Gillespie interviewed a neighbor, Bryan Smith,
and learned that on the 24th of January, before he reported
Maria missing and the day before he told her sister, Sharon,
that he expected her back from Saint John, David had sold
Maria's three-wheeler and her helmet to Smith. When Smith
had asked for a receipt and the registration, David went home
and came back with the two documents necessary to convey
ownership to Smith, both signed by "Maria Tanasichuk." The
following day, David sold Smith, who operated a TV repair

business, the Tanasichuks' television. Smith later bought other items from Tanasichuk.

Warrants were prepared. The registration and transaction records for the sale of Maria's vehicle were subsequently seized from the New Brunswick Department of Public Safety in Fredericton. A forensic handwriting examination determined that the signatures were not Maria's.

Conducting an investigation in a complex case, especially one where the facts need to be established by circumstantial evidence because the victim has simply disappeared, is like putting together a difficult jigsaw puzzle by committee. Everyone is working on a different section. Periodically they get together and share information to see how each piece contributes to completing the overall picture.

On February 2, while the apartment search was still going on, Cummings interviewed Donald Malley, son of the Tanasichuks' next door neighbor and father of Amanda. Malley told the detective that on the 16th of January, in the middle of the afternoon while he was driving through the industrial park area of Chatham, he had seen David Tanasichuk on his distinctive three-wheeler (David's vehicle was unusual because he had mounted a motorcycle front fork on his machine) coming along the old railway line that is groomed as a snowmobile trail in winter. Donald said that he had known David for many years and so, as he passed, Donald slowed his truck, blew the horn and waved.

According to Donald, although David could not help but see him since he was only a few yards away, David did not respond, wave or make eye contact, but stared straight ahead. After Donald had passed, he watched in his rear-view mirror as David crossed the highway and headed on into the woods. Not only was David's behavior strange, in refusing to acknowledge a friend he couldn't help but see, but Donald reported that David had a peculiar bulge beneath his jacket, approximately the size of a water jug, which made him look twice his normal size. At that time, Donald was searching for a part for his truck and he was able to confirm, through receipts, his certainty of the time and day.

Investigators could only speculate about what had been under David's coat and why he might ignore Donald Malley's greeting, but speculation is a fundamental part of any criminal investigation. They would soon hear another story of peculiar behavior on David's part that meshed with Donald's, deepening their certainty that the clues to Maria's whereabouts lay in the surrounding woods.

Sometimes, information comes to the police in unexpected ways and from unexpected sources and an investigator must always be attuned to the possibility of receiving such information. It might be in the grocery store or a fast food line or anywhere where someone with a story to tell feels comfortable telling it. As Cummings said, "Any place and any person has the potential to crack something huge for you. I always tell the guys that going to get groceries is an excursion for me 'cause I meet everyone in the community, and I can spend an hour going to get a box of crackers or something. I've solved an awful lot of crimes off duty in the grocery store because someone will stand in an aisle, leaning on a grocery cart, and talk to you about things that they might not come in and talk to you about at the police station."

A few days after the search of the Tanasichuks' apartment, still on the trail of Maria's jewelry and other possessions, Cummings went to see another neighbor of the Tanasichuks who lived around the corner. Cummings had heard the neighbor had bought a ring from David.

During that visit, Cummings ended up in a conversation with the neighbor's father, Ralph. Although uncertain about the date, Ralph told the detective that sometime during the week of January 12–18, Maria had stopped in at his house, trying to find David. David wasn't there at that moment, but later that evening, David did come by and was told that Maria had been looking for him. David had shrugged it off, complaining that she was always hounding him. Very late that same evening, Ralph, who was a night owl, had seen David Tanasichuk go by on his three-wheeler, heading toward Princess Street, where there is a connection to a major snowmobile trail leading into the woods.

About ten minutes later, Ralph related, he saw David drive past again, going in the opposite direction. And then, David went by a third time, heading toward Princess Street again. In all, David would pass the house six times, making three trips in each direction. Ralph was certain that it was David Tanasichuk he was seeing, since David's vehicle was so distinctive. Ralph stated that he had never before seen David do anything like that and found it odd that he was making so many trips so late at night.

Cummings related, "I actually went to his house to get a statement from Ralph's son about the ring that David sold him...and Ralph actually volunteered that about three weeks prior, he'd seen him making the round trips. And I was sitting in the police car, Greg Scott was sitting to my right...and we knew how significant what Ralph was telling us was...and there was always that element of...he may be willing to tell us this verbally now, but is he willing to go on the record? And one step further...he might be willing to go on the record, but is he willing to testify? Because you're talking about David Tanasichuk in February, 2003. I remember scribbling out this statement really fast and keeping Ralph talking and getting all the facts down on the clipboard in my lap, and I remember passing the clipboard over the seat to Ralph, and Greg's sitting there with his fingers crossed and I said to Ralph, "Just sign the bottom, Ralph," after I read it over for him, and I remember Ralph saying "...Is this one of those 'Gotta signs' or do I hafta?" And I said there's nothing in life that you have to do. And he said, "Aah, fuck it, give me the pen," and he signed his name. And after we let him out and drove away, Greg looked at me and said, "How the fuck did we just get that?" I said, "I don't know, but hang on tight."

"And Ralph knew...he didn't have to sign it if he didn't want to...but that little spark of goodness in him made him do it. And I will always have time for Ralph because of that spark."

The pieces were starting to come together on a couple that had seemed happy and devoted on the outside, but how committed was David? As Maria's sister, Sharon, put it, Maria's was a blind love. Many witnesses, including Sharon, described David flirting with them, but Maria wouldn't hear of it.

In their interviews with Maria's close friend, Darlene Gertley, investigators had learned that in 2001 David had taken a job as an assistant instructor in the carpentry department of the Progressive Learning Center. There, he had become close to one of his students. Eventually, he had told the student that he was attracted to her. He had admitted that he was in a relationship and he told her that the relationship was not going well. A few weeks later, he told her that he was no longer in a relationship with Maria, though David was still living in the same apartment until he found another place to live.

Between March and June of 2001, the two of them had had a relationship, based on the girl's understanding that David was no longer part of a couple with Maria. The two of them celebrated her graduation from the program

by spending the night together at a motel. According to
Darlene Gertley, Maria had become suspicious of David's
behavior and, one day during the spring semester, she had
asked Darlene to drive her over to the college. They drove
around the campus until they found the student's car, and
there was David in it. When he saw them, he hopped out
and jumped in Darlene's car like nothing was going on.
Darlene drove them back home and just went on into her
house, not wanting to hear David's excuses or his explanation to his wife.

After that, the student called the Tanasichuks' apartment. Maria answered and told the girl that she and David
were still very much a couple and she loved her husband. She
asked the student to stay away from David and the girl ended
the relationship. She also agreed to give Maria some letters
that David had written to her. The girl would later learn from
people who knew David Tanasichuk well that David had said
he was very unhappy with Maria but he could never leave her,
because Maria possessed secret information which could put
him behind bars.

Then Darlene Gertley, whose love for her good friend
and her concern about Maria's fate had made her the first to
suspect David, and the person who was the most certain that
he had done her friend harm, finally overcame her awful fear
of David and told the investigators what that "secret information" was.

It was a revelation that was enormously painful for
her to make and one she felt deeply guilty about not having
revealed years earlier, knowing well that had she come forward, her dear friend might still be alive. She told Cummings
that she had not come forward for two reasons: her desperate need, as a shy and lonely woman living far from home
and family, for a close friend, whom she had found in Maria,

which caused her to want to keep Maria's secrets; and her fear, based on her knowledge of Maria's secret and Darlene's observations of him, of David Tanasichuk's potential for violence.

One day, Maria had told Darlene that David was very upset because he had heard a rumor that she, Maria, had slept with a man named Albert "Abby" Brown (David's former common-law father-in-law), during the period when David was in prison from 1993 to 1995 for possession of a prohibited weapon. Maria told her friend that the rumor wasn't true, but that David was very angry and despite her protests, insisted that he was going to speak with Abby.

The following day, when they met as usual, Darlene asked Maria whether David had, in fact, gone to speak to Abby Brown. Maria's response was shocking: "Oh, he spoke to him all right," she said. "He killed him."

At the time of Maria's disappearance, the Abby Brown murder was still unsolved. The police had had a female suspect, but despite finding some potential evidence and uncovering a possible motive, they had never been able to charge her with the crime. After he was killed, Brown's body had lain undiscovered in the basement of his house for five days.

Darlene Gertley went on to tell the investigator that she had been so upset by Maria's revelation that she had called her husband, who was attending a conference, and told him that he had to come home. When questioned, her husband confirmed that Darlene had told him about a murdered man in a basement several days before the discovery of Abby Brown's body. This event occurred before B.J.'s death and before the change in relations between Maria and the police had occurred, and Darlene went on to report that both David and Maria were happy that David was not a suspect and had gotten away with the murder.

In one of those instances that go directly to Brian Cummings's observations about how you never know where or when you'll gain valuable information, at that same time Darlene told him that a few months after Abby Brown's death, in early 2000, she had seen Cummings in line behind her at a restaurant next to the police station. She said she had come within a breath of asking him to go outside that day and telling him what she knew about Brown's murder, but decided against it.

When Darlene Gertley made her painful and shocking disclosure, Cummings knew immediately that she was telling the truth, even though it had been over three years since Brown's death and they were focused on a different suspect. It was a painful, sobering disclosure. Such stunning revelations, rare in any investigator's career, can remain embedded in the mind forever.

That revelation would have been shocking enough, but there was more. Constable Gillespie had also conducted an interview with Darlene shortly after David had reported Maria missing, and she had told him a story which potentially tied David to another homicide and provided an additional reason why David might have feared the consequences of an estrangement from his wife.

Within the past few weeks, Darlene told Gillespie, David had appeared at her back door one night as she was making dinner and asked to speak with her. He was in a highly agitated state. The blood and water stains on his pants suggested to her that he had been injecting himself with drugs on the walk from his house to hers.

By that time, Darlene and her husband were no longer such close neighbors of the Tanasichuks, but had moved a few streets away. They'd moved because of increased tension between the couple after B.J.'s death and because some of

David's disturbing habits made them feel it was an unsafe and unpleasant place to raise small children. He would, for example, string up animals that he'd shot, in or out of season, and butcher them right there in the yard in front of her children who were out playing. Once he'd hung up a deer's head on an outbuilding and left it there. It hung there, decomposing and disheartening both to Darlene's children and to the little children in the church nursery school next door, until finally the church asked him to remove it.

Another of David's behaviors that was frightening to a mother of young children was that sometimes he would lurch out the back door, gun in hand, and shoot birds from the trees while her children were playing out there, leaving dead birds on the ground and hanging from the branches. Darlene found the bird carcasses distressing and the gunshots terrifying.

Not wanting to converse with David in the state he was in before her young children, Darlene stepped out onto the back porch and quietly closed the door. As she stood nervously in the winter darkness, an agitated David told her that Maria had been asking about her brother, Robert Breau, who had lived in the apartment above them until he mysteriously disappeared one frigid February night in 1999 after an evening of heavy drinking.

David said, "Do you know what Maria said to me?"

Darlene said, "What, Dave?"

He replied, "Maria asked me if I had anything to do with what happened to Robert."

Darlene told the investigator that she had just made her eyes wide and said that no, Maria had never, ever said anything like that to her and asked if David was sure that was what Maria was asking.

He responded that he was really pissed that she would ever think that about him.

Inside, Darlene's stomach was churning, because she and Maria had long suspected that David was probably responsible for Robert's disappearance. Maria had clung to the hope that she was wrong, and David had strung out those hopes for years with the occasional reported sighting of Robert by someone in a distant city or another province. But realistically, based on the circumstances of Robert's disappearance, the friends had thought that it was likely that handsome Robert Breau was dead.

The night Robert was last seen, Darlene had been visiting with David and Maria, and Robert, who lived upstairs with his mother, was there and he was drunk. Robert had made a pass at Darlene, which infuriated David. By the time the evening ended, Robert Breau was so drunk he could barely get himself up the stairs. The next morning, Robert was gone and David said he'd gone away because he'd ripped off a drug dealer. At the time, he was too drunk to stand, it was the middle of the night in winter and he didn't have a car. He left without taking his wallet or any of his belongings. He was on social assistance, but never cashed another check, worked another job or spoke to another human being.

On a previous occasion when David had been mad at Robert, Dewey Gillespie learned in an interview with the Tanasichuks' neighbor, John Paquet, that an infuriated David had beaten Robert unconscious and would probably have continued until the beating killed Robert if Paquet hadn't pulled him off.

What Darlene told the investigators provided very strong reasons why David would have wanted Maria to disappear, instead of simply leaving her. Maria already had knowledge of one murder he had allegedly committed; now, as things frayed between them, she was beginning to question his involvement in a possible second. According to numerous reports, their once deeply loving and envi-able marriage had deteriorated to the point where Maria despaired of being able to save it. She had told her sister that she was tired of fighting and shared with others that she had given David an ultimatum—stay off the drugs or they were through. He'd already had one affair. If David left, took up with another woman, and Maria was angry, what was to ensure that she would continue to keep his secrets? And if they separated, David would be homeless, for numerous wit-nesses had told the investigators that Maria would not leave the apartment where she had lived so long with her lost son.

This new information suggested that they were not just looking at a domestic homicide where the victim's body had been hidden. They were dealing with a suspected serial killer.

Part 2

Cat and Mouse

Chapter 8

Let the Games Begin

Later in February, the three investigations—the one into Maria Breau Tanasichuk's disappearance as well as the others into the brutal murder of Abby Brown and the sudden disappearance of Robert Breau—were all merged together. As the investigators realized the full extent of what they were dealing with, they became ever more determined to do whatever it took to find Maria and charge David with her murder. At the same time, this new information, coupled with their knowledge of his criminal history, made the detectives very much aware of how dangerous their suspect really was.

The importance of trying to get a suspected serial killer off the streets became their everyday—and every night—reality, because one of their principal concerns was that David would find a way to dispose of his wife's body in some manner that would mean the police would never be able to find it and formally establish her death. And they were hopeful that if they could find Maria, it would not only confirm their certainty that she was a homicide victim, but her body would also give them more vital evidence which would help in prosecuting the case.

The task of watching David became critically important. The detectives wanted to know where he was as much as possible, so that if he entered the woods, someone would know it who might be able to intervene and prevent him from moving the body. This was a nearly impossible mission. Ask any investigator about surveillance, and you'll get stories about techniques and tactics, the necessity for using a hopscotch weave of multiple officers. Then ask about the challenges of doing surveillance on foot, and it becomes more complicated. Then ask them to imagine doing surveillance in an empty town on an empty street in the middle of winter, on a suspect who traveled by three-wheeler or on foot and was as likely to disappear into the woods and travel on groomed woodland trails as to drive on paved roads. Then ask them to do it at night. That was the level of the challenge the Miramichi investigators faced.

David was an experienced woodsman who had spent thousands of hours of his life moving through the woods around the city, fishing, hunting with guns—whether he was allowed to have them or not—and hunting with a bow, both in and out of season. If he went with Maria, she carried the guns on her three-wheeler, wrapped in a tarp, until they were in the woods. If he hunted with friends, they carried the guns. It might not just be Maria's guns, either. Investigators had learned from those who'd hunted with David that he was known to stash guns wrapped in plastic tarps in convenient spots in the woods, just as he'd done when he was plotting to kill the judge and prosecutor in an earlier case.

Even the toughest officer is only being reasonable to be concerned about a suspect who may have killed three people and especially someone whose past anger at being charged with a crime led him to plot the assassination of law enforcement officials. Tracking David into the woods at night, stopping by to speak with him or even getting a phone call from him could make the hair stand up on the investigators' necks. He was volatile and dangerous, given to impulsive acts of terrible violence, yet also, as the assassination plot showed, calculating. There was always the possibility of a bullet from the darkness.

Sometimes, in police work, an officer will learn something that suddenly places a past experience in a startling new light. That was the case for Detective Cummings when he reflected on the information he'd gotten from Darlene Gertley. He remembered a time during the investigation into Abby Brown's death when he had sat in the living room of the Tanasichuks' apartment, talking with David as an information witness about a possible suspect in the case. Now, given David's potential for violence, he reflected on what must have been going through David's mind as Cummings queried him about a murder they now believed he had committed. Had David been complacent, content to have gotten away with the crime and enjoying the game of toying with the investigator? Had he contemplated taking steps to ensure that Cummings didn't get suspicious and didn't take things further? How truly dangerous, in retrospect, had that situation been?

The general public, in a case like this, will read in the newspaper that a woman has gone missing and that the police are looking into it. Rarely will they have much sense of what "looking into it" means. What are police looking into and how are they going about it? What is going through their minds when they wake in the morning and when they're trying to get to sleep? What are their days and nights like—are they different from the way they were before this woman disappeared? Even those who are cooperating with the detectives or have a relationship with the victim will have little idea of what an investigation really entails.

Even before the public had read anything in the papers, the police had taken a missing person report, obtained material information and photographs of Maria and prepared news releases and announcements about her disappearance which had been sent to the local and regional news media, giving a description of the missing woman and some available details about her and when and where she was last seen. They had also distributed press releases about Maria at taxi stands and bus and train stations throughout the province, looking for anyone who might have seen her leave Miramichi or arrive in Saint John or elsewhere. They interviewed personnel at the bus stations in Miramichi and Saint John and spoke with local taxi drivers who might have picked Maria up.

They had been working with the news media to keep Maria's disappearance constantly in the public's mind. Ensuring continuing news coverage served many investigative purposes. It fostered public investment in the disappearance of a fellow citizen, it served to nudge witnesses who might know something to come forward with what they knew and it helped pressure reluctant witnesses to tell them the whole story. Those stories also helped to keep the pressure on the suspect.

Another effort that helped keep pressure on the suspect, which police frequently use, was simply their continual presence: The patrol car that slowed when it passed the suspect and the car parked at the curb near the suspect's house were just a regular presence to remind the suspect that the police were keeping an eye on him.

When investigators began to strongly believe that the story David Tanasichuk was telling them was largely a bunch of lies and that the behavior he was attributing to his missing wife was a significant and implausible departure from her usual ways, the investigators then focused on constructing a different narrative—one that involved domestic violence, David's slide into deepening drug use, David's personal history of angry outbursts, including his statements to his drug counselor that sometimes he got so mad he wanted to kill someone and the fact that his wife, Maria, knew his secrets.

As the investigation went on, it truly did become a 24/7 thing, a complex investigation that proceeded on two fronts—on the one hand, trying to find helpful witnesses and usable evidence against their suspect and on the other, searching for Maria's body and watching David to see if he would lead them to it—an investigation made especially difficult as their suspect turned out to be nocturnal.

Maria was reported missing on January 26, and, as Paul Fiander put it, "Up until March 22, there weren't a whole lot of nights when any of us had a whole lot of sleep."

Surprisingly, in a discipline viewed from the outside as a "just the facts, ma'am" kind of occupation, the ability to imagine has critical significance in police work. Investigators, working with a constantly shifting kaleidoscope of facts, would merge those facts with their training and experience, their victimology—that deep understanding of the missing woman that they had developed from those who knew Maria—and their suspect analysis, to imagine scenarios which would help them solve the crime.

In the case of Maria's disappearance, two narratives from witnesses became very significant in getting the investigative team to imagine what had happened between David and Maria. They knew, from witnesses familiar with the couple, that one of the greatest pleasures the Tanasichuks shared was hunting together; another was riding together on their three-wheelers, or going riding in the woods together on David's three-wheeler, Maria behind him with her arms wrapped around his waist. It was an image witnesses constantly repeated—seeing the happy couple go by on their three-wheelers or together on one three-wheeler, heading out into the woods. David and Maria's love of hunting was an activity that bonded them.

Sometimes, they'd been told, when David hunted by himself he would kill an animal deep in the woods and then need Maria's help bringing it home. Maria had special clothes she wore for hunting and for three-wheeling. Even in her house-bound and depressed state, especially with the increasing tension between them about David's disturbing absences and inattention to their marriage, there was little that would have roused Maria to leave the apartment like an invitation from David to go out riding with him or a request from him for her help.

The second narrative involved witness reports of David's strange nocturnal trips into the woods around the time Maria disappeared, and his peculiar behavior the following day when he encountered Donald Malley as he was coming out of the woods. Now that they had established that her body was not somewhere in or around the apartment, they took the neighbor's story of David's three mysterious round trips into the woods on the night of January 15 and began to imagine what the rest of that tale might be.

Their knowledge and experience led them to surmise that late on the night of the 15th, David had convinced Maria to go for a midnight ride somewhere out in the woods surrounding the city. Once they were out there, he had lured her away from the vehicle and off the trail, killed her and then hidden her body. The neighbor's story not only gave them a likely date for Maria's murder, but the duration of those trips also gave them a timeline that would help them to narrow the search area. Assuming that David was passing the neighbor's house in one direction and then returning at fifteen to twenty minute intervals, Maria's body must be somewhere within a seven-to-ten-minute travel distance on a three-wheeler from the neighbor's house.

The weather that night had been clear, with the temperature rising as the evening grew later. There was a little snow on the ground and it was a bright night, just a couple days shy of a full moon, so there was good light for traveling in the woods. The night of the 15th, or early on the 16th, was also a date that made the greatest sense as the murder date, because the 16th was when David began openly pawning and selling Maria's possessions.

Initially, the investigators had wondered whether David's sale of Maria's jewelry was evidence of a temporary slide into drug use that was impairing his judgment. As they learned more they realized that his own behavior contradicted that assumption. There is a saying that investigators use to test the veracity of information given to them in an interview: *liars lie with specificity*. Liars tend to have a single story and stick to that story verbatim or close to verbatim—like, for example, David's oft-repeated story of the addiction counselor saying that he and Maria needed to spend some time apart. There was a shred of truth in it—she had told them to give each other an hour or so a week to allow each other space—but she hadn't given the advice David reported.

Because it has actually been lived, the truth is easy to remember, though remembered stories often change and become clearer as details of the event are recalled. Lies are hard to remember over time, so liars tend to ground them in something that did happen. Or, because their version of the events is not real and they didn't live through the experience, they tend to embellish their stories, filling them with authentic-sounding details so they will sound like something that really happened. Thus David had told an elaborately detailed story about the events leading up to Maria's departure—his call from the grocery store on the 11th, asking Maria if they needed dog food, the point at which she had announced her intention to leave the following day for Saint John and the color of the suitcase she'd packed and of the jacket she'd worn. He'd listed what was in the small pile of clothes that she had laid out to pack. He included the tender moments they had spent on the morning of her departure when he brought her coffee and their promises to be good to each other.

Those lovely, touching details made the story sound authentic, but Maria had been seen by friends and her neighbor at the apartment for three days after the date of this supposedly tender separation, and she had spoken with others on the phone when they called the residence, something David had never tried to explain, other than his comment that Darlene must have taken too many prescription pills if she imagined she'd seen Maria on the 15th.

And then Maria was never seen again, although over the next two weeks, David told her friends many different stories about her absence. He told Darlene on the 16th that she had gone to a baby shower, an event he later changed to a christening. He told others that she had left on the 19th or the 20th. He told Sharon Carroll that she was returning on the 25th and he would have Maria call when she got in. He even attempted to convince Darlene that she was mistaken in her statement that she had had coffee with Maria on the 15th, trying to get her to agree to a date when she was actually away on Prince Edward Island.

Records secured by a search warrant showed no calls to the Tanasichuk apartment from the phone in the lobby of the grocery store. No taxi driver had driven her to the bus station. No one had seen her at the terminal or on the bus. No friends in Saint John had seen or heard from her. There were no calls from the Tanasichuk residence to make arrangements to visit with anyone in Saint John.

The investigators turned their attention to strategies for locating a body somewhere in the woods. The area was vast and there were many possibilities—Maria might be tucked up in one of David's bear stands, hidden in some other shelter or buried under what was now almost two feet of snow. Detectives fanned out, some searching for hunting companions who might know the locations of David's bear stands or the areas in which David usually hunted. Some got in touch with search and rescue groups in the region, both to learn about winter search techniques and to begin the process of organizing some searches once the most likely areas were identified.

As part of setting their search parameters, they drove ATVs out on the major trails on timed journeys of between seven and ten minutes, taking note of how far these timed journeys took them. It gave them a search area that was still huge, but at least it had a focus. The most likely place to search, given their knowledge of the area, information from the places Tanasichuk had gone during his nocturnal wanderings and the timeline, was an area known as the "industrial park" that contained businesses, open areas, an old dump and the sewage treatment plant.

While the investigation focusing on David Tanasichuk was still in its early days, things began to happen which would dramatically change the character of the investigation for those detectives most intimately involved. The first events occurred late at night on February 4, following the search of the Tanasichuk apartment. Detective Cummings was sound asleep in bed, grateful to be getting some rest after the long days spent preparing the warrant, searching the apartment and conducting interviews, when his phone rang at around 12:40 A.M. As a detective, Cummings was used to calls at all hours. But this call was not from dispatch or another officer. The caller was David Tanasichuk, violating Cummings's boundaries and the unspoken rules of police/civilian interactions by calling him at home.

During that phone call, David was rude and insolent. He angrily demanded that the investigator make the Miramichi police department return the eight hundred dollars they had taken from his wallet, which had been left in the house during the search. Tanasichuk said that he needed the money to pay his bills. He then complained that when the police left, they had left his heat on too high, causing him expense and discomfort, and that as a result of the mess the searchers had left, he'd had to go to a motel.

Cummings told him that he had personally had little to do with the actual search, and that if David had a complaint, he should contact Detective Sergeant Fiander the next morning after eight. The following morning, Fiander called Cummings at home at 7:30 A.M. and said that David had also called his house during the night, around 1:00 A.M. Fiander had told David that police business was conducted during business hours and made clear, in no uncertain terms, that David was never to call Fiander's house again. Fiander also told Cummings that his wife had been very concerned by the call, because in all of Fiander's years in police work, nothing like that—a suspect being so intrusive, personal and provocative—had ever happened.

It was clear to Cummings, from both the tone and the timing of David's phone calls, that they were about more than an aggrieved citizen's complaints. Underlying what David had done was a message and a threat: I've got your number, Mister Policeman, and I know where you live. If you insist on making me your suspect in this case, I am going to haunt your dreams. I am going to disturb your sleep. I am going to be a force to be reckoned with.

By making the phone calls to the detectives' personal numbers at a time of night when it is never appropriate to make non-emergency phone calls to a residence, David Tanasichuk had made the investigation personal—a conflict between himself and the police—in a way that it had not been previously.

Friendship and familiarity—and the cops' perennial hope for reform—might have gotten David the benefit of the doubt early on in the investigation. Now, that familiarity became a reminder of the many ways in which the man couldn't be trusted and how important it was never to lose sight of how dangerous he was. Cummings considered the call to his home threatening enough to his family's safety that he immediately added a "call waiting" feature to his home phone, so that he would still be able to reach his wife, who enjoyed lengthy conversations, if she was on the phone.

Then, as the department maintained surveillance on David, hoping that he might lead them to Maria's body, he began to play cat-and-mouse games with the detectives. His primary source of transportation, when he wasn't traveling on his three-wheeler, was getting rides from his friend Donnie Trevors in Trevors's car. Knowing that he was being watched, David had Trevors drop him places, such as around the industrial park area not far from his house, where he would disappear into the woods and wait to see if the police followed him. He did this night and day, sometimes walking for hours, sometimes on groomed trails and sometimes not. Then he used his cell phone to call Trevors to come pick him up. Sometimes, Trevors drove down an accessible trail and emerged at the other end without David in the car.

The Miramichi detectives were outdoorsmen. But David took "outdoorsy" to a whole new level.

Around the time that Cummings installed call waiting, David called him in the afternoon at the office and left a voicemail saying he was going out skiing with some of his buddies; he was just calling to let the detective know. Of course, because they had him under surveillance, the police knew that David never left his residence and when Cummings returned the call and asked where the ski trip was, David said he was going out skiing behind the Portage Restaurant, which was out at the limits of the industrial park in the area where all the local gossip said that he had dumped his wife's body. The investigators understood that the call was their suspect's way of playing with them and of asserting that he knew he was smarter than the cops. David had always been very cocky and arrogant, certain that he was more intelligent than his adversaries. And he already thought that he'd gotten away with murder.

Another part of David's cat-and-mouse strategy, as a way of testing who was talking to the police, was to drop in and visit with people he suspected were giving the police information. He told them something—like the day he told Maria's friend Betty that he was going to go skiing behind the Portage—and then waited to see how the police would respond. Then, because they had to take it seriously, the police had to sit down and analyze the information and decide how they ought to proceed.

While they were hoping that their surveillance of David might lead them to the body, they also pursued every other avenue they could find. They were using every resource they could think of to locate Maria. They called colleges and universities throughout Canada, asking about new methods which might be employed to find a body under the snow. They tried people in British Columbia, who had experience with avalanches, to see if they knew of some useful technology to locate buried bodies. They contacted the science department at the University of New Brunswick. And time after time, they came up with nothing.

Constable Jody Whyte had been calling search agencies and military installations throughout the provinces, trying to find some sonar or other military device that might help them locate a body hidden in the snow. They borrowed a bunch of metal detectors to help with the search, thinking they might pick up zippers on her jacket or metal on her boots, but everything worked against them. The area they were searching was an old dump, and it was full of discarded bits of metal. The machines ran on batteries, which functioned poorly in the cold, forcing them to spend a fortune on batteries. After exorbitant expense and many frustrating hours in the cold, they had uncovered a lot of trash and were no closer to finding Maria.

It was discouraging, but cops are a determined lot. During another search, they were probing into the snow with long poles, looking for spots which might show a different depth. Day after day, they walked or rode along the trails, stopping and walking the edges of the trails or going out into the woods, looking for differences in the ground or the faint traces of old tracks. Everyone was constantly searching. The language they used, to themselves and to others, was that they were *haunted* by Maria's absence and the unanswered questions it created and driven by a sense of urgency—to get to her and the secrets her body could reveal—before David or wild animals found her and destroyed her.

Animals were a very real concern. There was a vast wilderness surrounding the city and all the investigators had had direct experience with hunters lost in the woods, suicides or people out walking who'd had heart attacks and their bodies hadn't been found until months or a year later. If predators had gotten at the body—which was common—they might get back only a small percentage of the remains. And in this case, that might mean that they would never know the cause of death.

There are many pieces of important evidence a body can provide. This begins with confirmation of death and expands to include clues about how the person was killed. Hair and fiber evidence might identify the killer. If tape is involved or the body is fresh, there is the possibility of fingerprints. Often, police will be looking for toxicology—evidence that the person was intoxicated or drugged prior to death, evidence which may be lost as the products of decomposition begin to mimic or mask drugs or intoxication.

They will be looking for gunshot residue, tissue damage, bullets, bullet trajectories, shoe prints or other tracks that might help identify the killer and ante- and post-mortem injuries which may tell them whether they are looking at the site where the person was killed or whether she was killed elsewhere. And every day that passes, decomposition advances and animal interference or weather events destroy the body, they may be losing critical evidence.

And too often, without a body, the pressure on the investigators is heightened because the suspect continues to walk the streets.

In order to spark the public's conscience and to keep the pressure on David, the investigators were very public about their searches. Their actions were constantly in the news and people in the community could see them out searching.

They chartered a small plane to do fly-overs of the area, looking for signs of a body, an artificial pile of branches that could mask a body or for clusters of crows or ravens that might signal the location. They looked for shelters, bear stands and anything out of the ordinary that suggested the need for on-the-ground follow-up.

Chapter 9

A Cold Night in Hell

Keeping track of David Tanasichuk continued to prove difficult as the investigation went on. Cummings said, "We even talked about whether there was any way we could get a warrant and put a tracking device in his jacket, because he always wore the same jacket, and see if we could follow him that way. We researched it and the tracking devices, they would weigh eight pounds."

One memorable night, with temperatures dipping down to -20 degrees Celsius (-4 degrees Fahrenheit), the investigation team was staked out along the trail, waiting to follow David around the industrial park. The night of the stake-out was chosen because of information they had received about David's movements. He had visited that area before and their information was that he would be heading there again that night. It was just before the date of an organized search and rescue operation in the area that had been well-publicized and thus a time when an agitated David might decide he had to move Maria's body.

Because there was now so much snow on the ground, they had augmented their usual heavy-duty winter garb by donning some white Norwegian Army snow camo suits, or "whites," that Jody Whyte had found in an army surplus store, camouflage which enabled them to effectively disappear against the snow. The detectives hid behind snowdrifts along the edge of the trail, communicating by walkie-talkies, while Greg Scott stood on top of a water tower on the roof of the feed mill, which gave an overview of the area, wearing night vision goggles. To help him stay warm, he was wearing a huge pair of white fluffy boots Dewey Gillespie had provided, which the rest of the team had dubbed "Sasquatch boots."

The investigators were once again balancing the necessity to watch because of a realistic fear that David might move the body with the knowledge that their suspect loved to play games with them. They didn't want to be out there. They wanted to be at home, with their families, where it was warm. They wanted peaceful evenings with the prospect of getting some rest—not that any of them were sleeping well.

They were tough men. Disciplined. Seasoned hunters. They were used to the rigors of the job and the patience that was required of detectives and to being tolerant of cold and discomfort, but the cold that night was nothing short of brutal, especially when they couldn't move around.

The icy night was so clear and still and the frozen snow so hard that any movement they made would have crunched loudly. So loudly, Cummings observed, that you heard the crunching fifty feet away.

Their bits of murmured conversation bounced between questions, strategy and profanity directed at the weather and their subject. They wanted a flask of black rum to help keep them warm. But they were working. They were there for Maria. For the principle that no human being deserves to be killed and discarded. For the idea that society needs order and justice. They were there to give Maria's family and friends closure.

Every day of the investigation was bringing them closer to exhaustion as they ran on adrenaline and caffeine and too little sleep. They were waiting and it just kept getting colder and later, and David wasn't showing up. As Cummings was rubbing Jody Whyte's feet, trying to bring some circulation back, Greg Scott's voice suddenly came over the radio, alarmed and desperate: "Help me. I can't feel my feet." Greg was way up in the air, with no shelter from the biting wind, clinging to the top of a tower.

"Keep talking to me," he told the others, "so I'll know I'm still alive."

They climbed up and guided Greg down from the tower, ready to pack it in, when *"He's here!"* came over the radio from two of the constables. Eddie Arbeau and Larry Matchett were staked out in some construction vehicles parked in the industrial park where they could monitor the road into the area.

As Cummings later remarked, "David came real close to getting shot that night. Larry Matchett...we'd pulled him off patrol and he was hiding in the cab of one of the dump trucks and unbeknownst to David, he walked right toward the truck and walked right toward him. And of course Larry didn't know if David had seen him or what, and I remember him telling me afterwards that he had his gun ready just in case."

A cold and miserable Greg went back up the tower and the frozen cops in their camouflage whites disappeared back into the snow, watching in frustration as David walked leisurely around the industrial park and headed off into the woods, rendering their efforts fruitless.

Decisions about how much pressure to apply were always balanced by countervailing forces: What was the suspect's breaking point? Were they pushing too hard? What would happen if the pressure backfired and David left Miramichi and went to some other city? And there was always the wild-card factor—his unarrested descent into full-blown addiction, with the accompanying volatility and unpredictability of an addict. Their strategies were based on their knowledge of his character and behavior. They didn't know how that might be altered by increased substance abuse.

In this particular case, there was a lot of game-playing on Tanasichuk's side, too, not just by the police. Much more than was common in most investigations. Paul Fiander described it this way, "It's like a chess game, too; you're always trying to stay one step ahead of him. And until he was arrested, that's what it was all about, you know...we were trying to keep a step ahead of him and he was trying to keep a step ahead of us, and he was playing his little games and we were playing ours. And that's how it works."

One of the most unusual aspects of this investigation, one that would imprint it indelibly in the investigators' minds, was the way that David's familiarity with the investigators, his friendship with them, coupled with his arrogant certainty that he was smarter than anybody, contributed to his game-playing. He went far beyond the usual boundaries of police/suspect interactions and testing, playing an annoying, persistent and sometimes unnerving game of "catch me if you can," more blatant and "in your face" than the investigators had ever seen before.

Because David was nocturnal, and because there was only a limited number of investigators available to work on the case—other police work, after all, does not stop because there has been a major crime—few of the investigators were getting any sleep. After a night rambling in the woods, David might be able to return to his apartment and sleep, but the detectives would be back in the office, handling other matters as well as strategizing about their case, plotting the next routes to follow in securing information about their suspect, and exploring new efforts they might make to find a hidden body. They spent very few hours in their beds.

David's impudent use of the telephone was a good example of game-playing. The night that he called Fiander and Cummings at home was only one of many instances of David contacting the investigators. Another night he engaged Cummings in a rambling complaint about how confusing their cell phone numbers were—how he'd call up Cummings and get Gillespie or call Fiander and get Cummings. David's comments, the investigator understood, were not about phone numbers. They were about letting the police know that Tanasichuk was out there watching them. That he had their phone numbers and felt entitled to call them.

On another occasion, he called Dewey Gillespie and asked if Dewey had sent him a letter, a not very nice letter. When Dewey replied that he'd sent no letter—for, indeed, it would be incredibly stupid for a detective in an active investigation to send a negative or threatening letter to a suspect—David went on to ask why Gillespie was telling everyone on the river that he was a murderer. Dewey replied that he'd told no one David was a murderer.

Even if the accusation hadn't come from the police, though, David was right in his perception that word had gone out along the river that he'd killed his wife. The police didn't need to work at that. Information always spreads quickly through the Miramichi. David already had a record and a reputation, and suspicions of murder are a riveting subject for gossip. David complained loudly that he no longer had a single friend on the river. He blamed the police, but he might as well have blamed the local newspaper or people sitting around idly gossiping over coffee. Or Maria's friends. Or his own behavior.

Many episodes in the frustrating, long-lasting game of phone tag revolved around arrangements for David's polygraph. On February 10, Cummings and Fiander surprised David at the home of Kevin Trevors, Donnie's brother and a known local drug dealer, one of the people David needed to see in order to support his habit. David was visibly shocked by the visit, according to Cummings, as though he thought they'd come to arrest him. At that moment, in Cummings's words, "You could have bought him for a nickel."

In the conversation that followed, David asked the police for an opportunity to take a polygraph test. The police were more than willing to set one up and arranged for a polygraph expert to be available in Fredericton on February 14. They called David and informed him of the date and place.

During a conversation on that same day, February 10, David asked Cummings if they were still friends.

A few days later, on February 13, David held his second news interview. Speaking with Dave Crase of Global News, David told the reporter that he had offered to take a polygraph test with respect to Maria's disappearance and it was scheduled for the following day. Then, on the morning of the 14th, David called the Miramichi police and canceled the polygraph, saying that his ride to Fredericton had fallen through. When they offered to give him a ride, he changed his story, saying that his brother was getting married in Saint John at noon, and he had promised to go to the ceremony. The detectives then offered to take him to Fredericton and drive him to Saint John after the polygraph. He refused the offer. Surveillance on David showed that he never did go to Saint John.

The polygraph test was rescheduled for March 4. On March 3, Cummings called Tanasichuk to remind him of the polygraph on the following day and David confirmed that he would be taking it. Later that day, he left Cummings a voice-mail saying he would not take the polygraph.

Then, as the investigators put plans in place for a major search effort using Miramichi area search and rescue, the investigation stalled. Extremely cold weather forced them to postpone the search until the following weekend. No new witnesses were coming forward and no new information was being developed. The investigators and the crown prosecutor were extremely frustrated and looking for ways to jumpstart the investigation.

Detectives were concerned because their suspect seemed to be drifting away from his friend Donnie Trevors and becoming closer to Trevors's brother, Kevin. Donnie's house, located on a road with only one way in and out, was easy to conduct surveillance on. When they learned from Jody Whyte that the drug unit was close to writing a warrant on Kevin Trevors, the problem solved itself. When the warrant was executed, the resulting find and Trevors's own state-ments put him behind bars.

With Kevin Trevors unavailable as David's drug sup-plier, the police increased the pressure on him by making other drug dealers on the river reluctant to deal with him. As Brian Cummings noted, "...On March 11th, Paul and I went to see a drug dealer that we knew David was frequenting, in Nolanville, and we told him in no uncertain terms that having David around or selling him drugs would warrant the kind of attention that we'd given Kevin Trevors on March the 8th, so we were trying to tighten the circle on David as much as we could and limit where he could go buy drugs, limit the people he could feel safe around, and I think that worked, because I don't think that guy sold another pill to David Tanasichuk."

As the date for the rescheduled search neared, David was back on the phone, calling dispatch on the 19th to see if Detective Cummings was working, then calling Cummings and asking questions about the search, rescheduled for the 21st and 22nd. The first area targeted for a search was around the industrial park. As the day of the search approached, David called Cummings and complained that the police weren't doing enough to find Maria. Cummings told him about the upcoming search and David asked if they were searching in Saint John. No, Cummings told him, they were searching in Miramichi.

"Oh, well, it doesn't matter where you're searching as long as something is being done," Tanasichuk replied.

Around the same time, David called Cummings and said that he wanted to come in to the station and give a new formal statement now that his head was clear. Cummings made an appointment but on the designated day, Tanasichuk called and canceled, saying his mother and brother were coming to visit. He later showed up at the police station, wanting to write out a statement and drop it off, saying he didn't have time to do a videotaped, formal interview.

He was told that it had to be a formal statement and the appointment was rescheduled. Once again David canceled, saying that his mother and brother had arrived in town. Cummings tested David's story, calling and reaching David's mother in Saint John. Yet another appointment was made for the taped interview; once again, David canceled.

On the day of the search, a caller who didn't identify himself but whose voice was identified by Cummings as David's, called Miramichi police dispatch to ask "if the snowmobile trails are closed because of that thing going on." That "thing" going on was police and search and rescue (SAR) personnel spending a long, arduous day searching five acres along the trail by planting dowels in the snow and looking for discrepancies in depth.

While the search effort was in process, the surveillance officers observed an agitated David being driven around the search area by his friend Donnie Trevors.

Chapter 10

Where Angels Fear to Tread

Even as plans got underway to work with the local search and rescue group to do a massive, organized search for Maria, the detectives got some news that ramped up the tension of the investigation significantly. The pressure of constant surveillance, police interference with his drug supply and the disapproval of people all up and down the river, resulting from publicity about Maria's disappearance and gossip that he was a suspect, was getting to David in a big way and making him extremely angry. Word got back to the investigators that David had stated that if the police didn't back off and leave him alone, he would *make* them back off by retaliating against them and their families.

Knowing David's reputation for violence and his lengthy criminal record, they did not consider this an idle threat. David seemed primarily fixated on Brian Cummings, that "bald-headed son of a bitch," because of their prior relationship and David's inability to convincingly lie to Cummings and manipulate the detective into believing his story about Maria's departure to Saint John. The threat was particularly

117

disturbing, because Cummings's family lived quite near to Donnie Trevors's house, where David spent a lot of time. But the threat was perceived as being against all of the detectives most visibly involved with the case—Paul Fiander, Dewey Gillespie and Cummings. Each man had children at home and Cummings's boys were very young.

David's ultimatum brought into play the downside of the detectives' abilities to imagine. Just as they were constantly imagining scenarios of the night Maria disappeared, based on the facts that they'd developed to help them locate her body, now they found themselves imagining scenarios involving their own families. Cops may be expert at putting the emotions of the job in lockboxes to avoid bringing them home, but this was something they couldn't lock out. It just wasn't possible to suppress the stories they'd heard over the years about David's propensity for violence.

They had seen firsthand the violence that was done to Abby Brown. As they conducted their interviews, the detectives kept hearing new stories involving David and violent acts. There was John Paquet's story of Tanasichuk beating his brother-in-law, Robert Breau. Darlene Gertley related a story she'd heard from Maria, about a time when David was hunting and had shot a deer but not killed it. Instead of firing a second shot and ending the animal's suffering, he had drawn his hunting knife and thrown himself on the injured animal, stabbing it repeatedly until it finally died.

Nor could they overlook Darlene's husband's story. David had always been obsessed with hunting. In the fall of 2002, he'd become particularly fascinated with bear hunting, buying and watching many bear hunting videos as well as putting out bait and spending time in his bear blinds, contemplating which animals he would ultimately kill. One day, he'd remarked to Darlene's husband that a skinned bear and a skinned human looked remarkably alike, except that the bear was heavier through the haunches.

And while it was entirely circumstantial, there was the information David was broadcasting through the art and words inked on his body. In addition to having guns tattooed all over his torso, he had four black teardrops tattooed beneath his right eye. Dewey had done research on those teardrops and learned that a teardrop tattoo is a permanent mark for each murder the wearer has committed. Canadian courts have allowed recognition of the significance of such tattoos in murder investigations. David also had another tattoo at the base of his throat, "смерть дилер," which he challenged Cummings to decipher. With the help of Dr. Allen P. Reid at the University of New Brunswick, the words were translated from Russian and Ukrainian as *Death Dealer*.

Prompted by the seriousness of the threat and by their deep concern for their families, the Miramichi police went to the RCMP and asked for help improving security at their homes. The RCMP installed security systems in each of the detectives' homes and provided their wives with security alarms to wear around their necks any time they left the house. From that point in the investigation, the tension levels rose sky-high for everyone concerned. The investigators' phones already rang constantly, with the Tanasichuk case and all their others. Now, each time the phone rang, they had a moment's pause as they wondered: was it a frantic call from home?

Suddenly, part of each day's to-do list included periodic calls to their wives to be sure that everything was okay, and if Cummings or Gillespie was out in the car, he might swing by his house just to check things out. In some ways, the threat was hardest on Paul Fiander, because his family lived twenty-five minutes outside the city, in an area patrolled by the RCMP. While the Mounties might be quick to respond, especially to a fellow public safety officer, they were thin on the ground. He took some comfort in the fact that he had a brother-in-law only a minute or two away, who could be there with a loaded gun if needed.

The threat had a significant impact on their families as well. In a community where popping in and out of each other's houses for a coffee or a chat was commonplace and where children ran freely in and out of neighborhood homes, the detectives' families suddenly found their lives drastically changed and constricted. No one visited for coffee. It wasn't safe. Neighborhood children couldn't play. It wasn't safe. Wives didn't leave the house without checking the yard. They never got in the car or loaded their children without first checking inside and under the car. Even a trip to the grocery store, school or work required remembering to wear the alarm and checking around before leaving the house or entering the car. Those aptly-named panic buttons weighed heavily on the hearts of the detectives and their wives.

While their wives and children were dealing with these newly changed circumstances, the detectives bore an added burden. Now they jumped each time the phone rang, never knowing when it might be a chilling message in a panicked voice saying, "Come at once. He's here."

As one of the investigators put it, he could live with the threat of danger to himself—he'd taken on that risk when he took the oath. But a threat to his family was a whole other thing. It really crossed the line. Cummings recalled that, for much of that February and March, even when he could get home he wasn't sleeping. When he was in bed, his loaded gun stayed at the head of the bed, an absolute no-no for anyone with small children in the house and especially for a cop. But it seemed like the only reasonable course of action. He wasn't taking chances with his family. "Every bump or thump, every time the motion-activated light comes on, I'm out there in the yard in my underwear and boots with my gun out."

In late February, Paul Fiander, aware that locating Maria's body was critical to their pursuit of the case and that none of the search strategies they'd come up with were working, began exploring the idea of using cadaver dogs. A lot of phone calls and online research later, he'd learned that trained cadaver dogs were a scarce resource in Canada. He'd located dogs that the RCMP had in Ontario and he was told that he could get a single dog to come to Miramichi if they were willing to provide first-class tickets for the dog and its handler.

Recognizing that a single dog was unlikely to be able to handle the task and that the expense was prohibitive for a small police agency, he began looking across the border in the United States. An internet search took him first to Andy Rebmann in Connecticut, a retired state trooper who had played a significant role in promoting interest in, and the training of, cadaver dogs in the region. Rebmann referred Fiander to the state of Maine and to a volunteer organization called MESARD (Maine Search and Rescue Dogs). Phone calls to MESARD's president, Keith Heavrin, elicited a positive response. The MESARD handlers wanted to help, but since they were a group of dedicated volunteers and a search of the scope Fiander was describing would need serious mapping and organization, MESARD then referred him to the Maine Warden Service and Sergeant Roger Guay.

Eventually, the back and forths between Fiander and Guay led Fiander to Lieutenant Pat Dorian, the Search and Rescue coordinator for the Maine Warden Service. Dorian, Fiander was told, would have the ability to assemble and coordinate a large-scale operation through his association with the Maine Warden Service's Incident Command Team, with their sophisticated mapping and GPS programs and substantial search experience.

The Miramichi detectives could not have found a better resource. Lieutenant Dorian told Fiander that he had been an incident commander for almost a decade, in charge of search and rescue for the state of Maine since 1995 and had extensive expertise in organizing and coordinating large-scale outdoor searches. Pat Dorian enjoyed the challenge of outdoor searches for homicide victims and understood the value of combining outdoor search and rescue expertise, including trained cadaver dogs and their handlers, with good detective work.

Two years earlier, Dorian had put the Maine Warden Service's search and rescue prowess on the map in a major way by initiating a search effort that found the buried body of a young Maine woman who had been missing for seven weeks. Lovely twenty-five-year-old Amy St. Laurent's disappearance had riveted the entire state. Because her body was recovered (buried bodies are extremely difficult to locate and are often never found), St. Laurent's killer was subsequently convicted and sentenced to sixty years in prison.

Dorian understood the dilemma the Miramichi detectives found themselves in—both the investigative urgency they felt and the frustrating complexity of conducting a large-scale outdoor search—and he sympathized. He wanted to give them the assistance they needed. Before Dorian could agree to help, however, he had to convince his superiors in the Warden Service to let him, his mapping expert and some of his experienced K-9 handlers and their dogs use work days to cross into a foreign country and travel many hours and hundreds of miles north to assist a small city police department, at a time when the Warden Service was facing budget difficulties.

Dorian told Fiander that New Brunswick and Maine had a mutual aid pact, which had been put into play in the past to allow Canadian and Maine agencies to assist each other in searches. He felt there was a good chance he would be able to persuade his agency to use that pact and consideration of prior aid that New Brunswick had provided on searches in Maine, to enable them to come to Miramichi and conduct a search for Maria Tanasichuk.

There was another, unexpected reason why he was eager to help. Pat Dorian was deeply familiar with the Miramichi region and it was a very special place for him. An avid salmon fisherman, Dorian had been coming to New Brunswick to fish the river for twenty-five years. He knew the area well and understood the challenges the terrain would present to the dogs and their handlers.

Before he set about getting permission for the search, Dorian spent some time on the phone interviewing Fiander about the case. Based on what he learned about the date of Maria's disappearance and the subsequent weather that winter, including the depth of the snowfall, Dorian knew that the body was almost certainly frozen and buried under snow, and therefore it would not be giving off scent. For a search effort using trained cadaver dogs to have any probability of success, it would need to be postponed until the snow melted and the body was thawed sufficiently to give off a scent which the dogs could pick up.

He also advised Fiander that with Maria's body frozen and buried under several feet of snow, it was unlikely that David would be able to move her. As Cummings put it, "They were very definitive about that. They didn't say 'well, he might do this, he might do that.' It was, he won't go near her until the snow's gone and she's not frozen. So that was a little bit of a comfort."

Dorian's assessment brought a huge sense of relief to the detectives. It meant that for the next month or two, they could put their constant fear that David would move the body, or that predators who worked on scent would find it and destroy it, to rest and focus their efforts on finding some way to get David off the streets and behind bars.

They didn't abandon their own efforts to find Maria and continued to plan for another search and rescue effort in a different part of the woods off the snowmobile trails, farther away from the Tanasichuks' apartment. As rumors of another search effort, and its location, swept the community, a very frightened witness came forward. She didn't want to give a formal statement. However, she had some information she believed they needed to know.

Lesley Allen was a tiny wisp of a woman who was the girl-friend of David's buddy, Donnie Trevors. In an interview with Cummings, she told the detective that she knew both David and Maria, and said that Maria used to visit her and Trevors at Trevors's house quite frequently. More recently, in the period just prior to Maria's disappearance, David had been coming by himself. When Maria called the house trying to locate him, Allen had been told to lie and say that he wasn't there.

She told Cummings about a conversation with David that she'd had the night before in Trevors's kitchen. She had been smoking marijuana, she said, and had gone into the kitchen where David was. He was blissed out on prescription pills, which tended to make him talkative. He was sitting down on the kitchen floor, and suddenly, referring to the rumors of another major search being planned south of the area previously searched, he said, "They're getting close. We have to go move the body or they're gonna find her."

Allen told Cummings that she had contacted the police because of the extreme seriousness of the statement, but insisted, because of her great fear of David—especially since he had confirmed for her that he was a murderer—as well as her relationship with his best friend, that she was unwilling to give a formal statement or to go on record as a witness.

During that interview, she also told the detective that David had given her a gold "90% Devil" pendant which she knew to be a piece of Maria's jewelry and she was quite certain that this gift had been made prior to the date that David had reported Maria missing. This was very significant to Cummings, because in his interview with David on January 29, he had specifically said that Maria was wearing the pendant when she left for Saint John. Cummings appreciated Lesley Allen's courage in coming forward with such important information and hoped that eventually they would be able to persuade her to go on the record as a witness.

The rumor mill soon generated another piece of news: even as he was tearfully reporting her missing, Maria's loving and worried husband, who had told Cummings in an interview that "there wasn't anyone on the river who doubted the love he and Maria had for one another," had gotten himself a new girlfriend, one he might already be sleeping with. The young woman was a friend of his deceased stepson, B.J., as well as a friend of Allen's.

On the same day that Cummings was speaking with Lesley Allen about what she had heard from David in the kitchen, Dewey Gillespie sat down to talk with the young woman rumored to be David's new girlfriend. Possibly because she was embarrassed about the relationship, she was not entirely forthcoming in her interview. That was a familiar situation—the challenges of getting information from a witness who is not candid because of shame about his or her behavior and is reluctant to be viewed in a bad light or who is uneasy about revealing too much about a person for whom he or she has, or had, serious feelings, despite his or her own suspicions about that person.

Witnesses like these put investigators in a difficult situation. They know it may take time and repeated interviews to build trust and elicit the full story. They also know that doing repeated interviews with a witness may backfire and result in charges at trial that they have harassed or coerced the witness. It would take a number of interviews with this particular witness and the passage of several years before the full story would be revealed. What they did learn at that initial interview in March was that David had tattooed the witness's name onto the webbing of his hands not long after he'd reported Maria missing and then, when she protested that it was inappropriate, he had literally chewed it off. David had told her that he was falling in love with her and that she was a very special girl.

The investigators, still running on little sleep and the debilitating effects of constant worry about their families, were desperate to get David off the street, especially when they received information that David was looking to acquire a gun. Then, in an interview with the Tanasichuks' neighbor, John Paquet, Dewey Gillespie learned that David was in possession of a shotgun that he was trying to sell. Getting his hands on a gun had been just too easy for David. It increased the urgency investigators felt about getting him off the street so that they could investigate the case without the constant worry that he would be coming after them or members of their families.

On March 14, as a result of the paperwork and warrants being completed regarding the illegal sale of Maria's three-wheeler and the forging of the sale documents, David was arrested. He spent the night of March 14 in jail. However, it was only a momentary relief.

They hoped that if David was behind bars, witnesses who were reluctant to talk to them because they were afraid of him—witnesses they *knew* were out there—might come forward. They anticipated the challenge of talking those witnesses past the risk that he might go to trial and get off, or, far worse in the imaginations of those living in Miramichi, that even if arrested, he might escape and, like serial killer Allan Legere, commit more brutal murders.

By mid-March, David had sold almost everything of value in the apartment to support his drug habit and was throwing items such as B.J.'s memorial Bible and family pictures into trash barrels on the curb. Neighbors who understood the sentimental value of these items were rescuing them from the trash and saving them for Maria, if she ever returned, and if not, for Maria and B.J.'s relatives.

Surveillance indicated that his rising drug use was rendering David erratic, unstable and, consequently, increasingly dangerous.

Tempers were fraying as the detectives sat down to discuss what other avenues they might pursue to uncover some offense that would enable them to put David behind bars for more than a night. That strategy session generated one important idea that would allow them to keep closer track of his movements. After applying for a search warrant to give them permission, the Miramichi police "stole" Donnie Trevors's car, which was known to be the primary source of transportation for David other than his three-wheeler, and installed both a tracking device to monitor the movements of the vehicle and a wire so that they could listen in on conversations.

Around the same time, they heard that David had sold the shotgun to a drug dealer on the river who, like David, was prohibited from possessing a firearm. As a result, a search warrant was written, the gun was seized and David was charged with illegally transferring a firearm. Now they just needed to find and arrest him.

For a few days they monitored the wire closely, hoping for a breakthrough and the chance to arrest David on the new charge. But just as they had their best-ever technology in place for keeping track of their suspect, David became more elusive and they lost all track of him.

Chapter 11

Pride Comes Before a Fall

David wasn't traveling in Trevors's car anymore, and he wasn't seen anywhere on the Miramichi. The investigators wondered whether what they had always feared had finally come to pass. Had the relentless pressure of surveillance and investigation driven him out of the region to some other city?

It was more likely, investigators thought, that David had learned that the police knew about his sale of the shotgun. If he knew that, he probably also knew that they were looking to arrest him on that charge. It was, in Cummings's words, "a chicken-shit charge," but David, who had served time more than once for possession of prohibited weapons, might not have known that. He also, they speculated, would be seriously afraid of being in jail, where he wouldn't have access to drugs. Given the apparent level of his drug use, he would have been in for a world of hurt.

David's drug of choice was an opiate. Jody Whyte, Miramichi's drugs investigator, described the effects of withdrawal this way: "When you're not using, it has the same withdrawal effects as any opiate. Muscle cramps, stomach cramps, diarrhea. As addicts have described it to me...it feels like you're going to die."

Whatever the reason, David Tanasichuk had disappeared and the investigators were very much on edge about it. Difficult and time-consuming as it had been to try to monitor their suspect, it was deeply unnerving to have him missing, not knowing where he'd gone, when or where he might reappear or what he might do when he did. And whether, when he reappeared, he would have obtained another gun.

Then, as suddenly as he'd disappeared, he reappeared in Trevors's car. The words he uttered over the wire were bloodchilling. He was heading to pick up a gun that someone was going to leave for him. From the overheard conversation and other information they'd received, the investigators believed that if he obtained that gun, David's next move would be toward one of their houses, with the intention of harming their families.

It was after midnight on a cold, dark mid-March night when David announced (to Dewey Gillespie, who was monitoring the wire) that he had found the gun, hidden behind a snowbank, and that he was traveling with that gun, hiding in the trunk of Trevors's car. Two cars full of investigators were now following and observing the car where they suspected David was lurking in the trunk, debating whether or not to make a traffic stop.

Traffic stops can be the most deadly aspect of law enforcement. Going in, there was no doubt in the detectives' minds that this one would be extremely dangerous. Trevors might, or might not, present a problem. David absolutely would. If they stopped the car, they would likely face someone who was armed, angry and either under the influence of drugs or suffering withdrawal.

While Trevors's vehicle drove through the take-out line at a doughnut shop, the two surveillance vehicles, one holding Cummings and Fiander, the other with Greg Scott and Jody Whyte, parked window-to-window in the lot of the superstore nearby and held a tense debate about what to do.

So much was riding on that decision. If David was out there in the night with a weapon and plans to harm the investigators' families, they had to take the risk. They had to move in and arrest him. But if they were wrong, if he hadn't gotten the gun yet and he was still traveling to get it, they'd wasted the wire and blown the whole operation and, at that point, they were just about out of other options. Blow it and they might be watching their backs forever.

They'd spent weeks with alarms on their houses, their wives and children isolated from their friends and panic buttons with their families anytime anyone left their houses. As the long weeks passed, the principal investigators—and targets of David's wrath—sat down together and seriously discussed the possibility of sending all of their families away to a place where they'd be safe and moving together into a single house in Miramichi until the case was over.

They had only moments to make a decision that night. Even as they were weighing their options, the car which held their suspect was moving toward the city limits. If it went straight, it would soon be out of their jurisdiction. If it turned and headed over the bridge, it was only a few miles from Cummings's house and his family.

Praying that Gillespie had correctly interpreted what he was hearing over the wire and that David did have that gun, they decided to go with their gut instincts, move in and conduct the high-risk stop of Trevors's vehicle. They picked an open spot away from the shopping center that would be safest for everyone involved.

A lot of planning may go into the lead-up to a major police action like the takedown of Trevors's car, but once the decision is made to go ahead, the team just has to hit the pause button on all the "what-ifs," on the swirl of emotions and the incredible weight that rests on the operation and the hundreds of questions in their minds. Would he have a gun and what gun? Were they potentially facing a .22? A shotgun? A sawed-off shotgun? Would they have to shoot him right there in the car trunk? Would he come out shooting or shoot right through the trunk? Would this be the night one of them got hurt?

What would carry the team through was their training and experience. Everything that transpired would be recorded by the wire, so this had to be a by-the-book arrest. Once the decision was made, they lit up their sirens and lights and moved in fast. Cummings pulled past the car and moved in front of it, surprising Trevors so much that he almost ran into Cummings's car. Jody Whyte and Greg Scott's vehicle was in the rear.

As they stopped the car and surrounded it, Cummings planted himself in front, gun drawn, watching through the windshield. First, they decided to get Trevors out of the car, wanting to get him under control and out of the picture so they could concentrate on David. They pulled him out of harm's way. He was stumbling around, confused by the lights and commotion, as Cummings was screaming, "Get your hands up! Get your fucking hands up where I can see them!" Not asking. Not just ordering. He was screaming. The urgency was to make it happen and make it happen fast, before they lost the element of surprise and without giving David time to respond. At moments like that, seconds can feel hours long and the world—and time—is suspended.

Once Trevors was cuffed, they asked him, "Okay, where is he?"

Trevors responded, "He's in the trunk."

Then they had to decide how to get David out. They had two choices. They knew, from having taken the car and installed the wire, that the car had a rear seat that flipped down. They could either go in that way or they could pop the trunk. Opening the trunk would give them better visibility and more room to maneuver than the small, cramped back seat; it would also give David a better opportunity to come out shooting. They opted to go through the seat.

Greg Scott went into action, starting to get in and flip down the seat, but Jody Whyte, their range master and coolest under pressure, called him back, telling him to wait until everyone was in place and they were ready.

Then, while Brian Cummings stood in front of the car, watching through the windshield, gun at the ready, they moved in fast, flipping down the seat as Greg Scott called out, "David, I want to see those hands." Then Whyte and Scott reached into the trunk, grabbed him and jerked him out of the trunk, out of the car and down onto the ground.

During the entire operation, David didn't say a single word or make a sound, except for a grunt as they hauled him out.

Once they had him on the ground and handcuffed, Fiander searched the trunk for the gun. There was a long, awful moment when he couldn't find anything, when they thought they'd blown it for sure. Then Fiander came out of the trunk and said, "I've got it. It's a sawed-off."

He'd found a plastic grocery bag in a corner of the trunk. Inside was a cloth drawstring bag decorated with a print of dogs and puppies. Inside that bag was a sawed-off, bolt-action .22 caliber rifle with a carrying strap, cut down to just twelve inches long, with a live round chambered and three more in the clip.

The number of bullets perfectly matched the number of occupants at Cummings's house, just a few miles away.

Also inside the plastic bag, they found what looked like a homemade abduction kit—two connected pairs of improvised handcuffs made from quick ties and two coils of blue plastic lawn trimmer string secured with black electrical tape.

Paul Fiander walked over to David, who was lying, cuffed, face-down on the ground with Detective Cummings pressing heavily on the back of his neck. Cummings bent low, speaking directly into Tanasichuk's ear: "You're fucked."

"You're off to jail!" Fiander added. "And now we're going to find Maria." Tanasichuk did not respond.

Standing in the frigid night on the dark city street, washed with the colors of their flashing lights, the investigators were pumped with adrenaline and flushed with exhausted triumph. The prohibited weapons charge that possession of the sawed-off carried would finally take David off the street and off their backs for a significant amount of time, freeing them to concentrate on finding Maria and building their murder case.

It was an incredibly emotional time for all of the investigators. Paul Fiander related, "Was it a good feeling when we found the gun? Absolutely. No doubt about it, because it confirmed what we had known all along. It probably saved someone's life, if not one of our own. We knew because of his previous record...and because we had him on such a serious charge, that was going to keep him in jail, it was going to buy us time to find Maria...I'll tell you. It was the greatest relief of stress, because, you know, we got him off the street. We can go home and sleep, and know where he's at. Our families know where he's at. I remember that night as if it was yesterday. It's burnt into the back of my brain and probably will be forever."

Brian Cummings said, "That audio tape of us taking that car down? Every time I hear that, my hands sweat, every single time, and I don't think that will ever change. Because I can remember the emotions that were going on at that time... and does he have a gun or doesn't he have a gun and are we going to have to shoot him in the trunk of this car?"

Jody Whyte affirmed, "The thing that strikes me, and I don't know how to describe it...is the sound...in [Fiander's] voice...when he said, "and we're going to find Maria." Brian said, 'You are fucked. You are going to jail and we will find Maria.' It was almost a combination of...I don't even know what term to use. Vindication is one. Relief. This guy's going to jail and we're going to have some time now to really concentrate on finding her and not really worrying about what he was going to do, and the certainty that we were going to find her.

"And I knew then...we were going to find her. Didn't know when and didn't know how, but I was certain then that we were going to find her, for sure."

They went back to the police station and put David in an interrogation room. Then they told Gillespie, who had been listening to the events over the wire, that he was going to conduct the interview.

Dewey Gillespie was surprised by the choice, since he didn't feel his interview skills were as appropriate to the task as Cummings's, but his colleagues were quick to point out that he was the only one of them left that David didn't actively hate, who hadn't gotten into the suspect's face and made it clear that he knew David was lying. Gillespie, the man who believed that everyone has some good in them somewhere, would have the chance to go into that room and reach David

Tanasichuk, to try for a confession and to get him to reveal the location of Maria's body.

There was little time for discussion or strategy. It had been a long day. It was well past midnight, but everyone was wound up, charged with adrenaline and eager to finish the job they'd started. They didn't want to lose the momentum of the situation. Rather, they wanted to go at David hard and hit him with their questions at the moment when he knew he was caught, when he was down and knew for sure that he was going away for a while on the gun charge.

They had a lot of ground to cover and were up against a statutory limit on the number of hours during which they could question their suspect. By law, he had to be brought in front of a magistrate before twenty-four hours had elapsed or he would have to be released.

Dewey Gillespie first asked Tanasichuk about the gun. "Of course I want to know what you're going—what you were going to do with the gun. And again, do you have to tell me? Absolutely not. Okay. But it's time to give it up, okay?"

"Time to give it up if I choose," David shot back.

They discussed how Tanasichuk had been thinking of turning himself in, and Gillespie asked: "Dave, if you were going to give yourself up, why would you go and get a sawed-off rifle? And a loaded one at that? I'm going to be really honest with you, Dave, 'cause you've got to be honest with me, okay. I think you have bad things on your mind with that gun, and it scares me. Okay. And I'm glad you got caught. Really, really I am. I'm—you know...happy that you got caught because there's hell coming down the tube with that thing. And you look me in the eye, David, and tell me there wasn't."

"There wasn't," David responded.

"Then what in the name of God were you going to do with that gun?" Gillespie inquired, "And the wrist restraints and cord and stuff? Geez, man, and it [was] loaded—what were you going to do with that? Hiding in the trunk of a car? Lord God almighty. You know, I'm glad you got caught so you didn't do something horrible, you know."[8]

Gillespie continued to explore Tanasichuk's intentions regarding the gun he had with him when he was found in Donnie Trevors's trunk.

David said, "Well, I can look you in the eye, Dewey, and I know you're probably going to call me a liar, it don't matter, but the only reason I wanted a gun was so I could shoot that little partridge or rabbit and whatever, just 'cause, well, you guys seen what little bit of food I had, so..."

After some back and forth, David gave up on the gun charge, taking full responsibility and letting Donnie Trevors off the hook: "Donnie was involved in nothing. Donnie was driving, that's all Donnie was doing."

For the next ten or eleven hours, Gillespie sat in that interrogation room with David, patiently and methodically asking questions, talking calmly and steadily as David repeatedly declared that he had nothing to say.

Gillespie was trying to get a confession. He was trying to get David to do the right thing for Maria, her family and friends: to lead them to the body or tell them where Maria was buried so that she could be laid to rest beside her son instead of rotting in the woods or being torn apart and eaten by bears. Trying to reach the man who'd loved his wife, not the one who'd lured her into the woods and killed her. The man who cared about what his son, his friends and family thought about him. It was eleven long, exhausting hours of sorting through Gillespie's bag of tricks and calling on resources developed over thirty years. He was trying to make a connection, trying to find some common ground and a way to touch something human and compassionate in David that would make him want to confess. In the conference room, the rest of the team watched the interview on a monitor.

From the very start, Gillespie had been trying to reach David's humanity, to touch his heart and make him want to cooperate.

At one point he told David, "We're simply asking you, you know...let us bring her home. Give her to us, okay. Just give her to us. You can do that, and I'll tell you something, Dave, it's the right thing to do. It has nothing to do with the law and the police...What are the rewards? No deals from the police promising—I can't do that, you know that I could never do that. I—that's way beyond me. I look at the rewards as something totally different. You look at the rewards as the impact it will have on people like your son, okay. Like family. Your mother, okay, and all those people."[9]

"And you can look at me honestly and say you really care?" David asked doubtfully.

"Well, absolutely I care, okay?" Gillespie responded immediately. "I cared right from day one...You can see no hatred and no animosity in me, not a bit. And I know that you...you don't have to talk to me. You don't have to tell me nothing, Dave. You can tell me to fly the Jesus out of here and what can I do? What else can I do except fly the Jesus out of here, okay? But you know we're looking for answers, and I'm looking for answers, okay? You're the guy that's got them, Dave."[10]

A little later, as the two of them discussed whether Gillespie was sincere in his concern for David, indicating that some connection had been made, David said, "Tell you the truth, right now you're the only fucking friend I got in the whole river."[11]

Gillespie's approach, developed from a seasoned interviewer's knowledge of the value of giving a perpetrator a reason for his actions, and showing an understanding of those actions, was to draw a distinction between the actions David might have taken because of his drug use, and the actions he would take as a decent man.

"[You wrote] an article on [prescription painkillers]. I never read the article, okay, I've never seen it, alright, but I understand that this article was about the effects that it had in your life, and I believe that [prescription painkillers] killed Maria Tanasichuk," Gillespie said. "Okay? I believe that [prescription painkillers were] responsible for the death of Maria Tanasichuk. And that the guy, David Tanasichuk, that's on the straight and narrow, okay, he don't do this, not on the straight and narrow, with steady legs under him, alright. But [prescription painkillers] knocked the legs out from underneath you, caused a lot of pressure and gained a lot of control, alright. Now, people out there know, I have never through this whole investigation met one person, not one, that said that Maria Tanasichuk didn't love you beyond anything, not one. Okay. They find it extremely hard, David, to think that you would let her lie, that—that animals would tear her apart, and that when we find her that there'll be a limb here and maybe no head and stuff, okay. 'Cause that is going to be really hard. Really hard for people to absorb. When David Tanasichuk is on [prescription painkillers], they say yeah, he'd do anything. [Prescription painkillers] will take control of him. But when you get your legs underneath you, okay, I find it—look at me, look at me, David; I find it really hard, I just cannot, I find it hard for me to even think in my heart that you would leave her there, and so do those people. When you get yourself straight, that you would leave her just like it was a piece of garbage or a piece of dirt that you throw away. I do—I will not believe David Tanasichuk is that kind of a guy. Am I wrong? Lord, no, because is that the David Tanasichuk that would take a human being that he's lived with what, eleven years, okay, and discard like a piece of garbage, okay, to rot or to be chewed and mauled and—and decay and decompose, okay, just as if it's nothing?"

A pregnant pause.

"I got nothing to say, Dewey."[12]

Gillespie was humble enough to routinely underestimate his interviewing skills, but Maine game warden Roger Guay, who would later have a chance to observe Gillespie interviewing some of David's hunting companions, and who has decades of experience watching other officers conducting interviews, said this about Dewey Gillespie as an interviewer: "I watched him do an interview. There were a couple of people we needed to have interviewed...and he had the best interrogation skills of anyone I've ever seen. He was an unassuming type of person, he carried no air about him, and he was instantly on their level...and he could get people to talk about anything. The last thing in the world they wanted to talk to anyone about, and when he was done, they would be talking. It wasn't in a threatening way...there wasn't any coercion...I mean, I've sat in on a lot of interviews, and he was just gifted at it. You know, just that way to bring people down, and calm it down and this guy, he had the bear baits, was David's partner doing the bear hunting, and he didn't want to talk at all, and Dewey was able to get him to chirp like a bird."

Eleven hours of excruciating roller-coaster emotions passed. There were those moments when Gillespie seemed to be coming so close; when it appeared, from the tenor of the conversation, both to him in the interview room and to the detectives observing, that David truly wanted to confess and tell them where to find Maria. And then it would be back to square one again. David would withdraw, declare that he had nothing to say and the process of persuasion and connection would begin all over again. Hopes would rise when David said he just needed some time to think, then plunge again as he repeated, "I've got nothing to say to you, Dewey."

Any lengthy interrogation, especially one where there is so much on the line, is an extremely tense experience, even for a skilled and seasoned investigator. Cummings talked about what he did to keep going, minute by minute, especially at those times when he felt like he'd reached the end of his rope: "It's suspenseful. It's mind-numbing. It's a huge game of cat-and-mouse, whether the person in front of you realizes it or not. When you get to that point where it's close, but you haven't got what's going to put us over the edge, you use what's called the Five Minute Rule. Which is: I'm at my wit's end. I'm almost done. I'm just going to give it five minutes. And then, at the end of five minutes, five more minutes."

They brought in the crown prosecutor to advise them and an attorney for David. At one point, they even brought in David's son, hoping that his presence might spur a confession, that having David's son see his father so degraded and charged with a serious crime might spur David to do the right thing and act honorably in front of his family, or that David's son might provide some insight that could help them move their suspect off the mark.

All the while, Gillespie was thinking as the hours ticked past, "What haven't I thrown at him? What hasn't been used in a prior interview? How do I get him to talk about Maria?"

Sometimes they'd leave the subject of Maria and talk about hunting—their common ground, because David was obsessed with hunting and Gillespie was also a hunter.

Sitting so close to David in the small room, Gillespie really sensed that David wanted to tell them where to find Maria, but that something was holding him back. He offered David possibilities: he understood how a man smothered by his wife might have lashed out in anger. Was it a blow and a fall? An impulsive shot? Gillespie continually reminded himself that, yes, David was a murderer, but he was also someone's son. And he kept hoping, kept at it, kept looking for the humanity in David, for the connection that would let the man do the right thing.

Gillespie finally asked straight out, "Do you see any hope at all, Dave, that we can resolve things?"

"In my heart?" David asked.

"Yeah," Gillespie nodded.

"Seventy percent," David responded.[13]

David told Gillespie he could keep talking, and the conversation continued. Because of their shared love of hunting, at times the dialogue veered off into hunting stories, especially Tanasichuk's tales of his bow hunting prowess. Gillespie eventually steered him back to the subject of Maria.

A few times during the interview, David suggested that Gillespie give him his business card, and some time to think, and he would call the next day to continue the conversation. While on its face it seemed a reasonable request, and evidence that Tanasichuk wanted to cooperate and give them what they were looking for, it was not a request the police wanted to agree to for a number of reasons. They knew they were dealing with a seasoned criminal who was very familiar with interrogation and the legal system. They understood that keeping up the pressure now, when Tanasichuk was most vulnerable, was their best chance to get past his practiced defenses and touch a part of him that wanted to confess. Later, those defenses would be back in place.

When continuing appeared fruitless, Gillespie voiced his frustrations and speculated that he was failing simply because he was the wrong person for the job: "We are all trying to rally around you, Dave, and say, lookit, Dave, do the right thing. But it just don't seem to be happening. And I know now, maybe I'm—I'm the wrong messenger. Maybe I'm not the guy to bring the message, I don't know. But I—I thought I was."

"You got further than anybody else did," David admitted to him.[14]

But while their instincts told them that a part of David Tanasichuk wanted to clear the air and give them Maria's body, in the end all of Dewey Gillespie's efforts failed. At long last, an exhausted Gillespie closed with a summary and an eloquent promise, a message that had a preacher's cadence.

"You have failed to take up the torch, okay, to lead the charge and do what's really your responsibility. It was yours to go and do it, so you could take the credit, but instead we will go and do it and we will take the credit, okay? Now we'll pride ourselves on bringing her home the way she should be brought. Because we will never stop, David, until we do.

"I felt for a few moments, quite a few moments as a matter of fact, that you would do the right thing. And I still believe that you have it in your heart to do the right thing, but for whatever reason, you won't. Okay. So I gotta do what I have to do, Dave. I gotta go do my job now...But I think it's a tragedy. I think it's an absolute tragedy, an opportunity came knocking...the opportunity to right the wrong. You know, to look at—look opportunity in the face and so much as say I don't give a damn, I just don't care. This is what I am and I don't give a damn. And I want the people to know that will be looking here at this, you and I, in this room, for them to know that the door—the window of opportunity opened up, Dave, and you slammed it shut."

David retorted, "They must also know that I have the right to say I have nothing to say."

"Absolutely, you do."

"And that's it," David Tanasichuk stated with finality.[15]

Dewey Gillespie reflected back on the interview: "At the end of it, I talked to David from my heart. I really meant a lot of the things I said to David, like, you know, that I cared for him. I mean, it maybe sounds crazy but at one time, he's a child, meek and mild, you know. Where did it go wrong and here he's sitting? And there's a million things going through your mind. If he admits, he's going for life. What can I give him that would make him want to talk to me? Where do you grab a theme that would make him want to talk to me? He always had a tough attitude, but there were times in there when I felt he was weak. When I told him I cared for him he says to me, 'Do you really mean that?' But you know, he's a human being and some day he's going to come out, and we'll have to live with that.

"But I didn't throw all caution to the wind. I mean, he's a killer. I go into the room with an awful lot of people who've done awful, horrible things. They all have a story. It doesn't mean it's right for them to do the things they did. But I always feel for people."

As time rolled on, the investigators found themselves on the downhill side of the adrenaline roller coaster. They went from the extreme high of catching David in an offense that would send him to jail, to the hour-after-hour tension of watching Gillespie come so close to getting a confession that they believed their murder investigation might be coming to an end, to the final, depressing realization that they weren't going to get what they'd hoped for. For some reason, even though they all felt that he wanted to, David wasn't going to give them a confession or tell them where to find Maria's body.

At one point during those long hours, the adrenaline dump left an exhausted Cummings literally sleeping on the conference room floor.

Earlier, when David was finally under arrest, Cummings had called his wife and said, "We've got him. It's done. He's going away for the next two to three years on the gun for sure." And he said, "I won't be home until the morning, at least."

Well aware of what the last weeks had been like for him, she told him that in the morning she was taking their kids to her mother's, so that when he did come home, he'd have a chance to sleep. As it happened, because of the length of the interview and other things that needed to be done, he didn't get home until the following afternoon.

The house was empty. He went inside, mixed himself a drink, then sat and watched some sports on television as he wound down. At six, he turned off the phones, pulled the blinds and went to sleep. When he woke the next morning at 8:00 A.M. he was in exactly the same position he'd been in when he went to sleep, the covers unrumpled. He hadn't moved in fourteen hours.

When Paul Fiander called him that morning at about a quarter to nine, Cummings was already out searching for evidence at a campsite where they suspected David had spent a few nights. Fiander wanted to know if Cummings wanted some coffee for their nine o'clock meeting. Cummings said no. After two long months of running on caffeine, he didn't want to taste coffee for a long time. Neither he nor Fiander have drunk a cup of coffee since.

Part 3

Just Give Us a Sign

Chapter 12

The Pressure Cooker

With Tanasichuk in jail, the investigators shifted their focus to firming up their case and putting search strategies in place to help them find Maria. Lieutenant Pat Dorian of the Maine Warden Service had gotten permission to bring some of his wardens up to Miramichi, and he was coordinating with the Maine Search and Rescue Dogs (MESARD) handlers to come and bring their highly trained cadaver dogs. A search operation was planned to take place in April or May, when the snow would have melted and Maria's frozen body would have thawed enough to begin to give off a scent.

But that was at least a month away. During those long weeks while the investigators waited for the timing to be right and for their important new resource to become available, none of them were idle.

It weighed too heavily on their minds that the gun charge against David was not enough. He might go away for two to three years, but he had gone away on gun charges several times before and, each time, he had returned to

Miramichi unreformed, unrepentant and still as violent and gun-loving as ever. If they couldn't find Maria and couldn't amass enough evidence to charge her husband with her murder, he would be out in a few years and they were certain that that meant they would once again be watching their backs and worrying about their loved ones.

If that happened, they genuinely considered finding new jobs and moving themselves and their families to other places where they could be safer from David's expected revenge. David's imprisonment meant they were less tense day-to-day than they'd been while he was on the loose, but there was still strong pressure to solve Maria's disappearance.

Nor was the likelihood of retaliation the only source of pressure. Maria's family and friends had bravely risked David's anger and potential violence to come forward to speak on her behalf. Both their courage and their need for closure weighed heavily on the investigators as the long winter weeks slipped by.

Part of their time was spent on follow-up interviews with witnesses to consolidate their evidence. They hoped that once David Tanasichuk was behind bars, where they were safe from his intimidating presence and fierce temper, people might come forward with information they had been reluctant to divulge. They also hoped that some people they had already interviewed would feel freer to share information or might be willing to go on record if they had previously been reluctant to do so.

Among those who disclosed additional information to Cummings was the young woman who had received a piece of Maria's jewelry from David. She revealed that the relationship had been sexual, something she had previously denied, and that it had begun not long after Maria disappeared. David had told his new girlfriend that he loved her and if

Maria returned, he would divorce her. In the end, it was a full year later that the young woman confided most of the details of the timing of her relationship and gave a statement for the record. And even then there were things she was too embarrassed to confide.

The original suspect in the murder of Abby Brown was invited to come in to take a polygraph test. She agreed to take it and passed.

For the most part, however, hopes that David might have talked to someone, and that someone would come forward, weren't realized. Cummings was quite frank about their hopes and their disappointment, as well as about the frustration of going out looking for Maria themselves: "We had hoped that people would think they could talk to us, now that he's in jail, and that didn't happen. Which, looking back on it now, shouldn't have surprised us too much, because it didn't happen on the other two homicides either, because this guy is a lot different from a lot of other killers. He's not out there talking to people and telling what he knows. And there were an awful lot of days, where we went out on the bikes, or we were out in the woods, and it just felt like an exercise in futility. And you know, you become defeated to the point where you get on the bike, you're heading to the woods, and you already know you're going to fail, because you've done it so many times and come back empty-handed. You're just going through the motions for the sake of going through the motions. And you can only do that five or six times before it gets old and you think, you know, we've got to change gears here and do something different, or we'll just spin our wheels forever. And that's where Pat Dorian and them came into play."

Much of the time, despite their sense of discouragement, when they weren't doing interviews, preparing warrants, consolidating their files or collecting potential evidence and transporting it to the various agencies involved in its analysis, whenever they had breaks in their other cases they felt driven to continue their search for Maria.

As Paul Fiander said, "The big thing was just us going out there walkin' it...but we had to do something, rather than just wait six weeks or eight weeks, whatever it takes 'til that day comes. You feel useless if you just sit there."

Brian Cummings agreed, "It's hard to explain. Really hard to explain. It just becomes overwhelming to the point where I stood out there and verbalized, 'Maria. Just give us a sign. Just give us something to start with and we'll take it from there.' And talking to nobody. Talking to the air. Talking to God. Just give us something."

Cummings described a time when he and Dewey Gillespie were out walking the snowmobile trails behind the Portage Restaurant. It was a cold, miserable day and the snow was so deep they were literally dragging themselves from one step to the next.

"...[Dewey] and I were out searching on our own time in the deep, deep snow and so looking forward to stopping at lunchtime and having a hot bowl of soup at the Portage because it was so cold out...and at 11:50 he stepped into a big hole and completely ripped the arse and crotch out of his pants! So bad that he refused to go to the restaurant to have a bowl of soup... and believe me...I WANTED a bowl of soup that day!"

A sample from Cummings's lengthy case notes recording the chronology of the investigation showed these activities for April:

April 1: On the snowmobile trails.
April 2: Make plans to do a fly-over...looking for ravens or
    crows. But there was a lot of snow, so it was postponed.

April 3: Updated Keith Heavrin from MESARD. Based on snow levels, Keith surmised it was three to four weeks before they could use the dogs. It was agreed they'd continue to stay in touch.

April 4: Gillespie and Cummings walked a portion of the snowmobile trail. Found the snow had not melted very much. No new tracks, etc.

April 4: Did a search warrant and general warrant at David's old apartment, asking for permission to rip up the carpets, looking for anything they'd missed, blood stains, etc. Warrant granted and search conducted.

April 7: Warden Roger Guay called to say that he had been speaking with Keith...Roger said they'd assisted in a number of homicide investigations where the victims had been buried and added that his service had a high skill level when it came to conducting cadaver searches. Talked about getting the agencies together to talk about a search.

April 8: Fiander and Cummings walked the snowmobile trails.

April 10: Cummings walked the trails with Constable Eddie Arbeau...purpose was to show Arbeau one of the areas they wanted checked from the air, for aerial search on the 11th with Jody Whyte. A flight planned for the 11th.

April 11: Flyover canceled due to high winds and snow.

April 11: Cummings and Fiander out walking in the woods found a recently constructed lean-to. Pieces of burnt wood were noted, and due to the depth of the snow, it was difficult to tell whether anything was buried under the lean-to.

The lean-to intrigued the detectives. It was an out-of-the-ordinary structure in an isolated spot and they determined that it needed further investigation. They marked out the area and, on the 13th, Cummings and Fiander traveled the trail to the lean-to with tools. They photographed and videotaped it and then began to excavate it. The site and the mysterious structure became more intriguing when, during a fly-over of the area on the 14th, observers in the plane reported that they could see Cummings and Fiander, but the lean-to was invisible from the air.

Cummings and Fiander shoveled out all the snow inside, right down to the bare ground. At that point, they debated whether it was worth trying to dig down farther into the frozen ground. Determined to exhaust every avenue, they returned a second time and spent a grueling, miserable, palm-blistering day chiseling down into the ground. It was, in Cummings's words, "a hateful day." But they had known Maria, had cared about her, and they weren't going to let her rot in the ground or be eaten by bears or other scavengers without making every effort humanly possible to recover her body.

And that was not the end of it. Since they didn't know the significance of the lean-to, and because of its unusual character, its location, its invisibility, the fact that it was hand-made and that the construction seemed to be quite recent, they couldn't dismiss its potential evidentiary value. To that end, the day after the hellish excavation, with palms still sore from all that shoveling, Cummings returned one more time with Jody Whyte and the two of them cut the ends off the logs that were used in the lean-to. They sent the ends, along with an ax they had recovered at the Tanasichuk apartment, to the laboratory to see if they could match the logs to the ax. The logs used to build the lean-to were held together with hand-knotted ropes, and those ropes were collected and the knots studied to determine whether they might yield any clues or information.

That was how it went, day after day and week after week. Discovering the lean-to sent Gillespie back to talk to

John Paquet to learn what John knew about David and axes. Another day, Gillespie was back talking to the upstairs neighbors, to see if there was anything new that they'd remembered. Day after day, when they could take the time away from other tasks, Cummings, Fiander and Gillespie walked the trails and studied the woods, looking for something they might have missed or something that the slow spring melt might reveal. Pausing again and again as they walked the woods to think: *Give us a sign, Maria. Give us something to direct us. Help us find you and we'll do the rest.*

They didn't get any signs but they didn't give up. It left them with an empty feeling whenever they walked the trails and found nothing, but they couldn't stop. Even though the community understood how the weather and snowfall was hindering the investigators' efforts, they didn't feel right not making every effort to find Maria, however exhausting and discouraging those efforts might be, because one of the key attributes that drives investigators is tenacity.

"I think you have to have hope," Fiander said. "And you know, coming up to that point, if you do lose that, then all you've done is for naught. It's easier to give up than forge on...To me that's the easy way out. That's too easy."

That attitude often is the difference between a successful case and one that goes cold. In any lengthy and complicated investigation, detectives can reach a point where there is one too many barriers and they give up and move on. These detectives who had known, and cared about, Maria were not going to do that.

Despite their limited budget, they were able to do additional fly-overs of the trails, because Eddie Arbeau was in a plane taking flying lessons. They used his lessons to send up another constable with him to study the trails, looking for signs of Maria or gatherings of ravens, crows or other predators. One day, when Greg Scott and Eddie Arbeau were in the plane, they saw a man in the woods burning something. When the plane flew over, he suddenly bolted into the woods. Relaying this suspicious behavior and his location to officers on the ground, they apprehended a thief who was burning the insulation off stolen copper wire.

Their plans for the arrival of the wardens and MESARD dogs and handlers kept getting pushed back due to the cold. From late April, it was moved to the weekend of May 9. As April ended, there were still eighteen inches of snow in the woods and lots of standing water. Fiander and Cummings went out and walked the trails again. With heavy rains predicted, the search effort was moved from the weekend of May 9 to the following weekend.

And they weren't getting encouraging news on other fronts, either. Gillespie was looking for David's new girlfriend to ask some follow-up questions and couldn't find her. The crime laboratory returned their analysis of David's computer: nothing useful was found. A few days later, the lab reported that David's ax had not been used to build the lean-to.

Until the search dogs came, there was little more that they could do.

Chapter 13

Going to the Dogs

Finally, after two months of planning and impatient waiting for the snow to melt and for the weather to be warm enough that a body might be giving off scent (the wardens, after conversations with the detectives, had surmised that Maria's body would be packed with snow and likely covered with brush or branches, which would act as insulation and further delay melting), the wardens and the Maine Search and Rescue Dog (MESARD) trainers and their cadaver dogs were coming.

The timing of the search was aimed at striking that ideal window of time when Maria's body might be found by scent but before predators would be drawn by that same scent. From his familiarity with the region, as well as decades of experience in the woods, Lieutenant Dorian had been concerned about going to New Brunswick too early, when it would be very wet in the woods and all the snow hadn't melted, as this would not be a good set of conditions for the dogs.

According to Lieutenant Dorian, for a successful search in springtime, ideally they wanted mild, rising temperatures, the snow to be gone and greenery to be just starting to grow—a minimum of about two inches. Along with air currents carrying scent from the body, that new spring greenery would serve as an additional source of scent, as the cadaver's scent would be absorbed by the vegetation, which would in turn give it off so that perhaps it could be detected by the cadaver dogs.

On May 15, four months from the last day that Maria Tanasichuk was seen alive and nearly two months after David Tanasichuk's arrest on a prohibited weapons charge, the wardens from Maine arrived to assist in locating Maria's body.

The search teams included both personnel from the Warden Service, who planned and managed the search as well as participated in it with some of their own dogs, and members of the volunteer search and rescue group MESARD. Led by Lieutenant Pat Dorian, the warden group included their mapping specialist, Kevin Adam, who was planning section chief for the Warden Service Incident Command Team, Sergeant Roger Guay and Specialist Deborah Palman. Guay and Palman brought their cadaver dogs as well.

The state of Maine is unique in that it has one agency in charge of search and rescue, unlike many other states where the responsibility may be divided among several different authorities. One significant advantage of that is its consistency—every search is run the same way, using the same mapping and computer work and the same management personnel. The result is that Maine Warden Service search and rescue personnel become highly experienced in organizing and conducting searches.

Accompanying them on this mission were six cadaver-qualified dog handlers from MESARD: Keith Heavrin, Chip Wadsworth, Jennifer Fisk, Kate Fleury, Michele Fleury and Spencer Fuller. These six volunteers were drawn from all over the state of Maine and many were traveling with more than one dog. All had driven many hours in unseasonable heat, a drive made longer by the need to take care of the dogs.

MESARD is a volunteer K-9 search and rescue group that supports search missions conducted by the Maine Warden Service, state police and other law enforcement agencies across Maine. A MESARD team consists of a highly trained K-9 handler and search dog that have completed extensive training and passed certifications. All the MESARD teams comply with the Maine Association of Search and Rescue standards. Handler and flanker training includes First Aid/CPR, day and night land navigation, radio communications, GPS, map and compass, wilderness survival, crime scene preservation, the incident command system and ground search techniques. Search dog certifications are in obedience and then one or more of the following: wilderness area search, tracking/trailing, evidence and land and water cadaver search.

Lieutenant Pat Dorian, who had been a warden for twenty-eight years, an incident commander in search and rescue for eighteen years and in charge of search and rescue for the state for eight years, was leading the effort.

If you passed Pat Dorian in a crowd, you might not notice him but he would certainly notice you, especially if you looked a little shifty. Average-sized, with dark, graying hair, he was a vigorous man who spoke twice as fast as most. He could juggle two phone calls, his e-mail and a conversation with the person in his interview chair, swearing creatively as he organized a nighttime effort to catch salmon poachers, answered a procedural question and studied a suspicious weed in a jar that might be invasive milfoil trying to gain a foothold in Moosehead Lake, without missing a beat on any front. He was energetic and righteous, and his uninflected, expletive-laden dialogue was brilliant but needed a marathon listener to keep up. He was a law-and-order guy who took the job of defending Maine's resources very seriously. In a part of Maine where law enforcement was thin on the ground, he once used his authority to make a traffic stop and took a drunk driver off the road, although the driver was surprised to find himself getting stopped by a game warden.

After two years of college in Florida, this Maine native who always knew he wanted to be a warden returned to Maine to join the Warden Service at twenty-two years of age. On his first assignment, he lived miles from anywhere with his wife in a cabin he described as having "running" water only because he had to *run* down to the pond with the bucket, chop a hole in the ice and then *run* back with it. The warden who trained him as a rookie made him walk miles in the dark without a flashlight to get him used to the woods at night. Sometimes they would walk all night.

He was passionate about the value of well-organized and coordinated search and rescue operations and was always looking for ways to make search and rescue more effective through training and technology. He arrived in Miramichi confident, after numerous phone conversations with Paul Fiander, that they would be able to mount a successful search to find Maria Tanasichuk's body. Part of that confidence stemmed from years of experience and partly from his familiarity with the Miramichi region.

Although everyone was eager to try to locate Maria, there was a significant amount of planning to be done before search missions could begin, and to facilitate an efficient and well-organized search, the wardens' "overhead" (incident management) team arrived a day early to begin to put that organization into place.

When the public hears on the news that they've "called out the dogs" or "brought in the search dogs," the image is too often that from old prison escape movies—a group of guys in uniforms toiling through the forest (usually at night, possibly accompanied by some local hunters) with a bunch of baying bloodhounds on leashes or ropes. The reality is far different.

For the search dog and handler team to be effective, hundreds if not thousands of hours have to be logged as the dog learns how to conduct different kinds of searches, from tracking and trailing following ground scent to the ability to use airborne scent to clear large blocks of land. The handler and the dog must learn to communicate with one another, and the handler learns to read and trust the information that his or her dog is providing. Despite the different personalities of the handlers, the many different breeds of dogs they use and the personalities of individual dogs, what makes a search team effective is the bond that time together and training together creates between the handler and the dog. It's teamwork of the finest kind, a deep and profound relationship that often begins when the dog is only a puppy.

Roger Guay, a warden who has been involved in search and rescue for over twenty-five years and trains search and rescue dogs, described the attributes he looks for when choosing a puppy with the potential for search and rescue work, "You know, you look at things like, are they really timid? Are they comfortable with who they are? Do they look you in the eye or are they always looking away? Do they have ball drive? Are they willing to chase a ball and play? And, if you pick them up and hold them, do they fight you or are they willing to let you hold 'em? Those are little signs."

Retired warden Specialist Deb Palman, former K-9 training coordinator for the Maine Warden Service and long-time training director for MESARD, has written extensively about training search and rescue dogs.

Palman has developed keen insights about choosing search dogs. In an article she wrote for the United States Police Canine Association website, she noted that "...selecting a dog for police K-9 training is analogous to selecting a recruit for training as a law enforcement officer. We all know that only a small percentage of the general population has the physical and mental abilities and personality to be good officers." She suggests considering dogs from "working lines" rather than "show lines," and offers the following analysis for selecting a successful K-9:

> Often the selection process starts with a temperament evaluation, because this test is usually the most inexpensive for a department...I will cover some of the general points in testing. One is that any dog used for patrol or detection purposes must be stable, comfortable and outgoing in environments which are new to the dog. Police dogs rarely work at home and must perform in places that are new to them and their handlers. Even if they work in the same area such as a prison, the situations they encounter are constantly changing.
>
> Confidence in new environments is shown in dogs of all ages, so puppies can be evaluated for this trait. Temperament tests must be done in a place that is new to the dog.
>
> Dogs used for police work must also show good "prey drive" or hunting drive. This is expressed in the desire to chase moving objects, seek out hidden objects and carry objects. This drive is essential to all scent work and off-lead apprehension work. Even young puppies should chase toys and follow moving objects. Dogs of any age which will chase and persistently search for objects in a new, adverse environment (like a slippery floor or climbing over unstable footing) make the best candidates for detector or other scent work.

Temperament testing for patrol work is best done when the dog is...approaching maturity...and shows most if not all of its temperamental traits. Maturity varies with breeds and individuals. Malinois seem to mature early at one to two years, German Shepherds at two to three and Rottweilers even later...Sometimes a dog which is not fully mature will not show a mature defense or dominance drive but would be suitable for training if trained carefully or allowed to mature before training. Even if this is so, enough of this drive should be present at 20 months to two years for an experienced evaluator to determine if the dog is a candidate or not. Someone familiar with the breed being tested will make the best evaluator.

Evaluating puppies and immature dogs is much harder because they tend to show submission to people and this will repress their defense and dominance drives. Someone who is familiar with the parents, ancestors and possibly siblings from earlier breedings and has raised and trained many puppies has the best chance of predicting whether or not a puppy will be a good working dog. The way a dog is raised also has a profound effect on its ability to work.

The best individuals show great confidence and drive even early in life, but most do not show significant defense drives until more mature. Insecure puppies or young dogs which show defensive aggression early usually grow up to be insecure adults. If a puppy from working parents shows confidence and stability in all sorts of environments, good prey drive and some indications that it has defense drive, it will probably be suitable.

A skilled evaluator can also determine by the dog's movement and gait whether the dog has any serious physical faults. Working dogs should have good conformation for their breed, good movement and agility. I prefer dogs with tight ligamentation and muscles rather than loose build because they seem to be less prone to injury. The size, color and overall looks of the dog are much less important that its soundness and ability to function. The high-drive and hard-hitting Malinois breed has proven that size and weight are not needed to be effective in bitework.

Smaller dogs are easier to transport (I once swore that I would never work a dog I could not carry out of the woods), care for and usually less prone to injury and fatigue. A small, agile detector dog can reach more places or be put in more places by its handler than a large, bulky dog.[16]

The dogs can then be trained in a number of different areas of expertise. They may be trained to work primarily on a lead with a handler or they may be trained to work off lead to quickly clear a block of land (a hasty search). Search dogs working with the Warden Service will be trained to do evidence searches, in particular finding hidden fish or game, firearms, ammunition, spent cartridges and clothing. Over the course of their training, dogs learn to discern a particular scent and follow that, despite working in an area where the scents of many people are present and the situation can be very confusing.

In her article, "Search and Rescue Dogs and the Ground Searcher," Palman offers this description:

> Search and rescue (SAR) dogs come in two basic types: air scent dogs or ground scent (tracking) dogs. Air scent dogs generally search for the lost subject or their fresh, airborne scent in a direct manner, so they are deployed at the direction of their handler in a hasty search mode or in grid searches designed to cover large blocks of ground. The strategy of the handler is similar to that of a ground searcher, except that the area covered by the dog is dependent on wind direction and other weather factors.

Maria Breau
at age
sixteen

Maria and B.J. messily celebrate
his first birthday

David and Maria
on their wedding day

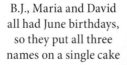

The Cyrillic "Death Dealer" tattoo on David's neck

A young David Tanasichuk, covered in tattoos, displays one of his shotguns

B.J., Maria and David all had June birthdays, so they put all three names on a single cake

B.J. on the night he died

This cabin was the site of the
off-to-college party where
B.J. was beaten to death

B.J.'s gravesite, faithfully
maintained by Maria

David's three-wheeler with the custom motorcycle front fork

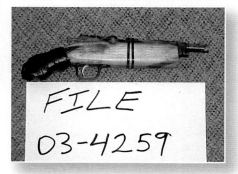

Above left, the pickup truck bed where the murder weapon was concealed.

Above right, the tarp used to wrap the sawed-off shotgun.

At left, a close-up of the gun used to kill Maria.

Body Location

Portage Restaurant

Portage Restaurant

Map showing the June search routes

Above, a close-up of the clear-cut area
where Maria's body was found

Miramichi Airport

NB Route 11

Deb Palman and Alex,
the team that found
Maria's body

The searchers meet
with, from left,
Brian Cummings,
Deb Palman, Michele Fleury,
Roger Guay, Spencer Fuller,
Dewey Gillespie and
Paul Fiander

With sincere thanks and gratitude from
The Miramichi Police Force
Miramichi, NB Canada

The Maine Warden Service officers and volunteer MESARD handlers
pose for a group photograph with their dogs

The author stands near the "Sentinel Pine," the only large dead
pine tree in the clear-cut area where Maria's remains were found,
possibly used as a landmark by the killer when he hid Maria's body

Maria's body was found wrapped up and concealed beneath a pile of brush and branches

David Tanasichuk, Maria's husband and suspected murderer

From left, Detective Constable Brian Cummings, Deputy Chief Paul Fiander, Detective Constable Greg Scott and Detective Constable Dewey Gillespie received Police Leadership Awards for their work on the case

Tracking or ground search dogs are utilized at or near the PLS (point last seen) or LKP (last known point) to follow the subject's track or path of travel that consists of scent left on the ground. Once the tracking dog acquires the track, the handler's job is to follow the dog and support the dog in its effort to follow the subject. Performing SAR tracking requires a dog well trained in scent discrimination that can follow old tracks that are often heavily contaminated by relatives and other searchers.[17]

The Maine Warden Service website describes rigorous standards for their search dogs and handlers:

Maine Warden Service K-9's and handlers train a minimum of 320 hours under the direct supervision of a Maine Criminal Justice Academy certified trainer and must complete a field test to get their initial certification with the Maine Criminal Justice Academy. They must continue to train under the direction of a trainer a minimum of 16 hours per month and complete a field test annually to maintain certification. Maine Warden Service K-9's are trained in the following areas:

1. Tracking—Following the trail of a person using that person's individual scent.

2. Evidence—Location of items containing human scent, gun powder residue or any other trained scent.

3. Hasty search—Using the air to locate persons along natural barriers such as trails, woodlines, ditches, streams and roads. The dog is trained to use the wind to follow human scent to locate injured and lost people.

4. Fish/Wildlife—K-9s trained in detection of fish or wildlife that are hidden by poachers.

5. Cadaver—K-9s trained in detection of human remains.[18]

There is a significant difference between the scents of live persons and cadaver scent. Alive, we all have our own unique scents. While there may be slight differences, cadavers generally all have the same scent.

According to the *Cadaver Dog Handbook: Forensic Training and Tactics for the Recovery of Human Remains* by Andrew Rebmann, Edward David and Marcella H. Sorg, "Cadaver scent differs from live scent. It is chemically generic and not specific to one individual. The chemical reactions associated with decomposition are essentially the same in all bodies. However, cadaver scent is not a single scent, but a range of scents produced during different stages of the decomposition process."[19]

Whether or not a search dog is being trained as a cadaver dog, it is generally a good training strategy to expose search dogs to cadaver scent as part of their training. Otherwise, a dog may search a sector and find a body but return without indicating. Explaining the problem of sending dogs trained in live search out on a search where the person turns out to be deceased, Guay said, "This is why, in the Warden Service, we ended up getting our dogs into the cadaver realm. Because we were getting involved in searches where the people we were looking for were deceased and what was happening, in a lot of cases, was...dogs have a natural aversion to dead humans. A lot of dogs. Not all. They don't like dead humans. They sense the badness of it and it creeps them out, in part from reading their handlers' negative reactions. So we were getting cases, and I was incident commander at the time and I was seeing a lot of stuff, search and rescue-wise, and I was seeing this pattern where dogs had been in that area and wouldn't go there (where the body was)."

Rebmann et al, confirm this phenomenon:

At the time of biological death, the individual scent emitted by a subject undergoes a transformation. This change is not immediately detectable by a human; however, it obviously affects the composition of the odor detected by the dog and the resulting behavior. A phenomenon that has been noted by many tracking/trailing dog handlers is that some dogs will follow a trail, often many days old, but fail to close in on the body if the subject is deceased. They may register the scent change and, whether from fear, difference in odor, or some other reason, may not approach...in reality, the dog is showing aversion to cadaver scent.[20]

While trainers can be coy about revealing the sources of cadaver scent they use to train their dogs, funeral homes and dentist's offices can be good sources and pulled teeth are useful because teeth are often what survives a fire and can be a good training device and starter model for dogs searching under these conditions. Sometimes trainers will get gauze pads from medical examiner's offices. Samples taken from sites where bodies have been found can be great sources of cadaver scent. It is this *adipocere*—sometimes known as corpse wax—a fatty substance that is often produced under anaerobic conditions and where there is moisture, that tends to go into the ground and become the lingering source of cadaver scent. Eventually that adipocere in the soil will be taken into the neighboring vegetation, which itself becomes a source of scent.

The availability of source scent varies in different parts of the country. Sometimes cadaver dog trainers will even trade scents to fill out their collections so that they can, in Roger Guay's words, "dial the dogs in to the age and type of scent anticipated in a particular search." Since it is generally recommended to keep scent samples frozen, it's possible to imagine a trainer's freezer filled not with ice cream or popsicles but with carefully labeled containers of scent objects to use for cadaver dog training.

Roger Guay says that he likes to store his samples in natural conditions, so his are hidden in an old military lock box somewhere in the woods, and samples used for a particular training event will travel with him in one or more old ammunition boxes.

Cadaver dogs are trained to identify and respond to many kinds of cadaver scent: old scent, fresh scent and sometimes even ashes. Air scent cadaver dogs are trained to search a block of land where the scent may be on the ground, buried under ground or even up in a tree. They may also have the additional expertise of being able to detect bodies that are in the water, either from boats or from the shore, (even, occasionally, from planes) by detecting scent molecules rising from underwater into the air. Trainers say that these molecules may be detectible within a few hours of death. Commenting on another search for the body of a missing New Hampshire girl ultimately found in the water, Lieutenant Dorian said, "They don't understand the dog world enough to know, if she was in the river system, within a couple of hours, if you got the right dogs you'd know automatically if there was a body there...but it is so difficult to break through that barrier, that wall of 'we know all' attitudes that a lot of police officers have. Why not try something new and different?"

Testing and training under different conditions and with different scenarios is essential to developing a competent search dog. But the most critical part is the time the dog and handler spend together creating that essential bond where the trainer can read the dog, the dog can read the trainer and the trainer learns to trust his or her dog's reactions and signals. And sometimes, a dog or a trainer may develop a bad habit that will require retraining, such as a dog's failure to indicate when it has made a find.

Not only are a well-trained dog and a strong relationship between the dog and the handler essential to a search, but handlers carry another responsibility as well: the importance of carefully documenting their dog's training, certifications and retraining at regular intervals, and the ability to adequately document a search event. Whether the search team is working in a professional law enforcement capacity or as a highly trained and skilled volunteer, depending on what result the search produces there may well be reports to be written and/or ultimately a court process involved.

Deborah Palman addresses this in a training article she wrote for MESARD:

All volunteer SAR dog handlers must keep records of their training and their dog's training. These records are needed to keep track of training progress, for planning future training exercises, and most importantly, to provide records for possible legal challenges to the team's work. Legal proceedings involving SAR dog teams may be criminal if the team becomes involved in a criminal investigation, or civil if the team or an entity the team works for is sued in civil court.

A proportion of missing persons are missing because of suicide, criminal activity or sometimes due to negligent actions by their caregivers. Any of these situations may lead to the criminal prosecution of suspects involved in the incident or the civil prosecution of someone who is deemed to be negligent. Unfortunately, sometimes the death of a missing or lost person causes the person's relatives to pursue the civil prosecution of those authorities who are responsible for the search, whether or not the suit is warranted...As part of the search effort, all search and rescue teams may share in the liability for a search, although the organizing entity ultimately will be held the most responsible.

If a SAR dog team ends up locating the victim and the victim is deceased or is the victim of criminal or negligent activity, the SAR dog handler will be called to testify in court if a court trial ensues, because the finding of the victim is an essential part of the investigative chain of events. Since the dog cannot testify, the dog handler has to testify to the actions of the dog. In order to testify to the actions of the dog and their meaning, the handler has to be established as having trained with the dog and as having the experience, training and skill to interpret what the dog is doing. This is the point in the trial where training records will be introduced. This is where certifications or other proofs of performance are valuable and can save having to testify to the details in training records.

Fortunately, most air scent SAR dog finds are pretty straightforward. The handler interprets what the dog does and follows the dog to the victim, a result that is immediately verifiable by the handlers and others. Meeting "industry standards" for training records and programs is more essential for the use of tracking/trailing dogs, which follow an unseen scent path, and detector dogs like cadaver dogs that may be used to establish probable cause to search or to say that cadaver scent was present. In this case, the handler may be called into court to testify to something that is not easily verified by a human.

Tracking/trailing and cadaver dog handlers must keep accurate and complete records of training so they can be prepared to testify in relation to any case involving evidence they "locate." The path a tracking dog takes when locating a victim may turn out to be essential to a court case. The cadaver dog that indicates on "scent" that cannot be verified by a find or forensic evidence may also end as an important part of the prosecution's or defense's court case. Sometimes being able to say that a track or other scent was not present becomes as important as saying it was present. This may be true with air scent dogs who clear areas or bodies of water. It goes without saying that these types of dogs should be training to, meeting and certifying to an industry-accepted standard.

Although it does not happen often, a SAR dog team may find itself being sued as part of a suit alleging that the team was not properly trained or deployed and harm resulted to the victim. This is yet another reason to keep good records and train and test to an accepted standard.

What records should a SAR handler keep? Everyone has different comfort and ability levels regarding records and organization. If going to court, be prepared to bring everything, including veterinary records if an attack on the dog's health is anticipated. All certificates and other proof of performance tests taken should be included.

Each time the dog is trained, a record needs to be made. The more detailed and organized, the better, but there is a minimum. The date, weather and terrain are important for SAR dogs working outside. If a trainer or other person who trains regularly with the team is present, they should be named in the record. A short description of what was done and approximately how much time was spent on each subject is needed. Tracking dog and detector handlers should keep some records of statistics like the age and length of the track, amount and type of scent material used in training, etc. "Find" rates are also important. A find rate might be a tabulation of the number of training samples present and the number of samples that were found by the dog or team. Courts accept the fact that dogs are not accurate 100 percent of the time. In fact, if the records show the dog never fails, the court and others will become suspicious that the records are inaccurate or fabricated.

A short summary of how the dog did, or a rating, should also be part of the record. Matt Zarrella of the Rhode Island State Police told me that what was essential was a description of "what went right, what went wrong, and what was being done to fix what went wrong." If the dog is only working at a basic level, be sure to mention this somewhere in the records and rate the performance according to the dog's level of training.

It is important that handlers design a system that works for them that they can complete in a timely manner. I make out handwritten records in a spiral notebook the evening after training or an actual search if I don't fill out a form after training is over. This rough, handwritten record is then transferred to forms in a computer file when I have time. The Excel worksheets I use allow me to total my training exercises, find statistics and hours in various subjects if needed, an added plus when using spreadsheet type programs.

Deployment records should also be kept. Documented use at searches by official agencies and actual finds on real deployments can be important to establish the team's credibility. It may also become important to have an idea of what the team did at the search if the area searched becomes more important later on. For example, Sgt. Roger Guay was called to testify in a murder trial because he did not find any handgun cartridge shells in a particular place. It seemed the defendant in the case was claiming that the victim fired many shots from a handgun at the suspect before the suspect fired back, killing the victim. What the defendant failed to understand however, was Sgt. Guay and his K-9, which had over a hundred actual finds of expended cartridges at wildlife poaching scenes, had searched the very area the suspect claimed the shooting took place and found nothing. Sgt. Guay was called to rebut the defendant's testimony.

In summary, design a system that works for you. You may choose to just put the date and weather down, who was there as a trainer and then a sentence about what was done if the exercise was short, or several paragraphs if more time was spent. Or you may design a standardized "check off" or fill-in-the-blanks form that can be filled out quickly and perhaps tabulated at a later date. Whatever is done, be sure that the basic information is preserved in case it is needed later.[21]

Game Warden Sergeant Roger Guay and Game Warden Kevin Adam gave a presentation at the 2004 NASAR conference, entitled "Search Techniques for Successful Missing Person/Homicide Investigation," that included details of the disappearance of a young woman from Portland, Maine, and the search for Maria Tanasichuk. Guay and Adam laid out some of the competencies that were essential to a successful search. With respect to training a handler, they noted that an experienced handler must be clue-conscious, comfortable in a wilderness environment, in good physical condition, able to pick up subtle changes in canine behavior, comfortable working at night and knowledgeable about using compass/GPS technology.

In terms of canine training, they identified some of the techniques essential for producing a dog that would be effective on a large-scale search. These included training the dogs with multiple-aged cadaver specimens, training in varied search environments, training the dogs to have a strong reaction to the find to adequately alert the handler and training for the fact that, in the real world, searches may include long hours, multiple environments and no finds.

They also noted the importance of trainer awareness of environmental factors that can affect the success of a search. These include the presence of ground water or surface water, the effects of weather, how different soil types and types of vegetation can affect scent, frozen ground, wind, animal contaminants and the condition of the body, including whether it may have been consumed by animals. Where there is a buried body, it may be in a shallow or deep grave. Many of these factors would come into play for the teams during the search for Maria Tanasichuk.

The whole matter of understanding terrain and airflow science plays a huge role in determining whether a search is ultimately successful. Time of day and rising temperatures, for example, can create a situation where the scent from the body is lifted straight up. This may mean that the dogs have to be closer to the source to effectively locate it. It may also mean that that scent will come down in another area and create a scent pool or pocket, an area where the scent is trapped by a barrier. In these situations, a dog may give a strong indication that the body is nearby, while not alerting on the source.

Once the area is cleared, the handler will need to read the surrounding area to determine what features might be trapping or condensing the scent and causing it to pool, what direction the wind is coming from and where the scent might be flowing from, and then redirect the dog. Sometimes, in complex terrain, handlers may even use smoke bombs to assess airflow to help them direct their dogs.

Scent pools away from the body's location can also linger from weather on previous days, creating conditions where several fringe scent pools must be cleared. Situations like this are frustrating for the dogs, as they are anticipating a find and a reward.

All of these factors separate most scent work—bomb dogs, drug dogs and many evidence searches—from wilderness searches for lost or injured people and cadavers. So it wasn't simply some handlers and a bunch of crated dogs that arrived in Miramichi in May for the long-awaited search. It was a highly-trained group of SAR professionals and volunteers who brought with them decades of experience in organizing, coordinating and carrying out a successful search and rescue operation.

The wardens arrived on May 15, to give them time to collect the data necessary for an effective search and to put the mapping in place that would enable them to create individual assignments for the canine teams and guide those search teams through the area. As soon as they arrived, the wardens went to work on many fronts.

As Dorian explained, the wardens' training and experience added a perspective to the investigation different from that of a regular police department. Because they do so many outdoor investigations, they think differently from a normal investigator. They're experienced in analyzing the geography of the potential search area in terms of where someone might get access to dump or hide a body, including breaking down the area into distinct zones divided by roads, rivers, tracks, wires, etc. Because people behave differently depending on whether the act took place during the day or at night—there's a lot of statistical information about how people's behavior is different at night—they also wanted to determine what the detectives might know about the potential timing of Maria's death so it could be factored into their planning.

In 2001, Lieutenant Dorian had attended SAR training taught by Michael St. John, from the Marin County, California, SAR unit. That training had focused on using SAR techniques for assisting law enforcement in locating victims of child abduction and homicide. Dorian had returned to Maine with this new knowledge and the question: How could the Warden Service, with its well-developed SAR and outdoor expertise, become a resource for law enforcement?

A case soon came along to test Dorian's question—the disappearance from Portland, Maine, of twenty-five-year-old Amy St. Laurent in December 2001. After reading news stories for six weeks about fruitless searches for the missing woman, Dorian contacted the Maine state police, offering assistance. A huge search effort was put into place, employing the warden's overhead team and the techniques Dorian had learned in that course. As a result, homicide victim Amy St. Laurent, buried in a carefully concealed grave in the Maine woods, was located, bringing closure to a family that had lived with uncertainty for more than seven weeks. Her killer was ultimately convicted and sentenced to sixty years in prison.

That case was pivotal in making the wardens a go-to resource for police agencies in cases where it was suspected that the missing person might be deceased and the body might be hidden in the woods.

Roger Guay talked about the difference between police investigators' expertise and what the wardens bring to the search: "The science of searching...In our world, because we did it every day, day in and day out, whether it was for a shell casing or a lost person or a poached animal, that's where our skills were. We were always looking for something...so when we started doing it in Amy's case...and some of these other high-profile cases we got involved with, we were realizing that, wait a minute, there's two different schools of thought here, we have this whole different track that nobody really pays attention to, that this (our knowledge of searching in the woods and of human behavior in the woods) is how you get to find that little square spot on the ground that you are looking for. And, you know, we just need to plug that into them. You know, we saw it in Miramichi when we went there... my perception when we had our first meeting, was that their thinking was: okay, here's the industrial park, we kind of want you guys searching around this. They weren't anticipating us to be able to say...we need to know what the suspect does, we need to know where his world is. We need to know the answers to these behavioral questions that we have. They weren't anticipating any of this. They thought we were going to come in and walk dogs and go home. They weren't anticipating the process."

Dorian knew that 72 percent of victims are found within 200 feet of where the murder took place, so they liked to search within 300 feet of a travel way. He also knew that once a killer realizes what he's done, there's a sense of panic and a need to get out of there as quickly as possible. He knew that a killer is unlikely to go far into the woods at night, and that people traveling in the woods at night believe they travel much farther than they actually do. That knowledge would be applied, and adjusted, in this case, to what they would learn about the suspect and the circumstances of Maria's disappearance by interviewing the investigators.

The interviews would involve information about David's familiarity with the terrain around the city, his hunting and fishing habits and his modes of travel. The interviews would reveal that many of the common assumptions about where a body might be dumped, hidden or buried had to be tempered by the knowledge that *this* suspect did not drive a car or necessarily travel along the roadways, but was more likely to have been traveling along the trail system, that he was unusually comfortable in the woods at night and by the fact that the trail systems around Miramichi were vast, complex and intricate.

As Dorian put it, "If you talk about a travel way...the situation in Miramichi was just unbelievable...the way they cut (timber, as much of these trails were logging roads) and the way it's laid out...I never saw anything like it."

And Cummings, having spent so many days searching the woods and, with his team, trying to devise strategies for locating Maria's body, acknowledged what a huge task it was, and how important it was to have the wardens' help: "I'm a hunter, but you don't realize how big the woods are until you're in the woods looking for something. You think of a person as pretty big, but it's like looking for a needle in the proverbial haystack. Because the woods are a huge place and if someone has secreted something in the woods, you need a lot of luck and a lot of good, dedicated people on your side, like we had later. And you're not going to find Maria without those people on your side."

Time was short, as they only had a limited time away from their jobs, so Pat Dorian and the other wardens had to act quickly to gather the necessary information to determine the search area. In an ideal search situation, two resources would be put into every search area—a dog and handler team, followed by a human ground search team. Here, they only had the dogs, and they only had a few days.

With limited time and resources, they needed to do everything possible to design the most effective search—one that would take into account everything the police could tell them about where, in the vast tracts of woods surrounding the city, David Tanasichuk might have hidden his wife's body. They needed to identify the highest probability areas so that those could be searched first.

Here, much of the information the detectives had gathered over the past months would prove useful. In a strange kind of role reversal for the detectives, they found themselves being the ones interviewed, as the wardens elicited the information their experience had told them they would need to shape an effective search. As part of this process, several very interesting aspects of inter-agency cooperation came into play. First, as the wardens were well aware, police are used to being in charge of information and their investigations, and they are wary about sharing that information. Often, case details are disclosed to outside agencies on a very limited basis, and that failure to fully disclose what the police know can be a significant handicap for the wardens designing the search. Sometimes that withholding is a control issue, as different public safety organizations can be seriously territorial. Often, though, the information is not offered because the investigating agency is unaware of its value and importance to the wardens.

Any warden and any cop can tell stories of cases whose success was impaired or delayed because of inter-agency territorialism or a failure on one part to appreciate the value of information held. But there was none of that game-playing or jostling for control going on in Miramichi. The detectives were aware that one aspect of those initial interviews was that they were being tested by the wardens to determine how open they were going to be.

The Miramichi detectives were willing to share everything they knew.

They detailed David's outdoor expertise, including his three-wheeling and his passion for hunting, to the wardens. They described his familiarity with the trails and the areas the surveillance team had seen him visiting after Maria went missing. Of particular significance, to the detectives and the wardens, was the neighbor's story of David's series of odd forays into the woods at night at the time Maria disappeared, coupled with Donald Malley's tale of David coming out of the woods on the following day, a peculiar "jug-shaped bulge" under his jacket, and refusing to recognize him.

The wardens were aware that it was part of their job to educate the detectives about what they needed to know. Not only what the police thought they needed to know, but the detailed information about the suspect's character and woodland habits that the wardens had learned, over time, could be essential to identifying the best areas to search. As Roger Guay noted, "Initially, the focus was on that industrial park area, but once we got on track of his other activities (bear hunting and other hunting) and where he had guns hidden, and we had the timeline and we'd run the ATVs, and we found out he'd grown marijuana in this area, all the pieces started coming together. And kinda like in the Amy St. Laurent case, when we started to rule out and identify highest probabilities, it started coming together right there."

Much in the way that a detective may have to do multiple interviews to get the whole story, the wardens ultimately acquired the information they needed for a successful search through a series of discussions.

Investigators told the wardens about David's habit of shooting an animal and then recruiting Maria's help bringing it home, that the Tanasichuks' apartment did not appear to be a place where something had happened to Maria and how Maria would likely have been easily lured out into the woods by her husband. The consensus was that whatever had happened to Maria had likely happened somewhere in the woods on the night of the 15th.

The search parameters had to be tailored to these new conditions and their mapping necessarily involved finding a way to upload the trail systems to their GPS devices so that the search of those trails could be broken down into missions and those individual missions—or the searching and clearing of a particular defined section of the search area—could be mapped and tracked to ensure that each section was systematically and thoroughly searched and all of the necessary ground was covered. As Pat Dorian often said, much of a search is elimination. You're obviously out there looking to find the person, but you're also carefully eliminating possibilities as the areas are searched, gathering and assessing additional information, then narrowing and refocusing the search as necessary. It's a process of trusting your resources—your dogs and the handlers—to successfully clear and eliminate the areas searched.

Dorian and his team were fairly sure, both from the time of year that Maria disappeared and their experience with people disposing of bodies, that Maria's body would be on the surface. It was highly likely, however, that David had packed the body with snow and further disguised it by covering it with branches or downed trees.

Lieutenant Dorian explained, "One of the things was... the simple fact that when she went missing the ground was frozen solid as the Rock of Gibraltar, so the probability of him being able to bury her was zero to none, so we knew more than likely she had to be on top of the ground somewhere, and it just depended on what the ground looked like whether we could actually find her."

For Kevin Adam, who was responsible for the mapping, his first assignment was to locate a GPS mapping program for Eastern Canada, which he could use in conjunction with local maps of the Miramichi area. He would then need specialized area maps with an overlay of the local trail system. This turned out not to be a simple task. Despite trying multiple resources, he was unable to find anyone who could tell him what mapping programs they used in Canada.

Eventually, Kevin found a resource with the forestry service who could provide a program, which he installed, and got forestry service personnel to give him a quick lesson in how to use it. Then they got some files and uploaded them, showing mapping of the area. Finally, he had to figure out how to upload the local trail system to the computer so they could map the trails and assign search sectors, and create a record of the areas covered as they searched and those which still needed to be searched.

It would be that constantly updated mapping of the areas searched which would ensure that they had thoroughly covered each section before moving on to the next. Each team of dog and handler would be recording their start and end points for each mission on a GPS device and uploading that to the overall map on Kevin's computer.

Uploading the trail system turned out to be a significant challenge. When he was unable to locate an uploadable map of the system, they used typical warden ingenuity and created their own. Because the city was essentially surrounded by forest, and they had limited time and resources, they set the parameters of the search using the information Cummings had gotten from Ralph about David's series of mysterious trips on the night of January 15.

As Kevin Adam described it, "We had geographic base maps and photos of the area, but no map of the trail system. We created that by putting a GPS on an ATV and sending someone out to ride and record on trails in the suspected area. Instructed them to drive normally...go out six to seven minutes from the [Tanasichuk] apartment, and upload those readings. By using aerial photos that the forestry department had, we could locate intersections and field edges and cuts. We then took digital photos of the area, and I synchronized their programs to the maps."

The process was nitty-gritty, "fly by the seat of your pants" mapping, but Kevin Adam was an expert who was passionate about mapping technology, and, having spent years facing the challenges of patrolling, all alone, vast tracts of the Maine woods, he *was* an innovator. Innovation, along with doggedness, stamina and patience, was the Warden Service way. They'd come a long way, they only had a few days and what they'd learned from the investigators about David made it clear how important finding Maria's body was.

In an ideal world, the wardens would have put dual resources into each search area—both dogs and handlers and a grid search team. They always liked to employ multiple resources. However, for this mission, they didn't have the grid search teams to follow behind the dogs. They had to go with the resources they had.

Dogs and handlers would set search limits of approximately 150 to 300 feet off the trails depending on the terrain. Data showing what terrain had been searched would be uploaded from each team's GPS device after each search mission was finished.

Once they had interviewed the detectives, the wardens rode out with them to survey the areas the detectives felt were the highest priority to be searched. Then they used this on-the-ground information and the GPS data to divide those high-priority areas into segments, create the mapping parameters for each segment and give the search teams their assignments for four days. On the 16th, the MESARD volunteer handlers and their dogs arrived and the searches began.

Team members were given a flyer that had been developed by Kevin Adam and Pat Dorian, describing what they were searching for and the tactics and hazards of the endeavor:

MIRAMICHI SEARCH

We are conducting a search for a white female 5' 4", 160 lbs. with long brown hair down past her shoulders. Currently there is no information as to what she may be wearing for clothes. All shoes that she is known to wear have been found in the residence. It appears from information that all jewelry she may have been wearing was taken from her. Information has determined that the victim was last seen in mid January 15 or 16. Around the same time the suspect in this case made three trips on a three wheeled ATV approximately 10 minutes long each trip at approximately 0100 hours. At that time there was 5–6 inches of snow on the ground. The main snowmobile trails were groomed.

Victim may be wrapped in a blanket or sleeping bag or covered with some type of material which may be blue or green for concealment. We do not believe that the victim is buried underground because of the ground being frozen and snow covered at the time of the incident. However it is highly probable that she is covered with brush, logs, small trees, and or stumps.

Information has revealed suspect is a hunter and very familiar with woods and ATV/snowmobile trails in the area. He has also in the past hidden contraband items in the middle of the woods for later retrieval. One of those areas is in the search area.

Search handlers should be aware that suspect may also be linked to the disappearance of a male subject in his late thirties in February of 1999. That disappearance occurred from the same residence, that person could also be located in the search area, as subject has never been seen again.

SEARCH TACTICS: Search along roadways, trails, hiking paths no more than 100 yards into wooded areas. Handlers need to be very clue conscious to their dogs as the scent may be diminished due to man made and environmental factors. Handlers need to check large brush piles and thickets thoroughly with their dog. Also small twitch or ATV paths into woods should be thoroughly followed and searched around those areas.

HAZARDS: Handlers need to be cautious of their dog's feet, as there are many old dumps the area with mostly old glass and sharp metal edges.

GPS UNITS: We are using Minutes and Seconds, NAD83 is the Datum. You need to change the time offset in your GPS to read (-03:00) as they are an hour ahead of us.

COMMUNICATIONS: If victim is found you may be able to reach one of the warden units on SWCC as there has been no other traffic up here on that channel. If you are unable to reach one of the warden units on the radio there will be wardens and police up on the snowmobile trail towards the Portage Restaurant. If you can still find no one go to the police station or call from a store.

MAKE SURE YOU TAKE A
GOOD WAYPOINT READING
SO WE CAN FIND IT AGAIN.
ALSO LEAVE A FLAGGING TRAIL.

Chapter 14

Fruitless

Not much went well for the determined searchers. While they had timed their arrival to miss the worst of the mosquito season, winter had been slow to release its grip on the region. The heavy snowfall had left the woods flooded and low areas still held patches of unmelted snow.

It was slow and uncomfortable going for the teams. They were also concerned that the presence of unmelted snow meant that Maria's body might not yet be thawed and might not be giving off scent. To make matters worse, the weather was hot and still, without wind to carry scent to the dogs. Roger Guay described the scene, "We had these really cold pockets with all of that snow...little pockets of ice-cold snow holding everything right in. You could see the mist where the air was being held...you'd have a place where the air was fifty degrees [10 degrees Celsius] and just a few feet away the air would be in the thirties [around zero Celsius]. Too much variance there to be really effective for using scent to search."

Search and rescue workers are used to working under difficult conditions. They train in the winter, in the rain, in swamps. They train at night. They train under all possible conditions so that when the call comes, they will be able to respond in a professional way with a dog trained to perform under those conditions.

The task was grueling. Not only were they working in difficult terrain for eight to twelve-hour shifts, but during the whole of that time, they were not just walking. They were searching. As they were covering their territory, they were constantly alert to the actions and reactions of their dogs so that they were aware of what the dogs were sensing and could read their dogs and give them support and direction. They were also constantly scanning the landscape themselves, looking for, in this case, David's distinctive tire track pattern, for footprints leading off the trail, for mounds of what might be disturbed earth, for a mass of brush that might have been used to cover a body, marks on a tree that might signal that brush was cut, bent or broken branches or other subtle signs that someone had gone that way through the woods.

It was so wet in the woods that Deb Palman had to change her boots and socks three times a day, taking care of her feet so that she could keep working. She alternated her two dogs, Hannah and Alex, for the eight hours they were out there. Being aware of the dogs' safety is always an important consideration for their handlers and in Miramichi's woods, the footing was treacherous for the dogs as well as their handlers. The long-standing country habit of dumping things in the woods meant that anywhere off the trail, the ground was likely to be littered with old cans and bottles, discarded pieces of metal, appliances, broken glass and other hazards. It meant the dogs had to be more careful in picking their tracks and the handlers more vigilant in protecting them and keeping an eye out for dangers.

Because of the timeline of David's mysterious searches, its proximity to the Tanasichuk apartment and the places David had gone when the police were conducting surveillance, much of the searching was focused on the industrial park area. Even when the searchers were ready to move farther out along the trail and deeper into the woods, Deb Palman's discovery of a set of David's unique ATV tire tracks drew them back toward the city. Further evidence that David had been driving there was that investigators knew the chain drive sprocket cover was missing on his bike. This exposed chain was located down underneath the motor, so when he was driving over a log, for example, the chain would leave a distinctive mark on the log as it was turning on the sprocket.

Although many parts of the woods close to the city contained dumped trash, appliances or junked vehicles, the area that was loosely designated as the industrial park area also contained part of an abandoned dump.

"I think it was in the industrial area there was a section of an old, old town dump. It was about as creepy a place as you'd ever find," Roger Guay said. "People were out there digging big holes down into it to get the old bottles. And they were digging way down inside. It was kind of grown-over with short brush, and you'd be going along searching and boom! There'd be this big hole that went down into the ground. Stuff you couldn't see until you were right on top of it. And there were people down in those holes. That was a tricky spot and we had to work carefully around it. And that was right on the fringe of the industrial area. So that was kind of why we focused on it."

Over the course of three days, Wardens Palman and Guay and the six MESARD cadaver-qualified handlers and their dogs conducted approximately forty search missions on foot and covered over one hundred and thirty-seven miles.

During those three days, Detective Cummings accompanied Guay on each of his missions. On the first day, due to the extreme wetness in the woods, Cummings decided, to his eternal regret, to wear his fishing waders. Guay, like Dorian and Palman, was used to spending many hours traveling through the woods in search of lost hikers or hunters, or tracking down illegal hunters or fisherman. After twenty years of covering the vast Maine wilderness around Greenville, he was a "plunge right in and get the job done" kind of guy. And one who, it is said, liked to test the mettle of presumably less outdoorsy police officers.

Trudging mile after hot, muggy mile in those waders left Cummings with a serious case of chafed skin on his legs. By the end of the day, he was in serious pain, but, just as he'd been determined earlier in the case to persist until David Tanasichuk was behind bars, he was going to persist until the search was over and they found Maria. Watching the handlers and their dogs, especially because of the time he spent walking the trails with Guay and his dog, and observing that interaction, Cummings came to share Dorian's certainty that they would locate Maria.

"I know I went with Roger and we went twelve miles," Cummings said. "It nearly killed me. Me in a pair of hip waders. I remember all the skin was wore off the insides of my legs. And I didn't complain because Kevin and Pat had told me that Roger took great pride in wearing cops down because they're not used to being out in the woods. And he (Roger) could walk forever.

"Roger was a dream. I really thought Roger was going to find that body, just because watching him work, and seeing the dog work...to me it was just a matter of time...watching the dogs and the handlers working with each other and the little nuances that the dogs would do that to you and I would just be a quirk or something, but to the handler, it was huge. I can remember specifically once, being with Roger, and I think it was with Reba, and she just stopped for a second and looked over her right shoulder at Roger...and as soon as they made eye contact, she just looked away and she was gone. And that was her way of saying 'I just smelled something. Follow me.' And Roger said that...he said, 'She's onto something' and that was just her way of signalling: I just smelled something. Follow me. And Roger said, 'She's onto something' and away we went. And just about 300 yards later, we were standing over a dead cow moose that somebody had shot. I was thinking...wow, because we would have to have been within twenty feet of that thing before we could smell it. Also, I was thinking: just that little look from that dog and him picking up on that and saying 'we're onto something' and away we went.

"And that happened a dozen times and very early, it was like...yeah, they're going to find her. It's just a matter of time."

For three days, May 16–18, they searched, returned to upload their data and get new search assignments, then went out and did it again. Although they covered a huge amount of territory and discovered numerous animal carcasses left behind by hunters, they did not find Maria.

As Palman later wrote in her report:

> The Maine dog handlers left, tired, footsore and thoroughly depressed. The Miramichi detectives were beginning to plan where they should move to keep their families safe when David got out of jail in a few years. Lieutenant Dorian, undaunted as always, was already talking about when the next mission would take place.[22]

The day they left was a hard day for everyone. The community had been aware of the searches and was waiting for the news to report results. The detectives, having exhausted all the avenues they could think of to find Maria, now faced the depressing possibility that she might never be found and that David would never be charged with her murder. Palman's words were echoed by Paul Fiander, talking about how it felt, watching the wardens and the MESARD volunteers driving away, taking the detectives' high hopes with them: "I'll tell you something, when they came and did that first search, and the day they left here, you talk about an empty feeling. [Brian Cummings] and I watched them drive out and we were over there by the back door. And it was one of the emptiest feelings we ever had. Because they had been here, they searched, didn't find her. David is in jail. And you just started thinking, are we ever going to find her? Not that you ever give up, by any means, but just where do you go from here?"

Cummings commiserated, "Time ran out on the weekend and they all had to go back to Maine. And they said they would come back. But I've been involved in enough investigations where something fails so you don't go back to it. And I can remember Paul and I being in the room, and Paul looking at me and saying: 'What do we do now?'

"Because I can remember them saying to us, day one, Kevin [Adams] and Pat [Dorian] sitting in that room after they'd peppered us with questions about the investigation, and I can remember Kevin looking at Pat, saying: 'We'll find her.'

"And at the end of two days: Gone. Deflated is...uh...a good term. Because we were asking, what do we do now?"

Chapter 15

Wonders Never Cease

T he months since her disappearance had been very difficult for Maria's close friends and her family. While everyone had become resigned to the likelihood that she wouldn't be found while there were several feet of snow on the ground, the detectives had stayed in close touch with those closest to Maria and they were aware of the impending search and its importance. Her friend Darlene, her former sister-in-law Cindy Richardson, her sister, Sharon, and Sharon's husband, Edmund, had all pinned their hopes on a successful outcome of that search. During the first search, all the while that the searching was going on, Sharon would send her husband over to the industrial park area to see what was happening.

While her husband was doing that, Sharon drove around, crying and praying that someone would come and bring her the news that her sister's body had been found. When the searchers departed without success, her heart sank just like the detectives' had. For more than four months, those who had loved Maria had waited for closure. For a chance to lay

193

Maria to rest next to her son, B.J., and to move on with mourning her instead of waiting in limbo. David Tanasichuk, in his jail cell, might have crowed in triumph but others were left as devastated as the Miramichi detectives.

In the week following the search, Sharon's husband, Edmund, troubled by the unsuccessful effort to find her and feeling a need to do something himself, both out of his affection for Maria and his concern about his wife's suffering, approached the Miramichi police and asked for permission to search for Maria on his own. He had done some searching before and he wasn't giving up. On that particular day, he felt a strong need to go out there and see if he could find Maria.

Sharon's husband was a simple man. He was attractive, hard-working, slightly hard-of-hearing and quietly religious. He had watched his family's anguish during the long wait for a result. His wife missed her frequent phone chats with her sister, and worried that there might never be closure and a chance to give Maria a decent burial. His daughter had been very close to B.J. and, later, to Maria. In Sharon's words, her daughter, Angela, and Maria had become "like sisters." Maria had stood up at her wedding, and she had asked Maria to be the godmother to her twins, an event to which Maria had been looking forward. Angela had been one of the last people to speak with Maria, in a phone call on the afternoon of January 15, the last day Maria was seen alive.

Edmund Carroll remembered happier times, when the families would get together, Maria and B.J. joining him, his wife and their daughters. Everyone had been strapped and struggling, but they had loved each other and managed to have some pretty good times. On one memorable day, Sharon recalled everyone had been kidding around and Maria, who had a bubbly, fun-loving nature, had started a water fight with Edmund. After chasing each other around the house,

Maria had trapped him in the bathroom, shoved him into the shower and put on the water. He then dragged Maria into the shower, Sharon had gotten into the game and all the grown-ups had ended up soaked and laughing.

On May 20, having gotten permission from the police to search in the area where the cadaver dog searches had taken place, Edmund Carroll borrowed a four-wheeler from a friend and headed out onto the trail system.

Several hours later, Carroll returned to the Miramichi police headquarters, asked for Constable Greg Scott and told him an amazing story.

After he got permission, Carroll had spent the next four hours slowly traveling along the trails without finding anything significant. He was heading for home, traveling back down the main snowmobile trail leading out of town, when he passed a light blue pickup truck bed that had been junked in the woods alongside the trail, just northeast of the Portage Restaurant.

He'd gone past it and driven perhaps a hundred yards down the trail when it seemed to him that he was hearing a voice. The voice was telling him, "The gun. Search for her. Go around. Search. Search."

Carroll hadn't gone out that day to look for a gun; he'd gone to look for Maria, so he was puzzled. But the voice persisted, telling him to turn around and look for the gun. He was not a man who heard voices, so this was deeply disturbing. He had driven past the truck bed without a second thought, but now, obeying what felt to him like a completely otherworldly compulsion, he heeded the call, turned the four-wheeler around and headed back up the trail.

This time, as he approached the truck bed, he stopped and got off his vehicle. As he walked slowly and warily toward the truck bed, he saw something green tucked beneath it. Going closer, he could see that it was the corner of a green plastic tarp. He felt underneath the truck, pulled it out and found that what he had spotted was something packed in a tightly-wrapped green tarp and secured with gray duct tape.

He loosened the tape just enough to see what was inside. It was a gun.

Hastily, he rewrapped the bundle and put it back under the truck bed, shoving it a little farther underneath to be sure it couldn't be seen. Then he drove back to police headquarters and reported what he had found.

Scott and Cummings returned with him to the site of the find. The area was photographed and the gun collected. It was a sawed-off .22 caliber rifle, 13.5 inches in length, a prohibited weapon that was remarkably similar to the gun that David had had in his possession the night he was arrested in the trunk of Donnie Trevors's car. It was found not far from where David had hidden the sawed-off shotgun he had planned to use on the judge and prosecutor back in 1993.

The weapon was transferred to the RCMP forensics section for examination, which, detectives hoped, would produce evidence that would directly tie David to the weapon.

In a subsequent interview with David's next-door neighbor, John Paquet, Paquet identified the tarp as one belonging to David, which he used to wrap guns in when he, or he and Maria, would go out hunting.

The detectives also did a thorough search beneath the truck bed, to ensure that there wasn't a body beneath there or signs of disturbed ground, but there was not. Although some of the search dogs that had been past that spot when they searched the area were trained to conduct evidence searches for items such as guns, shell casings or personal items, they didn't find the gun because they were working on commands to do cadaver searches and not instructed to do an evidence search.

Warden canine handlers will have a series of commands they give their dogs to instruct them on what type of search is wanted. These commands are designed not to alert or alarm people around them, so that a handler who is going on a search will not say "find body" in front of the missing person's family, nor instruct a dog to look for fish in the presence of a suspected poacher. Often, when a handler is starting a cadaver search, they will "warm up" the dog by doing an exercise with some cadaver scent.

Police detectives often feel that divine intervention plays a role in solving their cases, particularly those lingering or complex cases where it can get discouraging waiting for a break. That was how Edmund Carroll's find felt to the Miramichi detectives. Only days earlier, they had been deeply discouraged by the failure of their massive cadaver dog effort to locate Maria. Now, it seemed they were getting a message of hope. Don't give up, they were being told. You're on the right track and you're going to find her.

It was a breakthrough, and a kind of reassurance, that they badly needed.

A quiet man's determination had paid off and everyone was the better for it.

Now the detectives were back to the waiting game: waiting for the wardens and MESARD handlers to return, waiting for results from the forensic analysis on the gun and waiting for a second chance to find Maria.

Chapter 16

Slow and Steady Wins the Race

W hen Pat Dorian returned a month later, at the end of June, he came with a slightly different—and smaller—team. Kevin Adam was there again to manage the mapping and search sector assignments. Deb Palman and Roger Guay were there with their dogs, along with Warden Tom Jacobs and his dog. Most of the cadaver-trained MESARD handlers and their dogs were unavailable, unfortunately, but Michele Fleury and Spencer Fuller came back.

Although everyone had left feeling deeply discouraged after the unsuccessful searches in May, Dorian was undaunted. Certain from the first that they would ultimately be successful in locating Maria Tanasichuk, he dove right back into the task. They began to search areas near those identified as high-probability and to clear areas not covered well during the first round of searches. While the woods were drier, making that part of the searching less uncomfortable, the boggy spring had left the area teeming with mosquitoes and entering the woods was a miserable task.

The weather was also unseasonably hot, making it a miserable slog for searchers who had to wear long pants and long sleeves for protection. With the temperatures hovering in the nineties, the conditions were brutal for both the handlers and their dogs. To maximize the likelihood of success and minimize the discomfort for the dogs, the group decided to reorganize their schedules. They rose early in the morning so that they could get out into the woods by 4:00 or 4:30 A.M. and conduct their first searches of the day before the midday heat.

Around ten, they broke to eat, care for their dogs, cool down, upload their data and strategize about the locus of the afternoon's missions. Then they went back out again in the late afternoon as the heat began to diminish.

The new search effort was also limited by the wardens' availability because of other work commitments in Maine. The tourist season was now in full swing, which put pressure on the state's search and rescue coordinator and wardens with trained search dogs to be quickly available in case they were needed for their primary search and rescue duties. They only had two days of actual on-the-ground search time. The teams completed searching the main snowmobile trail running from the area behind the Miramichi Dragway to Craigville Road, including the paths and roads leading off it. A search was also planned for the power-line right-of-way that ran from the Chatham industrial park area to Napan Road.

As much of the area initially identified as high probability for David to have concealed Maria's body, based on the timeline of his strange nocturnal trips, was searched and cleared, the detectives and the wardens were wondering whether they needed to expand the search area. Was it possible, given his familiarity with the area, that David might have placed her somewhere near his friend Donnie Trevors's house or in a more remote section of the woods? Was it possible that he'd traveled off the trail system and across the highway toward the airport, opening up a new and vast tract of land to be searched?

The wardens re-interviewed the detectives, looking for information that might have been omitted or overlooked that might help guide the search. Dorian said, "There's not one of these [searches] where we didn't have a hard time. On every case we ever worked on, Kevin [Adam] and I and Roger [Guay]…when we'd go into a room with these guys, we'd reaffirm many times: 'Tell us everything you know about this individual,' because we usually ask some questions that they don't have the answers to, because they don't think of asking that question. When we delved into his background, of course he had a lot of outdoor experience where he hunted all the time, and that stuff about bear hunting and all…there was some stuff about they had found some guns that had belonged to him, he'd been hiding stuff in the woods. And we didn't learn it all at that initial meeting, and I can remember Kevin coming back and saying 'Why didn't they tell us that in the beginning?' You know there were some things…like we didn't find out about him taking them on chases and these false leads that he was purposely doing until we were pretty well into it. Maybe not until the second time we went.

"In the conversation with Kevin, he gets a little frustrated and says, 'You know, we tell them to tell us everything, yet they didn't.' Because little things that may seem insignificant to them might mean a lot to us."

The wardens also wanted to know about David's hunting habits and the locations of his bear stands. Ultimately, they asked the investigators to locate several of David's hunting companions and interview them about the areas where he hunted and his customary practices when hunting. That, in turn, led them to questions about bear-baiting and how he might have transported a heavy volume of smelly bear bait to the sites, something they felt he could not have done on his three-wheeler, especially since the bike was extremely clean and showed none of the signs that might have indicated he'd transported bait.

Once again, the wardens' outdoor expertise came into play. The wardens accompanied the detectives as they interviewed, or in some cases re-interviewed, men that David had gone hunting with, or with whom he had operated his bear stands. The detectives asked a number of questions: where did David like to hunt? What were his hunting habits? Where were his bear stands and how had he been able to transport bait to them?

As they interviewed, they were also alert to the possibility that if Maria's body wasn't somewhere where David could have transported it himself, if their theory that he'd lured her out on the bike was wrong or if he'd subsequently moved the body after the night she was killed, was there someone who might have helped him?

The wardens and MESARD volunteers were also aware that when someone familiar with the woods hides a body, he is likely to hide it in a spot that will be easy to locate again, in case he wants to move that body in the future. Therefore, they were constantly alert, as they conducted their search missions and their interviews, to the likelihood of a sentinel tree or rock or some other significant marker that would help their suspect find the spot again.

During the second round of searching, Brian Cummings's father also accompanied the police officers who were walking with the dogs and their handlers. Cummings stated, "From January till June my mother told me numerous times that my dad was worried sick about the ongoing investigation and was particularly worried about [my wife] and the kids because of everything that was going on. When the gang from Maine left empty-handed after the first search in May, he had asked me if they ever came back if he would be able to come up and help search. My parents live about two-and-a-half hours away. Of course we told him yes, because we could have used all the help we could get at that point, and I think he wanted to just be involved in some way to help alleviate that feeling of helplessness. So he participated in the searches on June 27 and 28."

On the first day of the June search, the temperature reached a high of 99 degrees (37 degrees Celsius) around noon. On the second day of the search, Cummings described the scene, "On June 28 we had been out since roughly five because it was so hot. And the hotter it gets for the dogs the harder they have to work and then you get less results. We started early and broke early. So, at roughly nine...we broke and had breakfast at the Portage, and while we were at the Portage, we were running out of areas to search because everything had been searched pretty thoroughly and we were talking about expanding the area to the other side of Route 11 toward the airport. And, I'm not ashamed to say, it was getting pretty frustrating at that point because we were running out of options. They had the laptop there; Kevin Adam, Pat Dorian and Deb [Palman] all looked at it. Kevin and Pat came up with the decision to search more thoroughly behind the Portage because on the map you could see there was a little pocket that hadn't been thoroughly looked at. There was no blue trail demarking a searched area, so Deb was assigned to that area directly after breakfast.

"That was a Saturday, I believe. We left the Portage and when Deb went out behind the Portage, we all returned to the office to get some equipment and to look at the bigger map that was on the wall down here and to try to regroup and come up with more assignments. I was with Roger Guay that day and I can remember Tom Jacobs, who was one of the wardens with the dogs that day was with my dad and he was on the west side of Route 11 out toward the airport, covering that area."

Dorian was uneasy about the possibility of extending their search area, still certain that they were on the right track where they were searching. As he put it, they'd already started some limited searches on the other side of the road, and "going into R.O.W." (the rest of the world) gave him a really bad feeling.

The temperature was cooler that second day and after their break for breakfast they decided that the conditions would permit a little more searching. Dorian and Kevin Adam had reviewed the GPS data to see if there were areas that had been overlooked, that hadn't been well-searched, where it might be useful to put somebody back in. From the mapping that they were studying at the Portage Restaurant, they could see that since the first search parameters were to search the existing trails and 100 yards off the trails into the woods along those routes, that there was an area in between the trails that had not been well searched—the center area about half a kilometer east of the Portage Restaurant, and south of the main snowmobile trail which contained an old gravel pit and a clearing. That particular section hadn't been searched because it was not crisscrossed by trails as most of the neighboring terrain was.

Deb Palman searched the area after breakfast. In an earlier search, she had used her older dog, Anna. She set out with her younger German Shepherd, Alex, to cover the "hole" in the mapping, because she knew Alex would fare better in the heat. Alex wore an orange vest, to signify that he was working, and which, along with a bell, would help her locate him if he disappeared from her sight. It was a fairly large block of land to cover, and she tried to cut through the area in a way that would allow the dog to smell every point.

Palman described what happened next in her report to the Warden Service:

> As is standard in air scent SAR work, they started out on a compass bearing that was perpendicular to the steady NW wind. After having to detour around a flooded, thickly grown-up gravel pit, Spec. Palman found that the block of woods was actually an area that had been mechanically clear-cut about fifteen to twenty years ago. Much of the area was grown up to twenty to twenty-five foot high birch and popple with thick clumps of fir and relatively open areas covered with bracken fern where the machines had traveled and packed the ground down.
>
> Spec. Palman noticed when Alex left, he was traveling upwind, in about the middle of the clear-cut. She could not hear the bell he wore and he did not return, so she turned up wind to follow him. After going fifty yards, she could smell decomposition but dismissed it as a moose carcass. [As the snow had melted, revealing them, and they had thawed, searchers on this second visit had found numerous moose and bear carcasses.] Alex eventually returned from the direction of the smell, made eye contact with Spec. Palman and turned back towards the smell to show her the source. Spec. Palman quickly lost sight of him again and heard his bell stop ringing another fifty yards away. She was still looking for moose parts when she spotted his orange search vest in a fir thicket. Alex wasn't moving.
>
> Approaching closer, she saw green cloth at his feet and immediately called him to her, praising him and securing him

on a lead. She gave him all the food treats she carried and, as he was busy eating them, stepped closer to the green cloth. A skull covered with brown, decomposed flesh was at one end of the cloth. The body, although very rotted, was undisturbed by large scavengers. It was deep in a fir thicket, covered with brush and about 300 yards from the nearest road. It was near the only large dead pine tree in the old clear-cut, a marker that would have been obvious in January.[23]

Then Deb Palman got on the radio to report her find to the other wardens and the Miramichi police.

Back at police headquarters, Brian Cummings and Roger Guay had just left the building. Paul Fiander and Dewey Gillespie were in another vehicle with a witness, a hunter, and they were about to head out to look at an area where the man had sometimes hunted with David. Cummings and Guay had just gotten into Guay's truck, with Cummings at the wheel, when Guay's radio crackled.

Cummings recalled, "Roger [Guay] and I picked something up and went back to Roger's truck, and I was driving his truck because I knew the area better, and we were in the process of pulling out of the yard with the dogs in the back and Deb came over the radio. Once you've been on the job long enough, even if you're not used to someone's voice, you can tell if there's panic in their voice when it comes over the air...and maybe panic's not the right word...maybe emotion and concern, and uh...whatever she was trying to convey was urgent. And she was trying to reach *somebody*. She was calling for *anybody* to respond. And of course, Roger and I had been out of the truck, so we didn't hear her first calls. So, Roger picked up the radio and said, "Go ahead, Deb", and she said, "10–4, I have a find."

"And I stopped the truck."

Cummings went on, "I heard what she said but I wasn't 100 percent clear on warden terminology and maybe my mind didn't want me to get my hopes up too much. But when I stopped the truck, Roger looked at me and asked, 'What did she just say?' And I looked at Roger and I said, 'She just said she had a find,' and Roger picked up the radio and said, 'Go again, Deb, we didn't copy,' and she came back on the radio again and you could hear the frustration in her voice, 'cause this time she said, '10–4, I have a find! I'VE... FOUND...HER!'

"And I immediately started whooping and roaring. I grabbed Roger and gave him a big shake. I put the truck in reverse and told Roger to hang on and peeled rubber through the parking lot and back to the office...because we were only fifty yards from the back door. And then all hell broke loose."

It was 10:40 A.M. on the last day of the second search. Maria Tanasichuk had been missing more than five months. Cummings rushed to share the news with Paul Fiander.

But when Cummings hurried to the door of the little Victorian building that housed the detectives' bureau, which was attached by an enclosed pedestrian bridge to the larger, modern police facility, eager to share Deb Palman's news, he ran up against an unexpected barrier: "I didn't have my keys," Cummings admitted. "I don't know where my keys were. I started banging on the back door, really hard. If Pat and Kevin and Greg didn't come when they did, I was going to kick the door in. And I could hear them coming down the back stairs and I could hear Greg Scott saying, "Just hang on, we're coming." You could tell he was frustrated with who-ever was banging on the other side of the door. And when they opened the door, it was Patty [Pat Dorian] out first and Patty just looked at me and I said, 'Deb just found her!' And I grabbed hold of Patty and lifted him about two feet off the ground and gave him a big hug and then we all started whooping and roaring, and then we all jumped back in the truck with Roger and Deb guided us right to where she was."

They let Fiander and Gillespie know about the find.

Fiander said, "Dewey and I, we were driving Pat [Dorian]'s van and we had this old man who had done some hunting with David. He was going to show us where some tree stands were. He was in the back of the van, and Deb Palman came across the radio, and Dewey and I looked at one another, because we weren't sure what we'd heard, and then she came across again. We looked at the old man, and we said, "We're going to have to drop you off." We were ready to drop him off right there by the side of the road, but we couldn't do that to him."

Arriving at the scene, which was within forty or fifty yards of places they'd walked in the prior months, they found a badly decomposed body that appeared to be female, lying face-up on the ground and covered with logs and branches. The body was wearing winter clothing—a green army camouflage jacket, ski pants, hiking boots and blue gloves. There was no hat or head covering and they observed two gold earrings in the right ear.

Dorian, assessing the scene from the search and rescue perspective, observed, "They cut that whole thing, and they'd left some pine and stuff to regenerate it. And we had done none of this rectangle piece. I had walked all along the road, all through this pit here, but see, we had done none of this area where the body was. And I walked out in this cut, 'cause one of the things we were thinking...one of the things guys do, that people do that dump victims, subconsciously, for whatever reason, they usually put them in some place where they can find them again, some sort of marker. And I kept thinkin', I don't know why I was doin' it, I kept thinking, "is there a big pine here somewhere, that...he could find his way back there easily?" And wouldn't you know, she's at the base of a great big *dead* frigging pine! And I was looking for a live tree." He added a note that was particularly telling, "One of the things he had done...and I think they do...I guess psychologists will tell you that if someone is close to somebody, a partner or whatever...that he had broke some fir boughs and put them over her face."

Once they confirmed the find, they did a quick first scan of the area, and then everything went to procedure. As Cummings put it, they went from search mode to police mode. It was midday. It was almost 90 degrees (32 degrees Celsius). They got out their phones and started making the series of calls that would put the crime scene investigation mechanisms in motion.

When Dorian and Kevin Adam reviewed the case, as they reviewed all cases to see where they might have done things better, one thing they focused on was all those nocturnal trips, phone calls and the cat-and-mouse game that David Tanasichuk had played.

Pat Dorian remarked, referring to the night-time trips that Tanasichuk had taken with the police attempting to follow him, said, "I told Kevin afterwards, one of the things we probably should have done was to look at all the areas that he led them on and plot them on a map and find where the hole is where he didn't go. And I'm sure one of the holes would be that area where she ended up being."

Chapter 17

Murder Will Out

Finally locating Maria meant that numerous phone calls had to be made to summon all of the essential personnel to the scene, many of whom had to travel to Miramichi from other parts of the province. Before they even started making calls, though, aware that the public knew about the search operation and would be alerted to any unusual activity, they sealed off the road into the area all the way back out to Route 11 by the restaurant. They called their chief and told him that Maria had been found. They made a call to the coroner. Wanting the most crime scene expertise they could get, they called the RCMP Forensic Identification team from Bathurst. Brian Cummings took some initial photographs of the scene.

Then, to provide scene security until the forensics officers could arrive, they left Greg Scott standing guard by Maria and stationed Dewey Gillespie at the entrance to the dirt road near the Portage Restaurant on Route 11. Then Fiander and Cummings drove across the river to give the news to Maria's sister, Sharon.

Police officers are deeply aware of the dichotomy that exists in such a situation. For them, the discovery was an exciting moment—the culmination of months of effort by the investigative team and fellow officers and hundreds of hours of searching. Finding a missing body was a beginning—the springboard for a new phase of the investigation, filled with possibilities for evidence uncovered and questions answered. There would be an autopsy and information, finally, about how Maria Tanasichuk died.

But the discovery of a body means an ending for the family. It means that their uncertainty is at an end and they can finally have closure, but it also puts an end to the hopes they might have held that their loved one was still alive and might one day return. Roger Guay, who has taken hundreds of bodies out of the Maine woods in his twenty-five-year career, became a warden, in part, because of experiencing a loss, and a search, himself.

"When you're a cadaver dog guy, it's the most bittersweet thing in the world because you have the success of the find," he said. "That's really good, but you realize now the family's got to deal with the reality of this thing, and that is tough."

Fiander and Cummings both understood that the living came first. Maria's body had been there for almost six months. It would take a while for the forensics people to arrive from Bathurst and for the coroner to get to the site. So they set out to honor the promise they'd made to Sharon Carroll many months before—that they would find her sister. They wanted to deliver the news and they wanted to reach Sharon before she heard something from the rumor mill or the media.

"That was so important," Cummings said. "And you can get caught up, doing the technical stuff and first thing you know, family members start hearing things and they haven't heard anything officially from the police, and that can leave a lasting impression on family members. That will be the one thing they remember...that the police forgot about us and didn't notify us. And it's easy to overlook because you get caught up in doing the things that need to be done. When in reality, one of the things that needs to be done is dealing with the family."

Sharon, alone while her husband drove Angela and their grandchildren home, was busy cleaning up the house. She'd scrubbed the floor and was washing the dishes when she heard a car drive into the yard. When she heard the two car doors closing, she *knew* that they'd found Maria and had come to tell her the news.

"Brian [Cummings] and Paul [Fiander] came up to the door," she recalled. "They said, 'Hi, Sharon, are you alone?' And I said 'Yeah,' and I looked up, and I said, 'You've found her, eh?' And they said, 'Yes,' and I asked if he'd shot her. In the back of my mind, I knew he'd shot her. I asked, 'Can I see her?' and he said, 'No.' Anyways...it was just like I was stunned. I had a glass of water in my hand, and they asked if I wanted them to stay here until I could get someone with me, and I said no. I can't even remember if I said goodbye.

"The hardest thing for me was that I couldn't see Maria. My sister had talked to Brian, before the body was found, and said whatever you do, don't let Sharon look. But I knew it was Maria because I know Brian and Paul.

"So then I went to the funeral home and made all the arrangements and the next day, Brian came over and he said, 'I've got to ask you something and you don't need to do it but we'd like to take Maria's skull and analyze it.'

"That was a big thing for me...too, because Maria's buried but her skull is in a box in storage."

Another important call that needed to be made before the news media got hold of the story or the rumors started flying around was a call to the prison facility where David Tanasichuk was being held. Paul Fiander called Supervisor

Brian Dicks at the Saint John Regional Correction Center, telling them they'd better keep an eye on their prisoner because he was about to get some bad news.

Keeping an eye on David, and ensuring that the authorities in facilities where he was being held were apprised of his dangerousness, was a continuing source of concern for the investigators. While an institution might be looking at him as a prisoner with some gun charges, the Miramichi police knew him as a suspect in multiple homicides and were well aware of the risk posed if he were ever to escape. They were certain that if he did, someone would be killed.

Furthermore, they knew that David had escaped from a penal institution before and that he admired and liked to compare himself to Allan Legere, the monster of Miramichi, who had escaped from police custody during a hospital visit, remained at large for seven months and committed four horrific murders before he was finally caught. They were careful to remind every institution where David was incarcerated that they wanted a phone call if he ever were to escape, and routinely left their cell phone, office and home contact numbers.

Shortly after the call was made, focusing official attention on David, wardens at the prison discovered that he had been slowly working on loosening the bricks of his cell and soon would have had enough loosened to attempt that escape.

It was a day of intense police work. It was also a day of incredible relief for the police and an intensely personal one for all of the families involved, especially Maria's. Brian Cummings described their feelings:

"After Paul and I had met with Sharon and brought her up to speed and then returned to the scene, we parked our car out at the perimeter and started gathering stuff to walk back in to where Maria was located. My dad was there waiting for us. He hadn't been there when Maria's remains were found or prior to Paul and I leaving for Sharon's; he'd been out on the west side of Highway 11 around the airport with Tom Jacobs and his dog, searching that area. You have to know my dad. He's a very quiet, incredibly hard-working and strong-willed man, what I characterize as a 'Man's Man.' I idolize him, and have always strived to try and impress him and live up to his expectations. As Paul and I approached him, I could see that his eyes were watery. He shook Paul's hand and congratulated him, and then he gave me a bear-hug and said, 'Ya's found her!' and told me he was proud of us.

"I couldn't talk. The lump in my throat was too big to swallow and I knew if I tried to say anything I'd break down crying, which was the last thing I wanted my dad to see his thirty-five-year-old, supposedly 'tough as nails' son do. But I am immensely proud of the fact that he was there that day when everything finally came together. We have a group picture that was taken later that evening of the twelve people who searched on the 27th and 28th and my dad is in it. That picture will hang in my office till the day I retire."

The rest of the day was a timeline of arrivals and departures, phone calls and consultations as the Miramichi detectives and the RCMP forensics officer worked the scene. It was a very long, slow day spent in terrible heat in clouds of mosquitoes, unable to escape the intense smell of decomposition. Despite the conditions, the crime scene was worked in the slow and careful manner necessary to ensure thorough processing and the collection, recording and preservation of every possible piece of potential evidence.

Working a crime scene doesn't go more quickly because of miserable weather. Detectives must still give the dead their due. Everyone involved had been heading toward this moment since David Tanasichuk's phone call had come in to dispatch on January 26. However hot and miserable they might be, they did it by the book, taking no chances that something vital might escape them or that a careless slip might come back to haunt them years down the road.

There is always that dichotomy at a crime scene. The detectives must be wholly present in the moment, observing what there is to be observed, noting what is there—and what is *not* there—and what the crime scene is telling them: in this case, a body heavily dressed in winter clothes, but without a hat. At the same time, while they are moment-to-moment intent on recording the scene with photographs and video and collecting any evidence that may be there, they also always have an eye to the future and to ensuring that their process is clean and their chain of evidence careful, so that a long time down the road, when the case comes to trial, or even to retrial, they won't lose whatever they've carefully collected and preserved because of flaws in the collecting process or the chain of custody.

By 2:00 that afternoon, Sergeant Guy Chamberlain, the RCMP forensics officer, had arrived from Bathurst and was briefed about the case. While Chamberlain and the detectives went to work, Paul Fiander consulted with Steven Tulle of the Department of Natural Resources and Energy about the branches that had been cut and placed over the body, and the possibility of matching them to David's tools.

Detective Cummings had strep throat and a fever that day, but just as he wasn't going to let discomfort keep him from walking the trails with the cadaver dogs and their handlers, nothing was going to keep him from working that crime scene. After initial photographs, the process began of removing all of the branches piled over the body to disguise its location.

"This was the first body that I'd ever had that had been out in the woods for six months, and I was interested to see what Sergeant Chamberlain would do as a crime scene officer," Cummings noted. "And it turned out he didn't really do anything more than what I'd expected.

"Of course he videotaped it. He photographed the scene. She was completely covered up with brush and branches. He had a mounted video camera focused directly on the body and his camera around his neck, and we would remove one stick, or one piece of brush that was intact, and as soon as it was removed, she'd be photographed again with that stick removed, and then we'd exhibit that piece of wood. Thirty or forty pieces. And eventually we had a sequence of photographs with one piece of wood at a time until it was just her on the ground. And all the wood came back with us."

All of those pieces were wrapped in plastic tarps and sealed. As the packages were sealed, they were placed in the back of Constable Eddie Arbeau's truck. Then they were taken back to the police station and placed in storage in an exhibit bay to wait for the trial.

As the slow process of uncovering the body continued, other essential people arrived at the scene. At 3:00 P.M., Coroner Fernand Martin arrived and consulted with Paul Fiander, and they both awaited the arrival of the regional coroner, Carl Jensen. By 4:00 P.M., Jensen had also arrived and both of them went to the scene, viewed the body and then left the area.

Arrangements were made for the removal of the body to Miramichi Hospital for storage overnight, and then for it to be transported to Saint John for an autopsy at 11:30 the following morning. The decision was made to actually pronounce her dead in Saint John, to avoid having to open the body bag at Miramichi Hospital.

It was arranged that a hearse from Northumberland Funeral Home would be coming to transport the body. Before that could take place, however, a path had to be cleared to allow them to carry her body out to the main snowmobile trail, where the hearse was waiting. To facilitate carrying her out, Dewey Gillespie and Eddie Arbeau used chainsaws to clear a path from the main trail closer to where the body was located.

To prevent any hairs or fluids contaminating the scene, the investigators wore white crime scene suits with elastic at the wrists and ankles, which only intensified the heat.

"It was the hottest I've ever been in my life," Cummings admitted. "We had those white crime scene suits on that have elastic around the wrists and the ankles that keep any... you know, you don't want body hair falling out or DNA. The bad thing about it is it also keeps the heat in. We called them bunny suits. I had one on...we all did, those of us who were working around the body, and I couldn't keep enough water in me; as quick as I was pouring it into me, it seemed like it was coming out. And at one point, when we were carrying the body out, I thought for sure I was going to faint and we had to stop. But there was no way I was gonna let that keep me from getting Maria into the back of the hearse. When we finally got her in, I just stepped away from the back of the vehicle, and I pulled the elastic away...and when I pulled it away, it was just like opening up a tap. The water just ran down my sleeve and out onto the ground.

"That was the hottest I'd ever been in my life. And I'd do it all again in a second if I had to."

At 5:50 P.M., the body was ready to be removed. By then, many of the investigators had spent several hours working through the heat of a day that had begun before 5:00 A.M. Finally, the hearse arrived to collect Maria's body. Because of the advanced state of its decomposition, placing the body on a stretcher and getting it into a body bag presented a challenging task. At that point, Maria was essentially held together by her clothes, so moving her was difficult and they needed to ensure that she was collected carefully, to preserve any possible evidence on or with the body.

Fortunately for the investigators, the funeral home had a lightweight metal stretcher that came apart in the middle into two pieces. They carefully shoveled away the earth underneath her until they were able to work the stretcher in beneath her from both sides, proceeding with painstaking care, in the process collecting a fair amount of earth and insects. The body was bagged with two body bags. Then Maria's honor guard—Paul Fiander, Brian Cummings, Dewey Gillespie and Greg Scott—began the slow walk to carry her body out to the waiting hearse.

The hearse left the scene, followed by Scott and Coroner Martin, who escorted it to the hospital. A constable remained behind to provide scene security, because the detectives planned to return in the morning to conduct further evidence searches of the area. Because of the risk of contamination by the curious, arrangements were made to have security at the scene throughout the night.

Working shoulder to shoulder on the search, the Miramichi police had come to regard their American counterparts as an integral part of the team. They knew that the day's result would not have been possible without the handlers and their cadaver dogs.

"Really, it was like...because of the fact that we first started talking to them in February, and you know, their passion and coming back a second time, it was like they were a part of the team," Paul Fiander remarked. "And we considered them a part of the team from the get go. I mean, no way, without them, would we have ever found her. We say no. It would have been someone stumbling on her, and the animals would have got her. There's no doubt about it. We're indebted to them for the rest of our lives. They helped us big time in solving this case, and we'll never forget that. We stay in touch with Pat [Dorian], and we'll continue to do that, because it means a lot to us. They went out on a limb by coming back...and out on a limb the first time.

"And we're talking two different countries. It's not like it's a neighboring province. We used the international cooperation between the state and the province.

"From a practical point of view it was very dramatic... what it took to make it happen. And, at the end of the day, it happened."

Even as their minds were already turning toward the morning, when they would search the site and surrounding area for evidence and possibly even the discovery of Robert Breau's body, Paul Fiander and Brian Cummings knew that it had been among the most unforgettable days of their lives.

"The day we found Maria Tanasichuk was by far the most memorable moment, if not in my life, then absolutely in my career," Cummings said. "And I always tell the classes [at the police academy] the same thing: With the exception of the births of my two boys, this was my most memorable day. For sure. Because finding her meant that we took a killer off the streets."

Fiander remarked, "I guess they say there's always one case in your career...and God forbid we have anything that tops that."

Later that day, the searchers and their grateful hosts gathered for a beer and pizza party. The next morning, the wardens and MESARD handlers gathered for a group photograph and then headed home to Maine.

Chapter 18

Execution

The following day, Maria Tanasichuk's remains were transported to Saint John, where Greg Scott observed the forensic pathologist, Dr. Marek Godlewski, performing the autopsy. Again, it was a lengthy and detailed process, complicated by the state of the body. During the course of the autopsy, the detectives collected Maria's clothing, including a heavy winter camouflage jacket with an orange lining, snow pants, long underwear, two pairs of socks, two shirts, gloves and hiking boots. They also collected several pieces of Maria's jewelry, two rings with diamonds in them, a cross pendant and some earrings which were tangled in her hair. When the body bags were opened, thousands of insects came pouring out.

Following the three-hour procedure, the detective remained in Saint John another two hours so he could return to Miramichi with X-rays of the body and the pathologist's report. The cause of death was determined to be gunshots to the head. How many gunshots and whether they could be matched to any known weapons remained to be determined.

A few days later, Scott returned to Saint John to collect Maria's skull, scalp and brain matter and transport them to the RCMP Forensic Laboratory in Halifax for analysis. Along with these portions of Maria's remains, Scott also provided the lab with the sawed-off .22 rifle that Edmund Carroll had found hidden under the junked truck bed, the .22 caliber ammunition which had been turned over to the police by David Tanasichuk along with Maria's guns and the ammunition he had not turned over, which had been seized by the police when they searched the apartment in February.

In real life, unlike on television, forensic examination can be a very slow process and frequently depends on overworked crime labs that must serve large areas and process material from many, many crimes. It wasn't a simple matter of looking at the skull, counting the holes and reporting the results. A competent analysis takes time to analyze the materials sent—skull, skin and brain matter—to determine the number of shots, to recover the bullets, to track, as much as possible, their trajectories by examining both entrance wounds and areas of impact and to examine the scalp material to determine whether the presence or absence of gunshot residue might be able to give an idea of how close the gunman was when the shots were fired. Following that, forensic experts at the lab needed to analyze the bullets retrieved from the brain and determine whether there were matches to the ammunition known to be in the possession of the suspect, and whether the bullets could be matched to any of the guns suspected of being involved.

Also at the lab were the tarp and duct tape that had been used to wrap the weapon Edmund Carroll had found. Stuck to the duct tape was human and animal hair. When these hairs were examined, it was determined that only one of them was large enough to provide a significant sample for analysis, and that hair belonged to a dog. Whenever possible, detectives like to have more than one source to establish a fact. In this instance, looking for an additional way of tying David to the weapon to augment John Paquet's identification of the tarp, they then set about locating David's former pet Rottweiler, Thor, to obtain hair and DNA samples.

Like the story of the detectives shoveling into frozen ground beneath the lean-to and carefully collecting samples of the cut ends of the logs and the knots in the rope, the effort to obtain a canine hair and DNA samples for potential matching is an example of the lengths detectives must sometimes go to in their efforts to secure the best evidence in a case. Locating the dog so that they could obtain a sample wasn't a simple matter.

In February, during the period after he reported Maria missing, David had been selling everything he owned. He had sold the dog to a man who later gave the dog to another man who then gave it to his ex-girlfriend. In April, having located the dog in Burnt Church, twenty miles away, Cummings and Greg Scott traveled there to get samples. The videotape of the process of Cummings obtaining hair and saliva samples from the dog demonstrates that Thor the Rottweiler was a reluctant and uncooperative witness. And like so many other efforts in the case—efforts they had to make—it brought an unsatisfying result. Cummings had taken a substantial risk with that dog only to learn, via a report from Dr. Amerarjit Chahal of Molecular World, that: "[The probability that] a sample from a randomly selected dog, unrelated to known dog, would have a mitochondrial DNA profile identical to the mitochondrial DNA profile from evidentiary 0016-AD ANIMAL HAIR is estimated to be 1 in 8."

Peter Richardson, the Miramichi animal control officer, estimated that 50 percent of the dogs in the city or an

average of 150 dogs per year were registered. Therefore, if
Richardson's numbers were assumed to be correct, there
would be approximately thirty-eight dogs in the city with the
same mitochondrial DNA as the hair found with the murder
weapon. If his estimate was low, there would be even more
matches. Thus, the hair would have no value in connecting
David to the weapon.

It's a sad fact of the investigative process—and one
that TV programs rarely acknowledge and thus the public
frequently fails to understand—that luck plays a big role in
obtaining forensic evidence. Sometimes the DNA is there.
Sometimes the fingerprints are there. Sometimes there is
hair or fiber evidence. And sometimes there is not. Equally
important, and rarely understood, is the problem of degra-
dation of evidence, particularly when a body is exposed to
weather, or simply due to the passage of time. Information
that might have been present at the time Maria was killed
and her body hidden might well be gone nearly six months
later, washed away by rain or snow-melt or degraded beyond
utility by natural processes.

An example of this would be the lab's examination of
her scalp for gunshot residue to help determine how close
Maria's killer was standing when he shot her. The lab was
unable to locate gunshot residue to establish that distance.
However, other information coming from the lab did help to
illuminate that point and provided significant information
for the investigators, who had been trying to imagine the circumstances of Maria's death. They had put together the information from the neighbor about David's nocturnal trips with
Maria's friends' information about him often soliciting her
help in dealing with a kill out in the woods, indicating how
eagerly she would have jumped on the bike with him for a
ride out into the wilderness.

After months of waiting, the detectives knew much more than the pathologist's conclusion that her death was caused by gunshot wounds to the head. Maria's skull was examined at the autopsy. Then, with her sister's permission, it was separated from the body and taken to the RCMP forensic laboratory, then collected later by Greg Scott and transported to the Ontario Forensic Pathology Unit where it was further examined by Pathologist Dr. David Chiasson and Forensic Anthropologist Dr. Katherine Gruspier.

The conclusions, after examination, were these:

Gunshot wounds to the head, three, with:

a) Right mid-frontal skull entrance wound, with multiple radiating fractures.

b) Right orbital entrance wound, with multiple radiating fractures.

c) Right posterior parietal entrance wound, with associated fractures.

d) Three .22 caliber fired bullets were recovered from inside the skull.[24]

The detectives now knew that Maria had been killed by three gunshots to the head. They also knew, because of information received from the Halifax laboratory in September, that two of the three bullets found in Maria's head had been positively identified as having been fired from the rifle Edmund Carroll had found wrapped in Tanasichuk's tarp and hidden under the bed of an old junked truck. The third bullet had been too damaged to match. When the detectives received that news, they could form a clearer picture of the events on the night Maria was killed.

Maria's body was found approximately 110 meters off the trail. Although she was bundled up for a night out in the

cold—heavy boots, winter coat, many layers, extra socks
and gloves—she was found without a hat or head covering
of any sort. Now the investigators could imagine the evolu-
tion of that evening. The Tanasichuks riding out along the
snowmobile trail, Maria happily accompanying her husband,
riding behind him, her arms wrapped around his waist. The
two of them parking alongside the trail, and David directing
Maria, walking before him, out to some location where he
needed her help with an animal, a deer perhaps, that he had
shot. He would be carrying his loaded and easily concealed
weapon—the entire rifle, with the barrel and stock sawed off,
was barely more than a foot long—ready for the moment to
execute his plan and protect his secrets.

It was a bright, clear night with plenty of moonlight
reflecting off the snow, making it easy for David to spot the
tall dead pine tree that was a known landmark in an area he
was very familiar with, both from his frequent hunting trips
through there and from a secret marijuana patch he'd had a few
years before, according to Darlene Gertley. This was a planned
event and he would need a marker—that sentinel tree—to
find the spot again so he could perhaps return in daylight to
conceal the body with brush and to erase his tracks.

Although no one will ever know for sure—there were
only two people there that night, and one of them is dead—
the three bullet holes in Maria's head suggest this scenario:
Maria's head was bare, because she had left her helmet back
with the bike. David came up behind Maria and shot her the
first time in the rear right side of her head. She fell, and either
landed facing up, or he turned her so that she was facing him
as she laid there bleeding onto the snow. What happened
next—though forensic examination could not determine
the order of the second and third shots—is cold, remorse-
less and brutal. He shot her twice more: once through her

right eye and once, execution-style, right in the middle of her forehead.

As the RCMP crime lab analysis reported, altering a gun in the manner that the gun David used was altered, by shortening the distance between the front and rear sight and the removal of the stock, makes it extremely difficult to aim and fire accurately. Thus it becomes viable only as a close-range weapon. He would have had to have been very, very close to Maria to carefully aim and place those shots as he did.

It was sickening to imagine the crime. To understand that it was not a crime of passion, a momentary explosion of David's known temper, but a planned execution, carried out in a cold and calculating manner by the "loving" husband who, the very next day, was out selling his wife's possessions to buy himself drugs, and only days later, according to Cindy Richardson (who had called him and overheard it), he was partying with friends in an apartment where his wife's clothes still hung in the closet and her purse sat in the living room.

Frequently in an investigation, the acquisition of a vital piece of information will have a backwash effect on information obtained earlier, making puzzling events or behaviors suddenly clearer. For the detectives, understanding the calculated brutality and violence of the crime, the cold manner in which Tanasichuk had executed his wife, suddenly made the circumstances of the interview after the take-down in Donnie Trevors's car make a lot more sense.

Throughout that interview, Dewey Gillespie and the detectives observing it had sometimes had the sense that David very much wanted to tell them where to find Maria's body, but something was holding him back. Now they knew what that "something" was. While Dewey had been offering possible scenarios of David suddenly snapping, losing his famous temper and striking out at Maria in anger, because she made him feel trapped, the knowledge of the actual crime that he'd committed made it clear why he couldn't confess, and why he hadn't given them the site of her body.

The caliber and placement of the shots was telling. A shot through the eye, for example, meant easier penetration into the brain, especially with a small caliber .22. That type of round enters but usually doesn't exit; instead, it spins around inside the skull doing a brain scramble and dropping the victim. There is not a lot of cast-off splatter, explosion of the skull or blowback onto the shooter. There was no logical way to read the three close-range, carefully placed bullets in the head from an unstable weapon as anything other than a cold-blooded execution.

Part 4

Wheels of Justice

Chapter 19

Making the Case

After the dramatic ups and downs of the investigation between January 26 and the end of June, followed by the wait for results from the various forensic analyses which needed to take place regarding the evidence, the investigators now settled in to work with the crown prosecutors to prepare the case for trial. Once David Tanasichuk was behind bars, they had taken a methodical approach to the case: putting the files in order, re-interviewing witnesses as necessary, meshing their witness statements with their evidence and copying maps, photos and videos of interviews. They had also done the paperwork necessary to explain their case to the prosecutors, including creating a detailed case summary and a timeline of actions before and after Maria's disappearance, based on witness accounts.

Doing these sometimes arduous tasks was vital. Over the course of a year, the Miramichi police had devoted over ten thousand man-hours to the case. They had interviewed more than one hundred civilian witnesses and twenty police and expert witnesses. They had produced paper transcripts of these interviews, records of their searches and logs of their phone calls. They had recorded more than forty hours of videotape of their interviews. Even though the investigators had worked closely with the crown prosecutor from the earliest stages of the case, shaping warrants, interviews and searches, they now had a room filled with documents which needed to be evaluated and summarized so that the best information could be provided to the crown. Only then would the prosecution be able to start putting together their most effective case.

As they consolidated their witness statements and began to prepare their witnesses for trial, new information was sometimes revealed. From the young woman who had been Lesley Allen's friend and then became involved with David shortly after Maria disappeared, they learned that even after he was incarcerated the relationship had continued via visits and phone conversations. This was troubling, because she had been a waitress at the Portage Restaurant during the period when the searches for Maria's body were underway. The detectives, the wardens and MESARD handlers had taken all their meals there and held many of their meetings there as well.

She reported that David regularly called and asked her for updates about the case, saying, "How did the fucking mutts do today?" He called her the day that Maria was found, and she told him that they'd found a body. His response: "I wonder how she was killed?" Brian Cummings, who was interviewing her, noted that David had not wondered "how she died," but knew the operative word was "killed."

After the loose bricks of his escape attempt were discovered, David was moved to a more secure facility. On July 31, 2003, he was convicted of possession of a restricted firearm with ammunition and sentenced to a term of thirty-eight months and fifteen days. He was incarcerated in the maximum-security Atlantic Institution in Renous.

Because of the slow pace of processing the evidence and therefore preparing the case, David Tanasichuk was not formally charged with first-degree murder in the death of his wife until May 2004. In part, it happened at that time because he had then served part of his sentence for possession of the illegal firearm and there was talk about transferring him back to a medium-security facility to serve the remainder of his sentence. The Miramichi police were adamantly opposed to this, continuing to believe that he presented a significant escape risk and posed a deadly threat to them, their families and critical witnesses if he were ever to escape.

Finally, in January of 2005, two years after Maria Tanasichuk disappeared, the multi-week trial began. But long before the crown prosecutors and the defense appeared in the courtroom before a jury, preparations had been taking place. First there were discussions between the prosecutors and the investigators about the witnesses and the stories they would tell. Documents, photographs, the detectives' notes and videos had to be copied and shared with the defense. Then the prosecutors took all the materials the investigators had developed, met with the principal witnesses and decided on the vital pieces of information, who would make the best witnesses and what order they would be presented in, in order to "tell the story."

The reality of trials is far different than movies or novels would have us believe. It is slow, often painfully so. The rules of engagement prevent the prosecution from leading witnesses, so that sometimes getting the story out can be a convoluted process. Prosecutors interview the witnesses, but the rules are quite restrictive about the amount of trial preparation or anything that seems like coaching the witness. The information comes in, not in a coherent and straightforward way, but in bits and pieces from multiple sources, so that the jurors must stitch it together for themselves with the help of closing arguments and the instructions given to them by the judge.

Nonetheless, it is still theater, a deadly real form of theater in which the stakes are not impressing the audience, but winning. And winning, for the prosecution in a homicide case, means getting justice for the victim.

What is often least known about the trial process is how much of what is uncovered in the investigation is never shown in a courtroom at all. Before the jury is chosen and the actual trial begins, the judge will have conducted an extensive *voir dire* process to determine the admissibility of evidence, whether each particular witness will be permitted to testify and what that witness will be permitted to testify to. In the United Kingdom, Canada, Australia and New Zealand, *voir dire* is a hearing where the judge determines the admissibility of contested evidence, the credibility of a witness or the eligibility of a potential juror. Since the *voir dire* often relates to matters that may cause bias on the part of the jurors, the jury is usually removed from the courtroom.

The jury in the trial of David Tanasichuk would therefore not hear about his lengthy prior record, his many gun charges, or his plot to kill a judge, a prosecutor and a police officer, because that would be prejudicial. They would not hear that during the period subsequent to Maria's disappearance and prior to his arrest, he was arrested for obtaining and selling a shotgun. They would not hear about his threats against the case investigators or their families, nor about the alarm systems that were installed in their homes or the panic buttons their wives wore for many weeks. They might hear about the gun charge he was arrested for in March of 2002, but not about the abduction kit he had with him in the trunk of Donnie Trevors's car on the night he was arrested, where he was believed to be heading at the time of that stop or what his intentions were thought to be.

They would learn very little about the affair he'd begun shortly after his wife disappeared. They would hear that his motive might be that he was feeling trapped by his wife's too vigilant attentions, but not that Maria was the keeper of his secrets, that she knew he had killed Abby Brown and increasingly suspected him in the disappearance of her brother. They would not hear that he'd told people he couldn't leave Maria because of what she knew.

There are two other things that the public is rarely aware of, yet which create powerful undercurrents in the courtroom process. First, it helps greatly for the family and friends of the victim to be present at the proceeding to stand as living witnesses for the deceased. They generally try to attend court each day, to sit in the room as visible physical reminders of who the victim was, demonstrating her ties to a community that still carried her in their hearts and remembered her with love and affection. In the case of David Tanasichuk shooting his wife, this meant the family and friends of the deceased had to rise early every morning of the trial to drive the winter roads to the courtroom, often missing work or facing the frustrating scheduling challenges of a process that was far from linear.

This was an important role for people like Maria's sister, Sharon, and her best friend Darlene to play. But it was a grueling one as well. Sitting in the courtroom meant they had to hear the wardens' sometimes graphic testimony about finding Maria's body, and forensic descriptions about decomposition and the bullet wounds. They might see the disturbing photographs that were placed into evidence. It also meant that each day, they entered that courtroom knowing they would face the accused. A killer. The person who had robbed them of something precious. And in this case, that killer would mock them.

A second aspect of the trial process that often goes unseen is the impact of that process on the police. As their statistics showed, the Miramichi police force had logged 10,000 hours on the case. It had been a central focus of many of their lives for a long time. This case had been deeply unusual. It involved the likelihood of multiple homicides. And it had flipped the normal investigative situation—it had become a case in which the hunters and their families had become the hunted. For nearly two years, the case had "belonged" to them. Now the men who had lived and breathed the case had to relinquish primary decision-making and control to the crown prosecutors, to the judge and, ultimately, to the jury. It was a hard thing to be so invested and to be relegated, to a great extent, to the role of support staff or spectator. Difficult to sit in the courtroom and watch vital testimony be challenged, excluded and diminished.

With a trial on the horizon, the Miramichi detectives and primarily Brian Cummings acquired a new role: witness wranglers. Lining up the witnesses for the particular day they were due to testify and making sure they had a ride to court was essential. It was also, often, a thankless and complicated task, for trials do not progress according to the timeline initially planned. It was January and there was snow and icy roads. There were witnesses who needed to come from two to three hours away when there wasn't ice and snow. Forensic experts had to travel from long distances, and the forensic anthropologist and forensic pathologist who had confirmed the third entry wound into Maria's skull had to journey from Ontario. Everyone had to be communicated with. Scheduled. Often rescheduled. And other criminals in the region didn't take a vacation because the Miramichi police were caught up in a trial, so the days were very long, often requiring Paul Fiander or Brian Cummings to hurry out of the courtroom many times during the trial day to take phone calls, advise investigators about how to proceed in other matters or rush across the river to handle other business.

Part of witness wrangling involved supporting the witnesses' spirits, especially for Maria's sister and her close friends. Because, while their love for Maria had given them the courage to come forward and tell the police what they knew about David Tanasichuk, they also knew that he had killed Maria, that he was a violent man with an explosive temper who had shown no signs of remorse about killing his wife. Despite their ongoing relationships with the Tanasichuks as a couple, and even though most of them had known David for many years, he had always been a person to tread carefully around. The only person who hadn't been afraid of him was Maria. With him charged with Maria's murder and suspected of at least two more, he had become, in their minds, a much more fearsome creature. And now they had to walk into a courtroom and meet him face-to-face, aware that the judicial system is uncertain and they might be testifying against a man—and before a man—who might explode with sensational violence in the courtroom, and who might, at the end of it all, walk free.

Sharon Carroll, Darlene Gertley, Cindy Richardson and Betty Schaefer were all quiet women, unused to the limelight, some of them timid around authority and intimidated by the whole judicial process. Amanda Malley was young. The women who'd had affairs with David would be testifying in public about deeply personal matters. They each entered that courtroom not only afraid of facing David, but uneasy about the judge and the process, about the questions the defense attorney would ask them and about sitting in the witness box before a room full of staring people.

It soon became clear that David was aware of their discomfort and wasn't going to make it easy for them. While the judge was leaving the bench or while he was turned away, David winked, waved and leered at them from the prisoner's dock. Arrogant and cocky as ever, sometimes he even blew them kisses. And although he was always accompanied by court security personnel and sat behind a Plexiglas shield, it seemed a very meager barrier to separate them from a man who had slaughtered animals with his bare hands and who had lured their beloved Maria, who had loved him more than life itself, out into the night and executed her, because she had become inconvenient and she knew his secrets.

The witnesses' concern about the prisoner's potential for violence was shared by the police. While the usual practice was for a prisoner to be transported from the prison facility to the courthouse in a prison van, the Miramichi police were taking no chances. Each day, when the van left the prison to bring David to court, it was accompanied by a Miramichi police vehicle and tactical officers armed with shotguns and rifles.

The story the prosecutors told through their witnesses was a simple one—a story of domestic violence, of a loving relationship gone wrong and a wife who had become inconvenient— one in which the husband had not fallen in love with another woman (even though there had been other women involved), but rather, where the man had fallen in love with drugs and been seduced by the pleasures that drug use could bring him. Seduced to the point where whatever scruples he might have

possessed—and his record suggests they were already few—
had fallen away. When his wife, who had weaned herself
from drugs and believed she could save him through love
and willpower, realized that her efforts were not working
and decided they were through, he chose to end the marriage in his own way, by killing her, rather than by divorce or
walking away.

It was a mainly circumstantial case but, as Crown prosecutor Jack Walsh told the jury in his opening, the Crown
would show motive, means and opportunity, and David
Tanasichuk's behavior after his wife's disappearance would
provide clues to what had happened.

There had been no witnesses to the crime. Despite careful scrutiny, the crime scene (or at least, the place where the
body had been concealed) had yielded no further evidence.
However, there were the bullets in Maria's head, which could
be tied to the gun found by Sharon Carroll's husband and the
gun was wrapped in a tarp identified by his next-door neighbor, John Paquet, as belonging to David Tanasichuk. They
had something close to an admission on the night in Donnie
Trevors's kitchen when David, stirred by the SAR efforts
and rumors of another search, had told Lesley Allen that the
searchers were getting close, that they'd have to move the
body. They had a timeline of when Maria had last been seen.
They had the neighbor's story of the mysterious nocturnal
trips and Donald Malley's story of David coming out of the
trail system with a peculiar bulge under his coat (quite possibly Maria's helmet, which he later sold) and refusing to recognize him.

Through testimony from her friends, the prosecutors
allowed the jury to envision Maria. Witnesses told the story
of a deteriorating marriage, with fights over money and
David's increasing absences from the home. They showed

her retreat from outside life after the death of her son and the resulting focus on her husband. They described her efforts to keep him from buying drugs, the way she watched him through binoculars, tried to keep dealers on the river from selling him drugs and how she tried to search him when he returned to the house, looking for drugs or drug paraphernalia.

Friends reported the rising tension between the couple over David's addiction and his use of the household money for drugs. Angela Arbeau, Maria's niece who regarded Maria as a second mother, testified about Maria's anxiety and agitation at Christmastime over David's lies and his drug use. She would tell of a depressed Maria reporting that she had attempted slitting her wrists but then decided she wouldn't take that route, refusing to give David the satisfaction of driving her to that level of despair. She also recalled David asking Maria for money to finish his Christmas shopping, claiming he'd spent more than he'd planned on a bow for his son, Adam. She described an agitated Maria searching the house after Tanasichuk's departure, saying that her husband was shooting drugs, and finding a syringe with fresh blood hidden under the cushion on a kitchen chair. Angela painted a picture of a woman reaching the end of her rope in her efforts to save her marriage and deal with her husband's lies and deception and sadly approaching the decision to move on.

Betty Schaefer testified that Maria had begun calling her often and sharing her worry about David's addiction. He was hiding his arms under long sleeves and staying away from home for long periods of time, while Maria would sit at the window, watching and waiting for him to return. Schaefer caused a stir of amusement in the courtroom as she patted her chest, testifying that after Tanasichuk stole $700 from

Maria, Maria had started hiding the household money in her bra. Maria's sister, Sharon Carroll, shared Maria's final, discouraged statements that she couldn't take it anymore; she was tired of fighting. Friends stated that Maria had given her husband an ultimatum and if he didn't comply, she was through. They testified that the only person likely to be able to get Maria out into the woods was David Tanasichuk.

They presented images of the happy couple riding off into the wilderness on David's three-wheeler. The house-proud Maria maintaining an immaculate apartment. The formerly bubbly and fun-loving woman spending days in her pajamas, huddled on her couch and tending a shrine to her son, but still regularly keeping in touch by visits or the phone with her friends and family. The prosecutor wanted the jury and those watching to see an otherwise informal, outdoorsy woman who was deeply attached to her gold jewelry, to hear of Maria's attachment to "Baby B," a little red devil bear, her last gift from her son, B.J.

Then they discussed Maria's sudden disappearance and the lengthy and implausible string of lies her husband told about her disappearance. They showed how unlikely it was, since Maria was a homebody who hated to travel and was tied to the apartment by her connection to her son, B.J., that Maria would have left for an undisclosed amount of time to visit a casual friend from years before. They showed all the things left behind in the apartment—"Baby B," her "sooky" blanket, her keys, her purse, her health card and her medications—and how unlikely it was that she would have left without them.

Although it is hedged with qualifiers, Canadian law allows a jury to consider "post-offense" behavior when evaluating a case. The principle that after-the-fact conduct may constitute circumstantial evidence of guilt remains good law. At its heart, the question of whether such evidence is admissible is simply a matter of relevance. As noted in *White (1998)*, "[e]vidence of post-offence conduct is not fundamentally different from other kinds of circumstantial evidence. In some cases it may be highly incriminating, while in others it might play only a minor corroborative role...As with all other evidence, the relevance and probative value of post-offence conduct must be assessed on a case-by-case basis... Consequently, the formulation of limiting instructions with respect to the broad category of post-offence conduct is governed by the same principles as for all other circumstantial evidence. Thus, while the term "consciousness of guilt" may have fallen out of use, it is still permissible for the prosecution to introduce evidence of after-the-fact conduct in support of an inference that the accused had behaved as a person who is guilty of the offence alleged—provided that, as with all circumstantial evidence, its relevance to that inference can be demonstrated."[25]

Because of this allowance, the prosecutors presented the jury with numerous details about David's behavior after January 15 to suggest that his conduct was not that of an anxious husband, deeply concerned about his wife's failure to return, but rather the behavior of someone who had no expectation that she would.

They played the video of David's first interview on the 29th, in which he detailed what Maria had worn and taken with her, affirmed that she had taken her jewelry and described some of the pieces to Brian Cummings. They produced the pawnshop receipts showing that David had sold or pawned some of those same pieces immediately after she was last seen. Lesley Allen revealed that David had given her a piece of gold jewelry—a "90% Devil" pendant—that she knew belonged to Maria, a pendant that Tanasichuk had told the police in his statement that Maria was wearing the day she left. Paul Fiander's testimony and official records confirmed that Tanasichuk had sold Maria's three-wheeler and her helmet before she was reported missing, and that the signature on the documents was forged.

Officers who conducted the search of the Queen Street apartment would confirm that drug paraphernalia was left lying around in plain sight, suggesting an inhabitant who had no fear of discovery.

Fiander testified about the items found in the apartment, including the little red devil bear doll that Maria had called "Baby B," the blanket and what appeared to be Maria's current purse, containing items she would have needed with her on a trip. He also described a sum of money found hidden in the closet, which David was apparently unaware of and which Maria likely would have taken with her if she were going away for any period of time.

Piece by piece, witness by witness, the prosecutors dismantled David's story and showed it to be lies. Sylvette Robichaud from the addiction counseling service testified about Tanasichuk's treatment history and stated that she had never advised the couple to spend time apart, except for a few hours from time to time to give each other some space. Records from the addiction counseling service at Miramichi Hospital confirmed that David Tanasichuk had stated that sometimes he got so mad he wanted to kill somebody, and that he took drugs to help him quell those urges. Detective Cummings testified that when he visited David the day after the formal police interview, David was not acting like a grieving or anxious husband. He was light-hearted and easy, apparently relaxed now that he had gotten over the hurdle of his interview with the police. Despite his earlier tears, he had mentioned his missing wife only in the context of asking whether her guns could remain in the apartment.

Many witnesses spoke about conversations with David after Maria disappeared. On the same day he had filed his missing persons report, David told Sharon Carroll that living with Maria was like having been in prison for eleven years. Amanda Malley testified to collecting some of Maria's special possessions and B.J.'s things when David threw them out and seeing the special angel ornaments people had given them when B.J. died broken and stuffed in the trash.

Further evidence cast doubt on Tanasichuk's statement that Maria had gone to Saint John. An affidavit admitted from Kathy Perry, whom Maria had known in Saint John, confirmed that she had only spoken with Maria once since Maria moved away, and that had been right after B.J. was killed. Cathy Penney, another friend from Saint John, testified that she had spoken to Maria on January 10 but they had made no plans for a visit. Maria's former brother-in-law and close friend testified via affidavit that Maria would have gotten in touch with him if she was visiting Saint John. Cindy Richardson, Maria's former common-law sister-in-law and B.J.'s aunt, stated that Maria remained close to her family members in Saint John and would never have traveled there without contacting them. She also spoke of Maria's attachment to the little red devil teddy bear, saying she would never be parted from it, because it was a link between her and her deceased son.

According to their neighbor, John Paquet, Maria was unlikely to have been the one who left because she had explicitly told him that if they were ever to part, David would have to be the one to move because of her attachment to the apartment where she'd raised B.J. He also revealed that David was familiar with the area where Maria's body was found, because during hunting expeditions the previous year, he had hunted with David in that region and David had often chosen the area where the sentinel tree was located. He testified that he had seen the Tanasichuks target practicing behind the Portage, each of them armed with a .22 caliber rifle. Police testimony later showed that when David turned over Maria's guns, there was only one .22.

Paquet also testified that he had bought some of the Tanasichuks' possessions, because David seemed to be selling everything. When he questioned David about why he was selling so many items, David told him he was going somewhere where he wouldn't be needing things.

Questioned about the green tarp in which the murder weapon had been wrapped, Paquet affirmed it was David's habit to wrap guns and bows and arrows in green tarps when carrying them on the three-wheelers to go hunting. The tarp resembled the one David usually employed but he couldn't be certain that it was the same one.

Paquet's wife testified about speaking with David as he emptied the apartment and asking what Maria would think coming home to an empty home. David replied that that was okay, he'd just get a divorce. When she offered to store some treasured possessions for David, he was indifferent, and when she asked what he thought had happened to Maria, he suggested she had started using drugs or run off with another man. Describing Maria's attachment to the apartment, Paquet's wife said that after Maria took a trip to Saint John in 2002, she said she never wanted to go back because all her memories were in her home. Later, Paquet's wife testified to a conversation with David when he called her from prison on the day of Maria's funeral seeking sympathy and saying the authorities wouldn't give him a pass to attend. She had told him straight out that he had killed the only person who had ever loved him. And she testified that David didn't deny it.

Asked on cross-examination whether she had any personal knowledge of the crime, Paquet's wife acknowledged that she didn't but stated that, in her heart, she knew.

Darlene Gertley testified to last having seen Maria on January 15, when they made plans to return some unwanted Christmas gifts together on the 17th. She described calling the house on the 16th and 17th, trying to arrange that trip, and finally going over there and being told that Maria had gone to a christening, when Maria had never mentioned any christening. She would say that later, when David called her and tried to convince her that the date she'd last seen Maria was the 12th, she reminded him that on the 12th she had been in Prince Edward Island visiting her mother.

Gertley testified that she had visited the apartment on the 19th and David told her that Maria had left for Saint John earlier in the day. She stated that Maria had been hiding her money, because her husband was spending it on drugs. When Gertley visited the apartment and saw the little red devil doll and questioned Tanasichuk about it, he had told her that it wasn't Maria's doll but belonged to the kids upstairs. She described Tanasichuk's insistence that she pay him the money she had borrowed from Maria for her trip to PEI.

Cindy Richardson, who had been B.J.'s aunt and Maria's friend since the two were very young mothers together in Saint John, testified regarding her increasing anxiety about Maria's disappearance. She had been envious of the Tanasichuks' relationship and fond of David, and had thought he was good for Maria. But the story that was unfolding as she began to question Maria's disappearance caused her deep concern. After a call on the 23rd from one of Maria's friends about being unable to locate Maria, Richardson had phoned her family in Saint John to see if Maria was there, but no one had heard from Maria.

The following day, the 24th, Richardson had called David and he told her that Maria had left on the 19th for Saint John. Later, she spoke with him and he told her he was putting up posters looking for Maria in Moncton, which made no sense to her since he had said that she'd gone to Saint John. Richardson also testified about having seen Maria at an event commemorating B.J. Breau in early January, how David wasn't in attendance and Maria looked sad. At that time, Maria had told her that David was back on drugs and was at home, passed out on the couch. She said she had spoken with Maria on the 11th and Maria had mentioned no plans to go away. Richardson identified the little red devil doll as Maria's last gift from B.J., stating that Maria always kept it close.

She agreed on cross-examination by Norman Clair, the public defender assigned to be David's counsel, that she had never seen David Tanasichuk yell at his wife or witnessed any signs of violence.

Possibly the most stunning moment during the trial came when Sharon Carroll's husband took the stand. As Edmund Carroll began to describe the circumstances that led to him finding the tarp-wrapped and duct-taped murder weapon shoved beneath the old truck bed, the entire courtroom fell silent. Everyone listened, mesmerized, as this simple, honest man told his story of that unearthly voice commanding him to turn around, to go back and to look for a gun.

He'd been out there for about four hours on a borrowed ATV, and he was heading down the road where that truck bed had been abandoned. After extensive questioning about the truck bed's location relative to the trail and how much of the green tarp-wrapped gun was visible, Norman Clair began a cross-examination taking Carroll through his search, the nature of the trail and where he was in relation to the abandoned truck box.

"Did you...I understood your testimony is you went by and then turned around?" Clair prompted.

"I was coming home that day," Carroll agreed.

"Okay," Clair nodded.

"Coming home that day, so I was going that way, going home—"

Clair interrupted and they spent a great deal of time establishing direction for the sake of the jury, showing Carroll heading away from the truck bed.

Carroll continued, "But on the day I found the gun, I turned back around..."

"Why did you turn around?"

"Just like something was telling me the gun—it's just like something—turn back around," Carroll admitted.

"Sensory perception?" Clair guessed.

"What do you mean by that?" Carroll asked.

"You say something was telling you...?" Clair led.

"It's just like something was telling me, like, turn back around and you know search for more, go around...search, search."

Later, Clair asked, "Why were you interested in looking at that tarp?"

"Well, the day I went to [search] for Maria, to search for the body, I figured maybe he might have—anyway I heard that there was—there could be a weapon involved too, I was just gonna check on that tarp and see what was in it," Carroll answered.

Carroll testified that he hadn't gone out that day to search for the gun. He'd gone out to look for his sister-in-law, Maria. He'd driven past that truck bed, he said, and had never stopped there, but when he turned back around, it all happened so fast. He could see a little corner of the green tarp. He opened the duct tape-wrapped tarp and saw the gun. Then he replaced it and drove directly to the police department.

Specialist Deb Palman, the Maine Warden who had found Maria, was in the courtroom, waiting to testify. She said that listening to Carroll's testimony was like something from *The Twilight Zone*. Palman felt, as did the Miramichi detectives, that there was some kind of divine intervention at work on that day, sending Edmund Carroll out there and leading him to that find. Everyone who spoke about being in the courtroom that day had the same reaction. It was eerie. It was spooky. And while the cross-examination tried to suggest there was something untruthful in his account, Edmund Carroll was such a decent, straightforward man that he was utterly convincing.

Later, Palman took the stand herself to describe the search protocol, the decision that had sent her and Alex out to search the area behind the Portage that day, and her interactions with Alex up until the moment when he made his find, returned to let her know that he had made that find and signaled her to follow him. She then described what she had discovered—a decomposed body dressed in winter clothes and hidden by branches and brush—and how she made the call to the Miramichi police.

In his cross-examination, Norman Clair tried to highlight the weakness of the prosecution's case: the lack of scientific or physical evidence linking David to the crime. He suggested that the police exhibited tunnel vision in investigating the case and, once they had fixed on David Tanasichuk as their suspect, they had not looked any farther. They had not examined other possible perpetrators. Clair's strategy was to show that David's lack of lucidity at the time he gave statements about Maria's disappearance to the police was not because he was intending to deceive them but was the result of his drug use.

His questioning of Maria's friends was meant to show that the Tanasichuks had a happy marriage, not a troubled one, and that there wasn't a history of violence in the relationship. He asked Angela Arbeau if Maria had seemed upset when she had seen Maria on Boxing Day, and Arbeau had said she was fine. He asked Sharon Carroll about their relationship and Carroll said they had a very good relationship. When asked what had changed, Carroll said that Tanasichuk had started taking drugs again.

The public defender's questions to Lesley Allen were designed to suggest that her critical testimony was suspect, because at the time that she heard David's statement about moving the body, she, like David, was under the influence of drugs.

Clair quizzed Maria's friends closely about whether they could be certain that various pieces of jewelry, and even the red devil doll, were ones that belonged to Maria.

As the trial proceeded, a major question loomed in everyone's minds: Would Norman Clair put his client on the stand? Would David speak in his own defense and attempt to explain his actions to the jury?

That question was answered on February 3, when Clair called David Tanasichuk to the stand.

"Did you kill your wife?" Clair asked bluntly.

David replied, "No, I did not."

In response to Clair's questions, David then attempted to explain the discrepancies in dates that played such a significant role in the investigation, stating that he had been using drugs at the time and his mind was muddled. On the 12th, he said, "Me and Maria worked on her bike." She had actually left on the 16th. On that day, she had found some pills in his pocket and accused him of buying them on the 15th when he was at his friend Donnie Trevors's house.

He testified that as he was leaving on the 16th to go to Trevors's house, she had hollered after him, "Don't expect me to be here when you get back and don't expect to buy any more pills on the river."

When he came home, she was gone. "I figured she went out with Darlene [Gertley] or to try and track me down." Then, because some of her things were missing—a pair of hiking boots, a bag and her money that she'd hidden in the bedroom, he figured she'd gone to Saint John. He said he'd made calls, looking for her, although the phone records showed no calls to Saint John until the 26th. He explained that maybe he had called from another location or used his brother's cell phone.

Asked by the Crown about Lesley Allen's testimony that she had heard him say, "They're getting close, we have to move the body, they're going to find her," he first said he was referring to rumors people were spreading, then added, "I heard what she said but, as far as me saying that that night, I can't verify me saying it or not saying it." He denied having called her the next day.

Similar to his response to Lesley Allen's statement, his explanations for testimony others had given generally came down to drugs. The affair with another woman had "just happened." He hadn't said he loved her, merely employed his habit of saying "God love you." He blamed the fact that he was using drugs for inconsistencies in what he'd told the police. His mind was clearer now and his memory had come back, to some extent. Responding to Donald Malley's statement about seeing him on the snowmobile trails, he simply said, "I don't know what to make of his testimony." And he reiterated that he did not kill his wife.

On February 9, 2005, the prosecution and the defense made their closing arguments. Prosecutor Jack Walsh urged the jury to apply logic and common sense, then summed up the Crown's evidence. Public defender Norman Clair countered that there was no scientific or physical evidence that linked David Tanasichuk to the crime, asserting that the only thing that could be known was that Maria had been murdered, that she had been shot three times by a .22 caliber, bolt-action, sawed-off rifle, and that her body had been found in the woods. No time or date of death could be established. Clair alleged that the police investigation had exhibited tunnel vision by focusing solely on Tanasichuk instead of on alternative suspects. He reiterated that Lesley Allen's statement about Tanasichuk wanting to move the body had been made under the influence of drugs. He noted that the burden of proof was on the Crown and insisted it had not been met.

Judge Roger McIntyre then gave his charge to the jury and they retired to deliberate.

Waiting for a jury to return with a verdict is an agonizing time for all the parties involved in a trial. The defense hopes they've raised reasonable doubt in the minds of the jurors. The prosecutors hope they've given the jury enough for a conviction. The family and friends of the victim hope for justice and closure. The family and friends of the accused hope for acquittal. The police walk the halls, wearing their professionally impassive faces, while inwardly veering from confidence that their work will bring the right result to wondering if there was something else they might have done, some other stone left unturned that might have given them one more fact, witness or piece of evidence that would have strengthened the case, to the almost unthinkable possibility that the jury would not be convinced of the suspect's guilt.

After nine hours of deliberation, the jury returned and announced the verdict: They found David Donald Tanasichuk guilty of first-degree murder in the death of his wife, Maria.

First-degree, meaning that there was premeditation and planning before the crime was carried out.

When the judge asked if the defense would like the jury polled, Clair said no, but David jumped to his feet and declared that yes, yes he *would* like them polled.

All twelve members of the jury, when they were questioned individually about the verdict they had reached, rose and said, "Guilty."

Maria's sister and her friends cried out and dissolved into tears.

In an interview after the trial, defense attorney Norman Clair said, "I'm disappointed, of course, because I felt that throughout, the Crown had a circumstantial case and that, even at the end, they hadn't really proven it, but obviously the jury felt differently." With respect to how his client was handling the verdict, Clair said, "...Very accepting. I've talked to him. He's not going berserk or crying or anything. He still feels that the community at large had it in for him, as he said before. I have no knowledge of that. He knows the Miramichi better than I do, certainly."[26]

Questioned by a reporter for the *Miramichi Leader* after the verdict, Sharon Carroll responded, "I said at first that justice will be done and I give all the glory to God for that—He came through. Justice was done. We're moving on now."[27]

Sadly, for Sharon and everyone else involved, that was not to be the case.

Chapter 20

Second Time Around

Indeed, everyone was ready to move on. Maria's sister, her best friend Darlene, her other close friends and her relatives wanted to finally grieve her loss in peace without the prospect of courtrooms, testimony and the awful, ever-present possibility hanging over them that her killer might go free. They wanted to let Maria rest in peace.

The boxes and boxes of evidence, interviews, videos, photographs and other case materials, including the sawed-off .22 and Maria's skull, were stored away. Thoughts about the case were shoved to the back burner, though efforts continued, when time allowed, to amass further information about the disappearance of Robert Breau and the brutal murder of Abby Brown.

The prosecutors and the investigators expected, though, that David would appeal the verdict and he did. Acting as his own attorney, he filed a handwritten appeal raising, in the words of the appellate court, "eight vaguely-worded grounds of appeal," raising a number of complex legal questions about the evidence that had been allowed in and challenging the judge's instructions to the jury. Subsequently, he filed three additional written submissions, "finally settling on eleven grounds."[28]

The appellate process was slow. The appeal was argued in the Court of Appeal of New Brunswick on November 30 and December 1, 2006, and on January 16, 17, 29, 30 and 31 of 2007, with John J. Walsh, Q.C. for Her Majesty the Queen, respondent and David Tanasichuk representing himself.

In November of 2007, Brian Cummings was teaching a class on interviewing and interrogation technique at the police academy when he got the call that the appellate decision had finally been handed down. Nearly five years after Maria Tanasichuk's murder, and two and half years after her husband was found guilty of that murder, the court had granted him a new trial. The police, the prosecutors and the witnesses would have to go through the whole thing again.

Cummings said, "It wasn't the evidence. It wasn't the testimony. It was legal error. And I sat there...and nobody in that courtroom who listened to Justice McIntyre's charge to the jury would think that man's rights were violated. You've put twelve citizens through a month of their lives, listening to horrendous stuff...and the appeals court says that doesn't matter.

"I remember getting the phone call while I was at the academy...that he'd gotten a new trial, and it was exactly the same feeling when I got the phone call that my grandmother died. You get that initial shot of adrenaline. Your body goes hot. You can't believe what you're hearing. Then emotion sets in, you feel like crying, you fight back tears. Then you get mad. You run that gamut of emotions in a very short time."

The 90-page appellate decision granting Tanasichuk a new trial raised six issues:

1. The trial judge erred in his charge to the jury regarding the evidence of fabrication;

2. The trial judge erred in his charge to the jury on the post-offense conduct of the accused;

3. The trial judge erred in allowing part of Paquet's common law wife's testimony to be considered as an adoptive admission;

4. The trial judge erred in admitting the testimony of Lesley Allen regarding an utterance by the accused without holding a *voir dire*, and in determining that the statement attributed to him was the product of an operating mind;

5. Counsel representing the accused was ineffective;

6. The trial judge misapprehended the evidence of certain witnesses and misdirected the jury accordingly.[29]

The decision, while finding there was a strong circumstantial case against David Tanasichuk, concluded that: "I am unable to say that the evidence against Mr. Tanasichuk is so overwhelming that a conviction is inevitable or would invariably result, such that he should be deprived of a proper trial on the grounds that there has been no substantial wrong or miscarriage of justice. As a result, I would allow the appeal, set aside the conviction, and order a new trial."[30]

Essentially, while all the issues were considered, the decision to grant a new trial was based on two of them. First, the appellate court found the trial judge's jury instructions on how to consider the issue of fabrication (the lies that he told to people during the weeks that Maria was missing and during his initial reports to, and interviews with, the police), and whether there was "independent evidence of fabrication" inadequate. Second, the appellate court considered the trial court judge's decision to allow David's silence to be considered as an adoptive admission when he failed to respond to Paquet's wife's accusation that "As far as I'm concerned, you killed her. You killed the only person who ever loved you."

Reading a trial transcript can be heavy going; much of the interest at trial that offsets the formality of the presentation requires being in the courtroom and observing the demeanor of witnesses, the manner of the presiding judge, the antics of the defendant, the often stately combat of the Crown and the defense, and the reactions of the jury. The tears, the expressions, the heartbreak can't be read off the page. Therefore, often, when the appellate court chooses to do so, the appellate decision can offer an excellent summary of testimony that sometimes gets lost in the back and forth of examination, cross and objection. Formal as it was, before getting into the legal aspects of its decision, the appellate court gave a good outline of the significant aspects of the original trial that were relevant to the subjects considered on appeal.

The Crown's case against David Tanasichuk was summed up as follows:

> The prosecution's case was circumstantial and it included evidence of motive, knowledge, means and opportunity. Prosecution evidence revealed that the couple's relationship had badly deteriorated, that Maria was last seen alive in the early evening of January 15, 2003, at her apartment, that Mr. Tanasichuk was in possession of a rifle that was similar to the murder weapon, and that Mr. Tanasichuk gave varying explanations to others as to when and where Maria had gone. The evidence also revealed that, after Maria's disappearance, Mr. Tanasichuk sold or pawned some of Maria's jewelry to obtain money for drugs and that, after his wife had gone

missing, he had a relationship with another woman. There was also evidence that before Maria Tanasichuk's body was found, Mr. Tanasichuk, under the influence of drugs, made a statement about moving the body because the police were getting closer. The prosecution also relied on what it considered evidence of fabrication, and on an incriminating statement the Crown claimed Mr. Tanasichuk had adopted as his own.

Mr. Tanasichuk testified in his own defense. He stated he had last seen his wife at their apartment on the morning of January 16, 2003, and that, at the time, she was very angry with him because she had found drugs in his jacket. He said that as he left the apartment she was cursing him, telling him "not to expect to find her there when he got back and for him not to expect to be able to buy drugs on the river." According to Mr. Tanasichuk, when he returned to the apartment around 1:00 P.M. that same day, Maria was not there. He testified that this was the last time he saw or heard from his wife. Mr. Tanasichuk offered explanations for the differing accounts he had given to Maria's friends and relatives and to the police, stating that these were largely the result of drug-induced confusion. He offered innocent explanations for his disposal of Maria's personal property, for the possession of a weapon similar to the murder weapon, for his sexual relationship with another woman following his wife's disappearance, and for the comment attributed to him about moving Maria's body. He was not questioned regarding the statement that the Crown maintained that he had adopted, that he had killed his wife.[31]

Then the court outlined, among other things, the couple's background; significant details regarding the Tanasichuks' marital situation before Maria disappeared; David's conduct after that event; the reporting that Maria Tanasichuk was missing; the police search of the Tanasichuks' apartment; and David Tanasichuk's conduct subsequent to reporting his wife missing:

The events leading up to Maria's disappearance:

On January 4, 2003, Maria attended an annual basketball fundraiser established in memory of her late son, B.J. Breau. Her friend Betty Schaefer drove her to the event. Maria told Ms. Schaefer that Mr. Tanasichuk could not attend because he was back at the apartment passed out. Maria also said that he had stolen money from her and that she now carried her money with her at all times. She told other friends that the reason her husband was not present was because of drugs.

Sometime during either the first or second week of January 2003, Maria called her sister, Sharon Carroll. Ms. Carroll noted that Maria "was crying, saying her nerves were bad, [and that] she was tired of fighting with Dave."

On January 9, 2003, Darlene Gertley, Maria's best friend, visited Maria and invited her to go to P.E.I. with her for a few days. Maria declined because she "wanted to stay home to be with Dave." Ms. Gertley left for P.E.I. on January 10 and returned in the early afternoon of January 13.

Laurie Eckert, one of the Tanasichuk's neighbors, visited Maria on Saturday, January 11. According to her, Maria was upset and waiting for her husband to come home. He had reportedly taken some of her money and was supposed to pick up a prescription for her. Maria said that she had called everybody she knew and didn't know where he was. Her mood ranged from worried and depressed to angry, saying "he did it again." The next evening, Ms. Eckert overheard Mr. Tanasichuk and Maria arguing loudly.

Darlene Gertley returned home from P.E.I. on January 13, 2003, and, that evening, visited Maria. Mr. Tanasichuk was present, lying on the couch. He was ill. The next day, Ms. Gertley spoke to Maria on the phone.

On January 14, Mr. Tanasichuk called the addiction counselor to reschedule his January 17 appointment. He also requested information on the methadone program.

John Paquet, another neighbor, saw Maria at 10:30 A.M. on Wednesday, January 13, 2003. She had come out of her apartment and had asked Mr. Paquet about the arrival of the mail.

At approximately 5:30 P.M. the evening of January 15, 2003, Maria telephoned Angela Arbeau, who lives in Fredericton. Maria said that her husband was out. Later that same evening, Darlene Gertley visited Maria at her apartment. Mr. Tanasichuk was not present. Maria told Ms. Gertley that her husband was "out doing junk" and told her about the argument she had had with him on January 12. She explained that the argument was about him "trying to take money from the house" and that she had "got in his face." Maria showed Ms. Gertley $1,700 in cash she had hidden somewhere in the bedroom. Ms. Gertley made plans with Maria to take her shopping on January 17. After visiting for approximately an hour, Ms. Gertley left the apartment.[32]

As derived from the testimony at trial, the court summarized the events following Maria's disappearance thusly:

Sometime after 2:00 P.M. on January 16, 2003, Donald Malley was driving his vehicle on a street in the industrial park. On approaching an area where a snowmobile trail crossed the road, he observed Mr. Tanasichuk on his all-terrain vehicle, stopped on the trail at the intersection of the road. Mr. Malley, who had known Mr. Tanasichuk for 20 years, stopped, sounded his horn and waved at him. Mr. Malley observed that Mr. Tanasichuk was sitting on his ATV staring straight ahead. There was no reaction from him. After Mr. Malley drove by, he watched in his rearview mirror. Eventually, Mr. Tanasichuk drove across the road onto the snowmobile trail in the direction that leads to the area in back of the Portage Restaurant.[33]

About Maria's friends' efforts to locate her, the appellate court noted:

On the evening of January 16, Darlene Gertley returned to the Tanasichuk residence to see Maria. Mr. Tanasichuk answered the door. In Ms. Gertley's opinion, he was "out of it on drugs." She asked for Maria. Mr. Tanasichuk told her "she had [gone] to a christening with a Pauline or a Sandy." Maria had two friends who lived together, Pauline Fowlie and Sandra "Sandy" Daigle. The evidence subsequently gathered in the investigation revealed there was no christening.

Between January 17 and 19, Darlene Gertley called the Tanasichuk residence numerous times and left messages on the answering machine for Maria to return the calls. On January 19, in the late afternoon, Mr. Tanasichuk called Ms. Gertley and told her that Maria "a few hours before, took a bus to Saint John to Kathy Perry's place." He said she went there to "take time for herself and to give [him] time to himself." When Ms. Gertley asked Mr. Tanasichuk why Maria had not called to tell her, he replied that, in the last few days, Maria had not wanted to speak to anyone. Kathy Perry had been a friend of Maria's when Maria had lived in Saint John, but Ms. Perry had not seen Maria since the late 1990s and had last spoken to her shortly after Maria's son died in 2000.[34]

...On January 22, Darlene Gertley went to the Tanasichuk apartment because she was worried. Mr. Tanasichuk was present...On the pretext of using the bathroom, Ms. Gertley got farther into the apartment. When she came up the hallway from the bathroom, she noticed the bedroom door was open. She spotted "Maria's B.J. devil doll" on the bed. Knowing the significance of the doll to Maria, Ms. Gertley exclaimed: "Maria went away without that doll?" At that point, Mr. Tanasichuk closed the bedroom door, telling her that it was not Maria's but rather a toy that belonged to a neighbour's child.

On January 25, Maria's sister, Sharon Carroll, called Mr. Tanasichuk, inquiring if Maria was there. He informed her Maria had gone to Saint John and would be back the next day. On the same day, Cindy Richardson called...[Mr. Tanasichuk] told her that Maria had left for Saint John by bus on January 19, explaining that "the addiction service worker had recommended that they have six or seven days apart because Maria wasn't letting him have any time alone."

Also on January 25, Lisa Trafton spoke to Mr. Tanasichuk on the phone, inquiring as to Maria's whereabouts. He told her that she had gone away to visit friends in Saint John. Ms. Trafton asked Mr. Tanasichuk when Maria had left, to which he replied, "Monday." Ms. Trafton said to him "January 20th? Kaleigh's birthday?" He replied "yes."... She called Mr. Tanasichuk again that evening. When Ms. Trafton commented it was "strange [Maria] didn't call," Mr. Tanasichuk started crying uncontrollably. He then became very angry, saying: "How the fuck would you like it if every time you went to the bathroom and you had to shit she was there or every time you had to have a bath she was there, every time the fucking phone would ring she would ask me who the fuck it was and what do they want?"

On the evening of January 25, Cindy Richardson telephoned Mr. Tanasichuk. He told her he was sick, but stated he would be going to Saint John the next day and that his brother's girlfriend was going to lend him some money to help pay the bus fare.[35]

Regarding David's disposal of Maria's possessions:

Sometime between January 10 and 16, Mr. Tanasichuk sold four rings to...a pawnshop owner in Miramichi. Three of the rings could not be worn and were purchased for scrap. The fourth was a lady's diamond channel-set ring. On January 16, Mr. Tanasichuk pawned a lady's gold bracelet and on January 17, he pawned numerous pieces of jewelry, including rings, pendants and chains. One of the pendants read "#1 Wife." Prosecution evidence adduced at trial suggested that most of this jewelry was the same as or similar to Maria's.[36]

On January 24, Mr. Tanasichuk sold Maria's three-wheeled all-terrain vehicle to [a male acquaintance] for $400.00, having first offered to sell both his and Maria's. [The acquaintance] insisted on a receipt. Mr. Tanasichuk left and returned shortly with a receipt and the registration, both signed in the name of Maria Tanasichuk. [The acquaintance] asked that a helmet be included in the sale, so Mr. Tanasichuk gave him a helmet, saying it was Maria's and that he expected it would be too small for [the acquaintance]. Mr. Tanasichuk advised that he would want to buy back the ATV, in a couple of weeks, for $500.00.[37]

On January 25, Mr. Tanasichuk sold a lady's diamond ring to [a neighbor] for $40.00. [The neighbor] gave the ring to his mother. The ring was later identified as similar, if not identical, to one belonging to Maria.

The court detailed David Tanasichuk's initial call that reported Maria missing:

> On January 26, 2003, in the midst of the first significant snowfall since January 13, David Tanasichuk contacted the Miramichi police and reported his wife missing. Responding to his call to take a missing person report, Constable Cheryl Seeley mistakenly said to Mr. Tanasichuk, "Hi, David, I understand you haven't seen your wife since January 12th," and he said "Yes." He then gave details surrounding his wife's departure.
>
> Later that afternoon, Tanasichuk called Maria's sister, Sharon Carroll, and stated that he had filed the missing person report. Then he began crying, telling Carroll that Maria was "following him all over the place; everywhere he went, she watched where he was going." He said Maria would "follow him to the store, she would watch him with binoculars," that it "made him feel like he was in prison in his own home."[38]
>
> On January 29, Cst. Cummings interviewed Mr. Tanasichuk and obtained both a videotaped and a written statement from him. According to Cst. Cummings, Mr. Tanasichuk was not impaired at the time. The information Mr. Tanasichuk provided can be summarized as follows:
>
> (1) Approximately five months earlier, Maria had started attending Mr. Tanasichuk's addiction counseling service meetings with him, as he had started doing drugs again and he felt it would be good if Maria was part of the process.
>
> (2) During the sessions, the counsellor suggested that they should spend some time apart for a while. As a result, 3–4 days prior to January 12, Mr. Tanasichuk told Maria he

was going to go to his brother Joe's in Moncton. He said
Maria did not want him to go to Joe's, so he suggested
that he could go to his mother's in Saint John. Maria
declined again, saying that she would go to Saint John
and visit with her friend, "Cathy." Mr. Tanasichuk did not
know who "Cathy" was, but had since learned that it could
be Cathy Penney.

(3) Between 1:00 and 3:00 P.M. on January 11, Mr. Tanasichuk
called Maria from the payphone in the foyer of [a local
grocery store] to see if she wanted him to pick up anything for the household. Maria said "no" and it was at this
time that she told him she would be leaving the next day,
by bus, for Saint John.

(4) Mr. Tanasichuk arrived home about half an hour later and
they talked about her leaving. Maria said that she would
be gone for about a week and that she would not call him
while she was gone until he contacted one of his family
members to get hold of her, so that he could have some
space. Maria talked about looking forward to seeing [her
brother-in-law] and Cathy. He and Maria went to bed
around 11:00 P.M., as usual.

(5) On the morning of January 12, Mr. Tanasichuk got up
between 8:30 and 9:00 A.M. and fed his animals. He ate his
breakfast and then made coffee and tea. He took Maria's
tea into the bedroom, at which time he noticed that she
had items packed on the floor. He made a comment to
the effect "So you really are going," and she replied, "Yes,
I'm leaving this afternoon." They then talked for about
twenty minutes while she drank her tea. He told Maria
that he had to go to Donnie Trevors's house to work on his
three-wheeler. Before he left the apartment, Maria made
him "promise that we'd always be good and stay away from
the drugs," and Maria repeated her promise not to call him

before he made contact with her in Saint John. Between 11:00 A.M. and noon, he left to go to Donnie Trevors's place.

(6) Mr. Tanasichuk spent the day of January 12 at Trevors' working on his bike until roughly 4:30 P.M. and then drove the bike home, arriving at approximately 5:00 P.M. Maria was gone when he got home. She did not leave a note and he had not heard from her since. He is certain the last time he saw Maria was on January 12.

(7) Mr. Tanasichuk started making phone calls about 6 days later to see if anyone had heard from Maria. He said nobody he contacted had seen or heard from her. He said that Maria left behind her prescription medication, her red devil teddy bear (what Maria called her "Baby B," for B.J., which was very important to her and which she kissed every night) and her "sooky" blanket. He said Maria would not go to sleep without having the blanket on her pillow. He acknowledged that the red devil teddy bear that Darlene Gertley had seen on January 22 was Maria's. Mr. Tanasichuk acknowledged that Maria was a homebody who did not go out much.

(8) Mr. Tanasichuk said that Maria wore a lot of jewelry and that she did not leave behind any of the pieces that she normally wore. He believed that when she left she would have been wearing 15–20 rings. He said he had not seen any jewelry that she would normally wear, or any rings, lying around the house. He presumed that she took all of her jewelry with her. He said that all of Maria's jewelry was gold. There was no silver and no pewter. He provided descriptions for some of this jewelry, including an engagement ring with six tiny diamonds surrounding a diamond and a "90% Devil" pendant which had been his.

(9) Mr. Tanasichuk started to get worried about Maria around January 16 and, as a result, made a number of phone calls,

both local and long-distance, in an attempt to locate her. He said that it was "really strange" for Maria to be away that long and not contact him, and that she had never been gone more than two days without contacting him, either in person or by phone.

(10) He related that things had not been "good" between Maria and him for quite some time, and it seemed like things got worse after August 2002, when she learned that she had Hepatitis C. He said that they never had any physical fights, but Maria was not happy about his drug usage. He admitted to being a casual intravenous user of [a particular drug] but also admitted to taking other painkillers. He confessed that the last time that he had used drugs was approximately one week earlier.

(11) When Mr. Tanasichuk last saw Maria on the morning of January 12, she appeared a little confused and worried about whether he would be alright. He said Maria's life revolved around him.[39]

The appellate court noted:

Several aspects of Mr. Tanasichuk's statement would later be called into question at trial by prosecution evidence. Sylvette Robichaud, the counsellor, testified that she "never recommended" that they leave one another, part or separate, other than recommending "some outings" to Maria, such as going to a movie or coffee with her friends. Prosecution witnesses established that, on January 10, Cathy Penney had called Maria from Saint John. She had not spoken to Maria for years. They talked for approximately 20 minutes but Maria made no mention of any plans to go to visit her. This was the last conversation Ms. Penney had with Maria. The evidence adduced at trial also revealed that there was only one payphone in the foyer of the [grocery store] and telephone records showed that no phone calls had been made in the month of January from that telephone to the Tanasichuk apartment. The evidence also revealed that the friend to whom Mr. Tanasichuk referred might have been a reference to Maria's former brother-in-law, who lives in Saint John. He and Maria had remained close friends, but he had not heard from her around the time of her disappearance.

Those of Maria's friends and relatives who testified stated that they had not received any calls from Mr. Tanasichuk inquiring about the whereabouts of his wife prior to his reporting her missing to the police. The prosecution evidence also revealed that there was a similarity between Maria's diamond ring and the one Mr. Tanasichuk sold to [a neighbor] on January 25, 2003, and between the "90% Devil" pendant Mr. Tanasichuk described and one he had given to Lesley Allen some time before Maria was reported missing.

In addition, telephone records introduced into evidence revealed that no long-distance calls were made from the phone in the Tanasichuk apartment between January 15 and the afternoon of January 26, that is, from the date Maria was last seen to the date when Mr. Tanasichuk reported her missing to the police.[40]

Other summarized testimony included details of the search of the Tanasichuk's apartment and what was found there, the finding of a gun which matched the bullets in Maria's head, and testimony about David using a tarp similar to the one in which the murder weapon was wrapped. There was testimony regarding David's affair begun shortly after his wife's disappearance, and testimony about him being arrested in possession of a loaded, sawed-off, rim fire, bolt-action .22 caliber rifle. Also:

(1) In the fall of 2002, John Paquet, a neighbour of David and Maria Tanasichuk, hunted on two occasions with Mr. Tanasichuk. On both occasions, Mr. Tanasichuk chose to hunt (with a bow) in the very section of the woods in which Maria's body was later found.

(2) In July and August 2002, John Paquet saw Mr. Tanasichuk and Maria target practicing in the area behind the Portage Restaurant. Both of them had .22 caliber rifles. He also saw them each operating three-wheeled all-terrain vehicles together in this area.

(3) In the early morning of January 2, 2003, Mr. Tanasichuk was operating a three-wheeled all-terrain vehicle and was stopped by a police officer at the location where Donald Malley later observed him on January 16, except that, on January 2, Mr. Tanasichuk was entering the intersection from the snowmobile trail in the opposite direction (i.e. from the area that runs to a location behind the Portage Restaurant).

(4) The distance from the Tanasichuk apartment to the area behind the Portage Restaurant, traveling on Queen Street and Howard Street, is approximately 3.2 kilometres [2 miles].

(5) Tamara Trevors observed Mr. Tanasichuk operating his three-wheeled all-terrain vehicle, with Maria on the back, heading up Queen Street toward Howard Street, sometime in the week of January 5–11, 2003.

(6) [The neighbor] lived on Howard Street, a couple of streets over from the Tanasichuk residence. He had known Mr. Tanasichuk for approximately 12–13 years and Maria for approximately 10 years. He testified that, sometime around the middle of January 2003, Maria had come to his home in the early afternoon looking for her husband.

She told [the neighbor] that she had not seen him for a day or two. When [the neighbor] chuckled in reply, Maria got mad, told him it was not funny and started to cry. [The neighbor] then sent his son to look for Mr. Tanasichuk on the snowmobile trails. Maria left. Sometime between 11:00 P.M. and 1:00 A.M. that night, Mr. Tanasichuk arrived at [the neighbor's] home on his ATV. It was a cold night. [The neighbor] testified that he told Mr. Tanasichuk that Maria had been there looking for him, to which he replied that "he had seen her and not to worry about it." Approximately 15 to 20 minutes later, Mr. Tanasichuk left on his ATV. [The neighbor] testified that approximately half an hour later, he saw someone he believed to be Mr. Tanasichuk on his ATV driving east on Howard Street, returning approximately 15 minutes later heading west, approximately 15 minutes later heading east and 15–20 minutes later heading west.[41]

The court then reviewed David Tanasichuk's trial testimony, including his explanation of the mysterious late-night trips past his neighbor's house:

Mr. Tanasichuk also remembered the incident testified to by [the neighbor]. He thought it occurred on January 11, but was not sure. Mr. Tanasichuk had been at a drug dealer's earlier. Someone had told him out on the trails that [the neighbor's son] was looking for him, so he went to [the neighbor's] residence. He denied having told [the neighbor] that he had seen Maria. Mr. Tanasichuk also denied that after leaving the [neighbor's] residence he had made the number of trips on his ATV that [the neighbor] had described. Rather, Mr. Tanasichuk's testimony was that when he left [the neighbor], he went home where he found his wife. He then noticed a part missing off his bike so he returned to the trails, driving past [the neighbor's] home to do so. He subsequently found the part and returned home, once again driving past [the neighbor's] home. He explained that the jewelry he sold was his, except for the ring sold to [the neighbor's son], and the jewelry he pawned was Maria's, which he intended to get back before she returned. He also testified that he planned to buy back her ATV.[42]

Having laid out the facts of the original case, the Court considered Mr. Tanasichuk's appeal, turning first to the question of fabrication. On that subject the Court wrote:

1) It is now a well established principle of law that, before any adverse inference may arise from an accused's exculpatory statement that is disbelieved, there is a requirement that the statement be shown to have been concocted.[43]

2) The circumstances in which an accused, or a person who eventually becomes an accused, makes an out-of-court statement which is found to be untrue may have an evidentiary value that is not present in the circumstance where an accused testifies and is disbelieved. False exculpatory statements made by a person upon being informed that a crime has been committed will in some circumstances be consistent with that person being conscious of having committed the crime, and may point to guilt in the same way that other after-the-fact conduct such as flight, a threat to a witness, or concealment of evidence can be probative of guilt. The circumstances in which a false statement is made may show an intent to mislead the police or others or an intent to deflect suspicion and may be evidence of a conscious mind that he or she has committed an offence. When a court is addressing the

admissibility of evidence contradicting an accused's out-of-court statement, it will be required to determine if there is independent evidence of fabrication, but in doing so, the court may consider the circumstances in which the allegedly false statement was made. If those circumstances tend to support a conclusion that the accused made a false statement because he or she was conscious of having committed the offence, then those circumstances may be used as independent evidence of fabrication.[44]

3) Statements said to have been concocted by an accused are treated as a type of post-offence conduct, which, in some circumstances, can lead to an inference of guilt. When ruled admissible, evidence of "fabrication" becomes a piece of circumstantial evidence for the jury to weigh in determining whether the Crown proved the accused's guilt beyond a reasonable doubt. This type of post-offence conduct is subjected to special admissibility rules, and, when evidence of fabrication is admitted in a jury trial, *it is imperative that the trial judge give specific instructions regarding how the evidence can be used.*[45]

When the appellate court considered the jury instructions that had been given in the first trial, it found that they had not been clear enough "to enable the jury to grasp the difficult concept that is the differentiation between evidence leading only to disbelief and independent evidence of fabrication. Nor did the judge explain that before these statements can be used as circumstantial evidence to be weighed with other evidence in determining whether the Crown has proven its case against Mr. Tanasichuk, the jury was required to find evidence of fabrication independent of the evidence showing the statements to be false. Without this critical instruction, the trial judge's charge to the jury could only have served to confuse the issue."[46]

In weighing the instruction to the jury, the appellate court wrote:

> I do not detect in Crown counsel's address to the jury any explanation of the need for the jury to find evidence of fabrication independent of the evidence showing the statements to be false, sufficient to cure the defect in the judge's charge. Crown counsel invited the jury to find that Mr. Tanasichuk deliberately lied to the police and, further, to conclude that the lies were fabrication to "cover his own guilt that he had murdered [his wife]." However, nowhere does anyone explain to the jury the difference between simply disbelieving the accused and finding, on the basis of independent evidence, that the statements had been concocted...Because the trial judge neither explained the need for independent evidence of fabrication nor pointed out that this requirement means evidence apart from the evidence showing the statements to be false, the jury was deprived of a crucial element that should have formed part of the analytical framework pursuant to which this potentially "extremely powerful" evidence was to be assessed.[47]

It was not that many of Tanasichuk's statements had been shown to be "fabrications," nor that independent evidence that they were untrue had been provided to the jury. It was that the instructions to the jury had not been adequate to help them evaluate the probative value of the information.

Turning to the second question of whether, by his silence in the face of Paquet's wife's accusation that he had killed his wife, Tanasichuk had admitted to killing her, the appellate court wrote:

> ...This ground of appeal requires this court to determine the following three questions:
>
> 1. Did the trial judge err in failing to hold a *voir dire*?
>
> 2. Did the trial judge err in concluding that there was sufficient evidence from which the jury might reasonably infer that Mr. Tanasichuk's silence amounted to an adoption of [Paquet's wife's] statement?
>
> 3. Did the trial judge err in his instructions to the jury with regard to the use that could be made of this evidence?
>
> [The court answered] all three questions in the affirmative.[48]

With respect to Lesley Allen's testimony about David's statement that the searchers were getting close and they'd have to move the body, the court concluded that, despite testimony that David and Allen were both "high," "there were sufficient indicia of consciousness to make Mr. Tanasichuk's utterance relevant and therefore admissible, and there was no need for a *voir dire*."[49]

Unquestionably, David Tanasichuk had showed himself to be an able jailhouse lawyer. Now, having inflicted untold misery on Maria's friends and family, he was going to put them through it all again.

The report of the appellate decision came in the fall of 2007. The new trial wasn't scheduled until the following fall. Between a lengthy *voir dire* process and scheduling conflicts for the new Crown Prosecutors, John Henheffer and Bill Richards, and Tanasichuk's new attorney, Brian Munro, the case did not finally come to trial until March of 2009, more than six years after the night Maria Tanasichuk disappeared.

One strange, sad footnote to this appeal was that Maria's silhouette, prepared by the Silent Witness Project to keep victims of domestic violence alive in the public's mind and a part of their traveling displays, was tagged with a note explaining that her husband's conviction was on appeal and was removed from public display. This was especially painful for Maria's sister, Sharon, who had worked closely with the project and found comfort in having her sister thus remembered and honored.

Retrying a case after so much time had passed was a nightmare and a headache for police and prosecutors. Memories had faded. The righteous and deeply credible John Paquet, the Tanasichuks' neighbor and the only witness who could connect David with the murder weapon because of the tarp it was wrapped in, had died. Vital witnesses had moved away and would have to be located and convinced to return for the trial. New prosecutors might take a different approach to telling the story; the presiding justice might not admit evidence that had been critical in the earlier trial. And all the old fears of entering a courtroom and confronting David were revived in Maria's friends, especially as it quickly became evident that David's new lawyer was forceful and tenacious and would be extremely aggressive toward the crown's witnesses. He would give no quarter in his efforts to secure a successful outcome for his client.

Before the *voir dire* got underway in the fall of 2008, David filed a motion for a change of venue, alleging that he would be unable to get a fair trial in Miramichi. To validate that assertion, he wrote in his supporting affidavit (as reported in *The Miramichi Leader*) that:

"Since the winter of 2003, I have been the subject of repeated rumors, gossip, and speculation concerning my wife's death. When I was eventually arrested and charged with her death, the media almost immediately focused its attention on me.

"It is my belief that I cannot get a fair trial in the Miramichi. This is based on the fact that I had a trial and that I was convicted during the trial by a jury from the Miramichi. In addition, I believe the newspapers and other media outlets have incorporated other investigations into their reporting which undermines the safeguards that normally would shield a jury pool from such sensationalistic reporting."

He went on to write that, having lived in Miramichi, he knew it was a close-knit community and could be negatively influenced by "...rumors, unfounded suggestions and sensationalistic reporting about tattoos, guns, and other things associated with the allegations against me.

"There are many examples in the media coverage in which the reporting is circulating a certain picture of me to the public. Almost everything they have been reporting concerning me is untrue and they leave an impression which I believe impacts any reasonable person or a reasonable prospect that I can get a fair and impartial jury within the Miramichi area. I believe I cannot!"

Drawing the court's attention to the fact that the police had merged the investigations of the death of Abby Brown and the disappearance of Robert Breau with their investigation into Maria's disappearance, he wrote:

"I believe this is a deliberate attempt to attach as many investigations to the ongoing murder trial, in an effort to paint me as some kind of serial killer or evil person. This assassination of my character makes it impossible for me to get a fair trial in this area, since they have previously heard details from the first trial and, now, with a second trial commencing in September, not even the safeguard of a ban on publication can assist me or cure the previously reported picture of me. Moreover, it will be impossible, given the amount of times the media have reported about other investigations, to disassociate me from other reported investigations and I believe, given the extent of the exposure from previous coverage, no juror in a jury pool will be able to objectively and dispassionately assess the evidence or presume my innocence.

"I believe justice is best served in the second trial if it is heard away from this community, whom I believe has been highly influenced by the reporting and events that unfolded over the last four years."[50]

Despite Brian Munro's argument that media coverage had painted his client as a "bogeyman" whom people had to fear, Justice Gladys Young, who was presiding over the case, denied the motion for a change of venue.

In the affidavit, Tanasichuk also took issue with portions of a report detailing the case and the search operation which Deborah Palman had written for the MESARD archives. In her report, Palman had stated (in part):

The suspect was a drug dealer, substance abuser, and convicted of weapons charges and other felony charges, including planning to kill a judge, prosecutor and officers involved in charges against him. The Crown prosecutor thus became personally involved in this case, something that is generally prevented by the Canadian system where prosecutors don't work closely with police during an investigation. The people in the small city of Miramichi feared the suspect and told police little or gave tips anonymously so they couldn't be followed up. The suspect, having been burned before by associating with an undercover officer, said very little to the few friends he had. His wife had devoted friends, however, and after she disappeared, they began to ask questions and the suspect was eventually forced to report her missing 10 days after she was last seen. He had already pawned all her jewelry the day after she was last seen.

Once he was a suspect, the detectives surveiled him 24/7. This included posting a detective on top of a metal tower a half mile from his house by the main ATV trail in minus 20 temperatures. The suspect, knowing he was being watched, complicated search planning by taking midnight forays into different parts of the woods all around town. These trips all turned out to be diversions.

During the investigation that was being aided by the wife's friends who finally had a compelling reason to reveal things previously hidden out of fear, the detectives learned that the suspect had probably killed the wife's brother and another man in 1999. The brother's body is still missing. The other man was found in his basement, stabbed and cut repeatedly and his throat slit from ear to ear. The suspect has tattoos of firearms on his body. He has a phrase in Russian that translates as "death dealer" or "people killer." In 1998 he had three tear drops tattooed below one eye, apparently following a Russian tradition of one drop for every person he had killed. In 1999, he had a fourth drop added. On his back is tattooed "Don't run, you will only die tired."

The detectives learned that he would hide guns wrapped in tarps in the woods around the city, miles away from his house. In the past, one of these guns had been revealed to an undercover agent. Another sawed off rifle was found after we left in May by one of the wife's relatives who was searching for her in an area not far from her body...

Very little of significance was found in May, and the
searchers left discouraged. Lt. Dorian was already talking
about when we would return as we drove home. The detectives
were wondering where they might move to to protect their
families and what new careers they might have by the time the
suspect was let out of jail.[51]

Tanasichuk characterized Palman's report as "entirely
fake things" that created a highly prejudicial picture of him.
He also took issue with her statements that he had a satanic
shrine in his basement and had told workers at the addiction counseling service that he used drugs to help control his
homicidal urges, insisting that "these things were entirely
untrue."

Ironically, while he complained about labels and sensationalistic reporting, some years earlier Tanasichuk had
actually labeled himself a satanist. In a letter to the *Miramichi
Leader* written while he was incarcerated at the Springhill
Institution, Tanasichuk took issue with those who didn't
know what satanism was, and wrote:

"You may ask then what Satanism is all about. Put simply, Satanism represents indulgence instead of abstinence;
vital existence instead of spiritual pipe dreams; undeified
wisdom instead of hypocritical self deceit; kindness to those
who deserve it instead of love wasted on ingrates; vengeance
instead of turning the other cheek; responsibility to the
responsible."

Tanasichuk also responded to concerns that satanists
condone virtually any bad behavior: "There are some basics:
do not harm little children; do not kill non-human animals
unless attacked or for food; do not take what does not belong
to you; do not bother anyone unless someone bothers you."[52]

There was also increased local tension, because at one
point during the *voir dire* process that had gone on for many

weeks during the fall of 2008, David had felt ill and had been transported from the prison to Miramichi Hospital. Hearing that he was en route, and knowing of his admiration for Allan Legere, who had used a hospital visit as a vehicle to escape and begin his violent murder spree, the Miramichi police scrambled personnel into action.

When Tanasichuk exited the prison transport at the hospital, he was met by police officers with K-9s and carrying shotguns. He surveyed the official reception waiting for him, shook his head and said, "I've seen enough." He returned to prison without entering the hospital, a decision that confirmed in the minds of the Miramichi police that he had something other than medical care in mind.

Another aspect of the *voir dire* process that was unsettling to the witnesses was defense attorney Brian Munro's aggressive style. The prospect of going back into court and facing David Tanasichuk was already terrifying. David had made the first trial a nightmare by winking, staring and blowing kisses to the witnesses when the judge wasn't looking. And, despite their courage in standing up and testifying, David had gotten himself a new trial. Now witness after witness was questioned about having bought drugs from David Tanasichuk, with some witnesses admitting marijuana purchases that surprised even the investigating detectives. Munro was particularly aggressive toward Darlene Gertley, who had been such a strong witness in the first trial, accusing her of using drugs and of having grown apart from Maria, rather than being the best friend she claimed to be.

The *voir dire* process was also difficult for both Brian Cummings and Paul Fiander. Through his attorney, David Tanasichuk made a concerted effort to paint them as liars who had targeted him as a suspect from the start, rather than reaching that conclusion after the interview and the investigators' meeting on January 29. He also sought to have them banned from the courtroom until they had finished testifying at the trial. According to Brian Cummings, Brian Munro quoted his client as saying, "I don't want those two fucking pigs in the courtroom." Even before the trial got underway, Cummings and Fiander both had the feeling that the pre-siding justice considered them liars. And Cummings, who would be testifying on multiple occasions, would be banned from almost the entire proceeding.

At last, the second trial got underway. Criminal trials are always competing narratives, with the prosecution trying to show that there is sufficient evidence for a conviction, and the defense trying to cast doubt on that and offer an alternative narrative to explain the story. Crown prosecutor John Henheffer opened with a description of the Tanasichuks' marriage at the time that Maria disappeared: how it had become troubled, stressed both by Maria's possessiveness and her obsessive desire to keep her husband away from drugs, and by David's increasing drug use. He then explained that while there were no eyewitnesses, there would be plenty of circumstantial evidence as well as the direct evidence of the statement made by David to Lesley Allen that the searchers were getting close and they would have to move the body. He reminded the jury that the accumulated circumstantial evidence would be very powerful and the only reasonable suspect in Maria Tanasichuk's death would be her husband.

Defense counsel Brian Munro offered the alternative scenario of a happy and loving marriage and the improbability in such circumstances that David would kill his wife. He then offered the alternative possibility that Maria was killed by another drug dealer on the river who feared that, in her efforts to keep her husband off drugs, she might go to the authorities. He explained the discrepancies in what David had said to others at the time of Maria's disappearance as the result of impairment from his drug use. He suggested that the police never looked at alternative suspects and mentioned the mystery of an unexplained third bullet (the one found in Maria's skull that was too damaged to identify) and other shells found near Maria's body.

Climatologist Gerard Morin was questioned closely by both sides—by the prosecution to show that David waited until the 26th to report his wife missing so snowfall would cover his ATV and foot tracks and hide the body; by the defense who tried to show that there was already enough snow on the ground to hide a body. In this trial, defense counsel Brian Munro pressed witnesses hard in an effort to establish that there might be other possible suspects. He tried to raise the specter of an alternative killer by questioning witnesses closely about Maria's efforts to dissuade drug dealers on the river from selling to her husband, including incidents in which she allegedly kicked down a door or lay in a field watching through binoculars.

Munro wove a theme of drug use and drug purchases from the Tanasichuks by the witnesses throughout the trial, trying to undermine witnesses' credibility. He jumped on discrepancies between their testimony during the first trial and what they were saying now. He questioned the investigators about whether they had ever seriously considered suspects other than David.

Tension was ratcheted up for Paul Fiander and Brian Cummings, who were intimately familiar with the case and had observed the previous trial, because they were sequestered along with the other witnesses. For Cummings, who was scheduled to testify at least five different times, that essentially meant he would be unable to judge the progress, lend support to witnesses he'd developed or quickly advise the crown prosecutors when a witness misspoke.

Sometimes they were able to send Jody Whyte and Greg Scott to observe the proceedings, but both felt deeply frustrated by being unable to be there to support witnesses they knew were extremely intimidated by the retrial process when they were bullied by the defense, or when David's attorney tried to use minor differences from their testimony from years before to make them look like liars.

In many criminal cases, the investigators have a sense that they are under attack, and their judgment, honesty and actions are on trial. Cummings said, "There's a saying that goes, 'The trial of the accused is a sideshow; the trial of the investigation is the main event.'" As trials become more complex, "the focus will be on the investigation, the methodologies and the technologies." Both Cummings and Fiander felt that the presiding judge was being swayed by Munro's characterization of them as dishonest, a characterization that the process gave them little leeway to confront, clarify or explain. Police officers have to take a lot of abuse and questioning of their characters as part of the job, but it was especially difficult here, to sit and feel themselves characterized as liars with no way to explain themselves. For a man with a deep sense of personal honor like Paul Fiander, it was a painful and frustrating experience.

Cummings stated, "The stress in the days leading up to testifying in the second trial, and during the *voir dire*, was huge. Sometimes you get to a point in your head where you feel like *you're* the accused...and when you get to that point, it's demoralizing. There were times during the second trial that Paul and I both felt like the judge was against *us*, for

Christ's sake, because of Munro's questions and her follow-up questions...there was a certain tone in her voice that suggested we were liars and were willing to say whatever needed to be said to put Tanasichuk away.

"All the while, we had to face that piece of shit sitting smugly in the prisoner's dock with that 'I'm gonna get off with this' look on his puss...and we couldn't testify to all the stuff that we *really* knew."

For Cummings, the challenges to his character became incidents that frayed his temper, until a moment on the stand restored his perspective and gave him back his focus.

"I remember a particular moment in the second trial when I was on the stand and I was introducing the booklets of photographs of Maria out at the scene where we found her," Cummings recounted. "And I can remember looking down at the picture of her after we had removed all the sticks and debris off her, so she was lying there exposed with her skeletonized head and green camouflage jacket and black ski pants...and there was a pause in the proceedings because [Justice Young] was putting a court exhibit sticker on her booklet, I think... and I looked at the female juror closest to me, and she was looking at the picture and there were tears in her eyes.

"And I had this moment of pure rage that came over me. And I looked over at that asshole in the dock and he met my gaze...and then he looked *down*, which he never did. And I can clearly remember that was when everything changed for me on the stand.

"I remember thinking, 'Fuck this! *We* are the good guys and *he* is not and I don't care what this arrogant asshole lawyer says to try and paint me in some different light, because I'm not letting it happen.'"

Something that is not shown in television show trials but is agonizing for all the parties in the real world is the slow pace of the process. Although an extensive and lengthy *voir dire* had been conducted in the fall, decisions had not yet been reached about the admissibility of some evidence and about whether some witnesses would be allowed to testify and/or about the extent of their testimony. The trial was repeatedly delayed while there were arguments about these issues, as the jury would have to leave the courtroom so the matters could be discussed.

The trial was postponed for a week when a juror became unavailable due to family illness. It was also delayed because David became ill, repeatedly raising the possibility that he would need to be hospitalized, and the risks surrounding that. Rather than running a full five days a week, it would run for four, or Justice Young would schedule half days on Mondays or Fridays. And all the while, the prosecutors and defense had to remain ready and available, staying in motels in Miramichi, some hours from home. The police had to reschedule witnesses, some of whom had to be picked up in distant cities and transported to Miramichi, and the jurors had to give up another week of their lives.

Maria's sister, Sharon, and the women who had been her dear friends waited in the lobby outside the third floor court-room, knitting or doing other crafts to keep themselves busy, staring out over the snowy landscape toward the river, or joining the group gathered on the chilly front steps to smoke, nervously comforting each other as they waited to be called, one after another, to testify. The *voir dire* process had given them a taste of how Brian Munro would behave, and they could only hope that they would remain calm enough to give their testimony in a clear and coherent way in the face of his loud, bombastic questions and the ways he would try to twist what they were saying and make them look like liars.

Angela Arbeau testified about the clashes she had wit-nessed between David and Maria during the Christmas holiday over how much he'd actually spent on gifts and was holding back money to buy drugs, and about whether he was using drugs. Munro then pressed her hard about her knowledge of drug dealing from the house. She replied that she had never seen it and that it had never gone on while she was there. And then, crying softly, the young mother who had been like a sister to Maria and who had asked Maria to be godmother to her expected twins, told of her last phone conversation with Maria, on January 15. The conversation had barely begun when someone had come to the door. Maria had excused herself, saying she'd call Angela back. And that was the last time they'd ever spoken.

At one point, Cummings picked up two of Maria's old friends—Cathy Penney and Kathy Perry—and Maria's former brother-in-law in Saint John, a long, stressful drive on slippery winter roads, and brought them up to Miramichi to testify, only to have the trial postponed when David fell ill. He then had to drive them back to Saint John and Maria's niece, Angela Arbeau, back to Fredericton, more than six hours on the road. Then he had to drive back to Saint John the next week and do it all again, with snow and freezing rain making the three-hour journey into four and a half.

The issue of drug dealing by the Tanasichuks came into play more strongly in this second trial, with the defense attorney aggressively questioning Maria's friends and neighbors about it. Maria's best friend, Darlene Gertley, had been the first to suspect foul play in her friend's disappearance, and she had been the recipient of many of David's lies as she attempted to learn what had happened to her friend. After she had testified about her interactions with David in the weeks after Maria disappeared, Brian Munro challenged Darlene, attempting to discredit her as a witness by proposing that she had been among those who sold David the prescription drugs he was abusing.

Munro asked, "Didn't the fact that you were trading him marijuana for opiates upset Maria?"

The question, and the accusation behind it, pushed Darlene's buttons in a major way. Despite being a shy and reserved woman who found Munro intimidating, and while getting up to testify was an ordeal for her, she had traveled back and forth from Nova Scotia several times for the trial, taking time off from work and sometimes taking her husband out of work and her children out of school. Maria Tanasichuk had been her best friend in the world. She was the one who had kept Maria's terrifying secrets. She was the one who had first suspected that David had killed her friend. She was the one who had tried to find out what was going on, bravely hiding her suspicions as she faced a man she believed to be a murderer. She had held it together then, and she was going to hold it together now.

Darlene was there in the courtroom to represent Maria and she wasn't going to let Munro intimidate her. She had readily admitted to occasionally buying marijuana from the Tanasichuks, but she was not letting this outrageous accusation stand. "No," Darlene replied, gathering her dignity about her and glaring at the man who was trying to call her both a liar and a drug dealer. "What you're saying isn't true. I never sold him drugs...I did buy marijuana from him for cash," she said.

The following day, when Munro's cross-examination continued, he questioned whether her relationship with Maria was as close as she had claimed. He showed her a photo of the apartment and asked her to pick out items she recognized. One such item was a gray blanket she pointed to and called "Maria's sooky blanket."

Munro challenged her, saying, "Angela Arbeau said her sooky blanket was yellow."

Darlene snapped, "I don't know what she thinks Maria's sooky blanket is, but I know that's her blanket."

"Do you know if they got a new TV for Christmas?" he asked.

"I don't remember that."

"Because you weren't there very often, were you? Because you and Maria weren't getting along?" Munro insisted.

"I wasn't there as often because she was going through a hard time and I was giving her space," said the faithful friend who had agitated relentlessly among Maria's other friends and relatives to raise concern about Maria's disappearance.

Munro then showed her photos of a couple on three-wheelers, challenging her identification of Maria by pointing out that Maria wasn't wearing a helmet and Darlene had testified she always did. "Well, they aren't driving," Gertley replied. "They're just sitting on them for pictures."

So it went with Maria's other friends, who would, one after another, bring Maria's spirit back into the courtroom as they spoke for the woman they still mourned. Lisa Trafton, the sister of Maria's sister-in-law, broke into tears on the stand as she spoke of calling David for news of Maria's whereabouts, and had to take a break to compose herself. Betty Schaefer, who had become close friends with Maria after B.J. died (B.J. had been friends with her sons), brought a hint of humor to the room when she testified about David stealing their money for drugs. Indicating that Maria had begun to imitate her, she told the jury, "she started doing like me," patted her chest, and said that she kept her money in her bra.

The little red devil bear that Maria called "Baby B" wove in and out of the testimony and, as the witnesses focused on it, it became a symbol for the absent Maria, for her loss, her grief and her determination not to lose the last bit of her family left after B.J.'s death—her husband, David. Cummings testified that David had told him Maria never went to bed without it, never let it be far from her and made him kiss it every night. Her niece, Angela Arbeau, testified that Maria had brought both the bear and her sooky blanket when she'd come to Fredericton for Angela's wedding: "She said she'd never go anywhere without them."

Darlene Gertley told how she was suspicious about the stories David was telling her about Maria's departure and how she went to the apartment and spotted "Baby B." When she asked David, "Did girlfriend go without her devil doll?" he had replied that it was a different toy, one that belonged to the children upstairs. He would later admit that the bear was Maria's. As she left the apartment that day, she testified that she saw Maria's keys still hanging on the rope with B.J.'s picture. She had given Maria that rope to hang around her neck because she was always forgetting her keys.

Maria's former sister-in-law, Cindy Richardson, had known Maria since they were both sixteen-year-old mothers struggling to care for their infants back in Saint John. Even after Maria's relationship with her brother had ended, Cindy had remained close to Maria and her nephew, B.J. She had taken B.J. in and cared for him when Maria went to jail, and shared Maria's devastation after B.J.'s death. She testified that the camouflage jacket Maria was wearing when she was found was one she only wore when she and David went hunting. She spoke about the love between David and Maria, and how she was very sympathetic to David when Maria became withdrawn and unavailable after B.J.'s death.

Then, in a powerful and dramatic moment that, like the testimony of Edmund Carroll, stunned the courtroom into silence, while she was being questioned by crown prosecutors about the little red devil bear that had been her nephew

B.J.'s last gift to Maria, she gripped it in its plastic evidence bag and began to cry. Expressing anger and frustration that the beloved object—a gift from the joking son to the mother who had called him "a little devil"—had become a piece of evidence sealed up in a bag, she tore it out of the bag as she told the jury that Baby B was not where it belonged.

Through sad and angry tears, she waved it at the jury and said, "It seems so sad to see it in this bag and not in her hands."

To the investigators' great relief, John Paquet's information, so vital for connecting David with the gun, was allowed in via the taped record of his testimony at the first trial.

When Cummings took the stand again as the last witness, Crown Prosecutor Bill Richards, meeting the defense's suggestion that Maria might have been killed by a drug dealer, asked Cummings whether Maria had been planning to rat on any drug dealers. Cummings replied, "Absolutely not."

A classic example of how a witness who has been carefully interviewed can still produce surprises involves the young woman with whom David Tanasichuk had an affair shortly after Maria disappeared. On April 2, 2009, when he was driving her to the courthouse to testify in the second trial, Dewey Gillespie asked her if she was sure she had told them everything, and she said that she had not. When she reached the courthouse, Gillespie reported that she had additional information to share. Cummings consulted with the crown prosecutors about how to proceed. On their instruction, he then sat down with her to review her testimony for the trial.

She told about events that had occurred on February 14, 2003, little more than two weeks after Maria was reported missing: "It was Valentine's Day, February 14th; I remember it right to a tee. I had just got off work from the Portage and I went right to Donnie Trevors's house," she reported. "David Tanasichuk had called me at work and told me to come to Donnie's, that he wanted to see me that night. I would have got off work at ten, so this was probably around 10:30 P.M. I went into Donnie's and David called me into the living room and he told me he had something specially made for me, and that there was only two that he knew existed, and that's when he gave me a 'bow and arrow' pendant. He told me to lift up my hair and he put it on the chain around my neck. He told me he had taken some of his old jewelry, got it melted and that's how they made it. He said hunting was his favorite sport, and this would be a way for me to remember him forever. Then he told me that he loved me, we kissed and he said I'd always have a place in his heart."

The information was significant, as witnesses had told Cummings about David and Maria having matching bow and arrow pendants. She went on to tell the detective that she no longer had the pendant, that she had thrown it into a swamp in shame and disgust on the day that Maria's body was found and had burned any love letters that David had sent her.

But she wasn't done. There was something else she hadn't told the detectives. One night around the same time, after he had gone into the bathroom and gotten high on drugs, she had found David out in the yard, staring up at the stars, crying hard with tears running down his face and saying, "I'm sorry. I'm sorry." When she asked him what was wrong, and who he was saying sorry to, he said he missed Maria. Then he asked for a hug and they went inside.

Brian Cummings returned and shared her revelations with the prosecutors. They advised him to sit down with her and get a supplemental statement, which he did. When this new information was revealed to the defense, along with her previous testimony about an intimate relationship beginning shortly after Maria was reported missing, the defense objected. A lengthy *voir dire* was held with the witness, out of the hearing of the jury. During that process, a tense exchange took place between the witness and the defendant in which she accused him of killing his wife and he told her to shut up.

Justice Young ultimately ruled that since the relationship began after Maria's death, it would be primarily evidence of bad conduct, which would be prejudicial to the defendant. To the crown's great disappointment, her testimony was deemed too prejudicial and wasn't admitted. Although she had testified at the first trial, all of her information was excluded this time. The jury did not hear how David had tattooed her name on his hand and told her that he loved her, or that he had given her gold jewelry just weeks after he had reported his wife missing.

The defense made a big fuss about Cummings having interviewed her about the new information, when both he and she were to appear as witnesses at the trial, despite the fact that he was instructed to do so by the prosecutors, and despite the fact that he was the police officer who had interviewed her previously and taken her earlier statements. The whole incident later caused a controversy about the appropriateness of Cummings's actions, which were ultimately deemed appropriate conduct by an investigator operating under the direction of the prosecutors.

Although one of the points made by the appellate court in ordering a new trial was that where "Mr. Tanasichuk put his credibility in issue by testifying, denying the charge and offering explanations for the evidence that militates against him...he is entitled to have his credibility assessed and all of the admissible evidence weighed by a properly instructed jury"[53] (Court of Appeal decision, pg. 89), in this trial, David chose not to take the stand. Through it all, though, he exploded, postured and engaged in elaborate gestures when he wanted to consult with his lawyer, and sometimes sulked in his cell, refusing to enter the courtroom. Neither maturity nor incarceration, it seemed, had had any effect on David's violent temper or on his need to be the center of attention.

During the second trial, vigilance by the prosecution kept him from blowing kisses or otherwise harassing the witnesses as he had during the first one. Vigilance by court officers kept his schemes to get his shackles removed from coming to fruition, a good thing in the minds of those who knew him best, especially as his counsel frequently rushed into the defendant's box for consultations without securing the door behind him.

The trial had begun in early March, but it was not until April 17 that the prosecutors and the defense presented their closing arguments to the jury.

Before he summarized the testimony for the jurors, Crown Prosecutor Bill Richards drove home the brutal, calculated nature of the crime. The sawed-off weapon used to commit the crime—the tarp-wrapped gun a mysterious voice had led Edmund Carroll to find hidden under a truck close to where Maria's body lay hidden—was a single-shot weapon that was easy to conceal. For the killer to shoot her three times, he would have had to aim, fire, open, reload, cock and fire again. Open. Reload. Cock. Fire again. Not a crime of passion, the forensic evidence showed, but a crime of deliberation. Before he summarized the evidence, he reminded the jury of how powerful circumstantial evidence could be.

Then Richards gave a long, careful, detailed summation of all the testimony that the jury had heard over the month of trial. He ended with a litany of the lies David had told multiple people, including the police, about Maria's trip to Saint John.

He spoke of Tanasichuk's statement about having to move the body.

"The Crown's position is this is an admission. He knew she was dead. Those looking would find her. And he didn't want them to find her," he said. "Why the need for a phone call if it was a joke? And what husband would make a joke in such circumstances?"

Richards added, "What if it was a joke? The joke just happened to predict what actually happened? Is that just bad luck?"

And on the subject of Maria's purse and things that were found in the apartment: "What didn't she take with her? She didn't take her purse, or her house keys, or the red devil bear, or her house coat. She didn't take her medication. She wasn't found with a lot of rings on her fingers. On the evening of the fifteenth, this woman was coming back home in her mind."

Richards closed by reminding them of the biggest lie of all—the one that David Tanasichuk told Maria to get her to go out with him on his three-wheeler.

Then it was Brian Munro's turn. The dynamic defense attorney was a strong contrast to Bill Richards's courtly, erudite, understated demeanor. Focusing on David's drug use, he urged the jury to consider many of the statements the Crown characterized as lies as simply the product of confusion. In an era when TV watchers are attuned to the "smoking gun," DNA and fingerprints, he reminded them of the lack of forensic evidence. In an area where hunting was common, he used the discovery of bullets found seventy feet away and the damaged, unidentified third bullet in Maria's head to suggest a possible second shooter was involved. He offered the upstairs neighbor's testimony about David's tears as evidence that he wasn't likely to be contemplating murder, saying, "Do you think if he were entertaining the idea of murdering his wife he'd be crying?" He suggested the couple had a happy marriage and there was no motive for murder, suggesting instead a mysterious stranger at the back door who had pulled Maria away from that phone call with her niece. "Someone was at the back door that night. We know that because that is where the doorbell was. Maria was leery about going back there. That's where the drugs were."

He suggested she might have been killed by drug dealers on the river who were fearful that Maria might rat them out. He stated, "We don't know her body was in the woods in January," despite the outdoor clothing, because there was no hunting in January.

It was painful for the investigators to listen to this, knowing all the information that had been withheld from the jury. David's history of explosive violence. Of plotting other murders. All the other guns. All the other *sawed-off* guns. The illegal hunting. The fact that dealers do not like to trade with customers who are falling deeply under the spell of their habits and becoming increasingly unstable and unlikely to be able to pay, and whose erratic behavior may attract the attention of the police. They worried about the "CSI effect"—and the way juries have come to expect dramatic forensic evidence, unaware of how fluky those discoveries can be, and of the effects of time and weather on evidence. They worried about the timing. About a jury that would have a whole weekend with Brian Munro's last words lingering in their minds before Justice Young's instructions on Monday.

They could only hope for a sensible jury, for men and women who could look through glib bombast and the specter of doubt and see that the prosecutors had revealed a solid case for conviction.

Chapter 21

Justice for Maria

O n Monday, April 20, Justice Young charged the jury, who had been instructed the previous Friday to come prepared with their pajamas and their tooth-brushes. The jury retired to deliberate. For both sides, then, the waiting began.

As the jury retired, the investigators speculated that they would return a verdict on Tuesday. But it would be two long and anxious days before the jury made their decision. On Wednesday afternoon, April 22, 2009, the jury returned with their verdict and David Tanasichuk was again convicted of the first-degree murder of his wife and sentenced to life imprisonment. Under Canadian law, this meant he would have no parole eligibility for twenty-five years.

After the verdict, Maria's sister, Sharon, hugged her husband and tearfully told *The Miramichi Leader*, "We lived our lives in misery long enough. It has been six long years. God held me in his hands; I would have broken without him."[54]

The paper also quoted Sergeant Brian Cummings (Cummings had, over the course of this case, been promoted from constable to sergeant, taking the job formerly held by Paul Fiander, who had been promoted to Deputy Chief), who had once been close to the Tanasichuks and had been the primary investigator on the case: "It is bittersweet that in order for this day to happen a life had to be taken. I just hope Maria is looking down and is happy."[55]

Deputy Chief Paul Fiander noted how stressful the trial had been for everyone, especially after so many years: "The biggest barrier was how much time passed. Sometimes witnesses lose those small details but the details are important. But we were confident the outcome would be the same as the first trial."[56]

It is sometimes the case that the efforts of law enforcement officials are not appreciated by those they serve, but Maria's friends and family felt a deep and sincere gratitude to the investigators and the prosecutors, who had seen them through the process and finally achieved justice, and, they hoped, finality for Maria.

The following month, David filed another appeal and asked for a third trial.

On May 27, in response to David's new appeal, Cindy Richardson wrote a letter to *The Miramichi Leader* that voiced the feelings of so many who had been involved in the case:

"Please allow me at this time to express my deepest gratitude to all the great people that assisted, in any way, with the triumphant outcome of David Tanasichuk's two trials."

Richardson then acknowledged the Miramichi Police Force Criminal Investigation Division, the judges, the prosecutors, the juries, the witnesses, the sheriff's department, the *Miramichi Leader* staff, family, friends, and God.

She lamented, "How disconcerting it is to see that David Tanasichuk is appealing again! Our hard-earned tax dollars will be wasted further, along with our time, lost wages and urgent court cases delayed further..."

She then suggested that Tanasichuk should find better things to do while incarcerated than to push for another retrial: "Does David really need a third trial to hear the verdict of guilty again? Why didn't he take the stand on his own behalf if he's an innocent man?"

Richardson continued by questioning the wisdom of holding David Tanasichuk in medium security at Springhill Institution, since if he managed to escape he would most likely exact revenge on those who "...got justice for Maria."

She concluded, "Who is the real victim here, anyway? My beautiful friend, Maria, who can't be left in peace even in death with her precious son, B.J.

"So many people know, for a fact, that no one in the world would hurt Maria but the person who was charged, tried, and convicted twice—David Tanasichuk!"[57]

Tanasichuk's appeal, alleging six grounds of error, was heard on February 16 and 17, 2010. The court considered three of those grounds. As summarized by the court, they were:

1. The trial judge erred in failing to provide a two-stage instruction to the jury, as it relates to post-offence conduct and other evidence demonstrating lies;

2. His right to a fair trial was breached when the investigating police officer, Sergeant Brian Cummings, who had already testified, a) interviewed a potential witness during a *voir dire*, and b) relayed information about the appellant to a potential witness; and

3. The trial judge erred in failing to hold a *voir dire* in order to determine whether there existed independent

evidence of fabrication before admitting post-offence conduct of the appellant and third-party evidence demonstrating the appellant lied on earlier occasions.[58]

It was not until late in September of that year that a decision finally came down, a carefully reasoned twenty-page document denying the appeal and affirming the verdict. The appellate court found Justice Young's jury instructions adequate, decided that the ultimate conclusions on the issues of fabrication and post-offense conduct belonged to the jury and that, since none of the potential witness' testimony was admitted at trial, Brian Cummings's actions in interviewing her while a witness himself had no impact on the fairness of the trial.

More than seven years after Maria Tanasichuk's death, the legal process had finally concluded.

Brian Cummings was in the woods hunting with his father, far from cell phone service, when news of the decision reached the Miramichi police. When he came out of the woods and back into cell range, his phone was jammed with calls, his e-mail was brimming with messages and his phone back at the station was ringing off the hook. After such a long process, it was hard to believe it was actually finished. When he returned to Miramichi, some drinks were had to celebrate. It was finally over.

Maria Tanasichuk is one of the victims of domestic violence memorialized by the Silent Witness Project. A life-sized red wooden silhouette bearing her name has joined a traveling exhibit of silhouettes of women who were murdered by a husband, common-law partner, boyfriend or intimate acquaintance. Because these women no longer have a voice, they are called the Silent Witnesses. The project's literature states: "Each silhouette represents a woman who once lived and worked among us. We eventually hope to craft a silhouette to honor every woman in Canada who has died tragically as the result of domestic violence."[59]

With finality, and the assurance that there would be no third trial, Maria's skull was cremated and buried with her body in St. Michael's Cemetery on June 28th, 2011, eight years to the day since she was discovered by Deb Palman and her cadaver dog, Alex.

No one who has been deeply affected by a murder walks away unscathed. Darlene Gertley lives and works in Nova Scotia, where she devotes herself to her husband and her two sons. Having already lost one best friend and her twin brother before her deep friendship with Maria had such a tragic end, she has never let herself develop another close friendship. Like Sharon Carroll, who lost a sister, and Cindy Richardson, who lost a friend she'd known for decades, Darlene cherishes her memories of Maria Tanasichuk, a bubbly, lively, life-of-the-party woman, a generous friend who stayed in constant touch and attended to the lives and needs of her friends, a woman lovely in person and in spirit. Ask any of them to talk about Maria and the photo albums will come out and the pictures will bring stories. Ask any of them what it was like to go through two trials, and they will shiver and grow silent.

Paul Fiander is the Miramichi Police Chief now. Brian Cummings has recently been promoted from leading the detective bureau to Deputy Chief. Dewey Gillespie still talks about retiring.

Every long-time police officer has a case that will always be with him. For Paul Fiander, Brian Cummings, Dewey Gillespie and Greg Scott, it is the Maria Tanasichuk case. Years later, they are still discovering the effects those weeks living with the threat of danger had on their families. The endless months of preparation and delay leading up to the second trial caused nightmares and devastating stress. Many of them can recite, word for word, what was said the night of the take-down. It is, in Paul Fiander's words, burned in their brains forever.

Lieutenant Pat Dorian has retired from the Maine Warden Service—Kevin Adam now has his job—but Dorian is still deeply involved in search and rescue matters. He is still a passionate fisherman and often returns to the Miramichi River to fish. The Tanasichuk case forged an enduring friendship between the Canadians and their American counterparts. When he returns to New Brunswick, Cummings, Fiander, Gillespie and Scott still drive down to see him. Over beer and salmon, they relive the case.

Without that unusual international cooperation—the result of a detective willing to think outside the box (and outside of his country) and ask for help and a warden who believed in the value of combining GPS, SAR and cadaver dogs—Maria's body would never have been found and David Tanasichuk might never have been prosecuted. Miramichi's "Death Dealer" might have still walked among us.

Epilogue

When the news about Maria's suspicions about her husband's involvement in Robert Breau's death came to the investigators from Darlene Gertley, Brian Cummings and Paul Fiander promised Maria's sister, Sharon, that someday they would find Robert.

In 2012, investigators discovered an area that they believe may contain Breau's body. Pat Dorian was consulted and, on his advice, brush and vegetation was cleared. Cadaver dogs and handlers once again traveled to Miramichi to search for Breau's body. Breau was a missing person who police believed to be a murder victim and they suspected that he had been killed by David Tanasichuk. Findings at the site and the behavior of the dogs indicating in the area that the investigators were searching suggested to detectives and the cadaver dog handlers that the site was significant. To date, though, Breau's remains have not been found.

Once again, Brian Cummings traveled to visit with Sharon Carroll to let her know that they had not found her brother...yet.

But the promise that Brian Cummings and Paul Fiander made to her is one they intend to keep.

Endnotes

1. From case summary prepared for the Crown Prosecutor by the Miramichi police.

2. Bonnie Sweeney, "Having Such a Weapon Can't Be Tolerated," *The Miramichi Leader,* October 27, 1993.

3. Vernon Geberth, *Practical Homicide Investigation,* 3rd Ed. (CRC Press, 1996), 269.

4. In eastern Canada, the term "sooky" or "sookie" is used to refer to someone who is weak, timid or a crybaby. A common insult would be "poor sooky lala." A sooky blanket is a comfort blanket, used to sooth or pacify.

5. Letter from David Tanasichuk to *The Miramichi Leader,* September 12, 2000.

6. David Simon, *Homicide: A Year on the Killing Streets.* (Ivy Books: New York, 1991), 36.

7. Mark McClish, *I Know You Are Lying: Detecting Deception Through Statement Analysis,* PoliceEmployment.com, (Winterville, NC, 2001), 53.

8. Warned Statement given March 22, 2003 by David Tanasichuk at the Miramichi Police Station, pg. 24–25.

9. Ibid., 73–74.

10. Ibid., 10.

11. Ibid., 15.

12. Ibid., 85–86.

13. Ibid., 126.

14. Ibid., 210.

15. Ibid., 287.

16. Deborah Palman, "Obtaining and Selecting Dogs for Police Work," http://www.uspcak9.com/html/training_toc.html

17. Deborah Palman, *"Search and Rescue Dogs and the Ground Searcher,"* training article prepared for MESARD.

18. "Canine Team," Department of Inland Fisheries and Wildlife, Maine Warden Service, State of Maine, http://www.maine.gov/ifw/warden_service/canine.html.

19. Andrew Rebmann, Edward David, Marcella H. Sorg, *Cadaver Dog Handbook: Forensic Training and Tactics for the Recovery of Human Remains.* (CRC Press: Boca Raton, 2000), 13.

20. Ibid.

21. Deborah Palman, "Record Keeping for SAR Dog Teams," training article prepared for MESARD.

22. Deborah Palman, *"Miramichi Search, May—June 2003,"* report to MESARD.

23. Deborah Palman, Region 9 Quarterly Award—Detector April-June 2003, Maine Warden Incident Command Team, Maine Warden Service K-9 Detection Teams, Maine Search and Rescue Dogs, 4–5.

24. Report dated February 23rd, 2004 from Forensic Pathologist Dr. David Chiasson to the Miramichi police.

25. *R. v. White*, [1998] 2 S.C.R. 72 quoted in R. v. White, 2011 SCC 13, [2011] 1 S.C.R. 433.

26. Aimee Barry, "Guilty! Husband killed Wife: Jury." *The Miramichi Leader,* February 11, 2005

27. Ibid.

28. Tanasichuk v. R., 2007 NBCA 76 24/05/CA Judgment, pg. 2.

29. Ibid.

30. Ibid., 3.

31. Ibid., 4–5.

32. Ibid., 7–8.

33. Ibid., 8.

34. Ibid., 9.

35. Ibid., 10–11.

36. Ibid., 8–9.

37. Ibid., 10.

38. Ibid., 14.

39. Ibid., 16–17.

40. Ibid. 17–18.

41. Ibid., 22–23.

42. Ibid., 28.

43. Ibid., 34.

44. Ibid., 36.

45. Ibid., 31, author's emphasis.

46. Ibid., 40.

47. Ibid., 41.

48. Ibid., 63.

49. Ibid., 75.

50. David Tanasichuk, supporting affidavit excerpted in *The Miramichi Leader*, April 24, 2009.

51. Deborah Palman, "*Miramichi Search, May—June 2003*," report to MESARD.

52. David Tanasichuk and Lawrence LeBreton, Opinion, "So-Called satansists don't know what writers are talking about." *The Miramichi Leader*, February 28, 1995.

53. Tanasichuk v. R., 2007 NBCA 76 24/05/CA Judgment, pg. 2.

54. Laura MacInnis, "Guilty Jury renders decision in first-degree murder trial of David Tanasichuk." *The Miramichi Leader*, April 24, 2009.

55. Ibid.

56. Ibid.

57. Cindy Richardson, Letter to the Editor, *The Miramichi Leader*, May 27, 2009.

58. Tanasichuk v. R., 2010 NBCA 68 Judgment, pg. 4.

59. http://www.silentwitness.ca/nb_honour.asp.